The Carpetbaggers of Kabul and Other American-Afghan Entanglements

GEOGRAPHIES OF JUSTICE AND SOCIAL TRANSFORMATION

SERIES EDITORS

Nik Heynen, University of Georgia
Mathew Coleman, Ohio State University
Sapana Doshi, University of Arizona

ADVISORY BOARD

Deborah Cowen, University of Toronto
Zeynep Gambetti, Boğaziçi University
Geoff Mann, Simon Fraser University
James McCarthy, Clark University
Beverly Mullings, Queen's University
Harvey Neo, National University of Singapore
Geraldine Pratt, University of British Columbia
Ananya Roy, University of California, Berkeley
Michael Watts, University of California, Berkeley
Ruth Wilson Gilmore, CUNY Graduate Center
Jamie Winders, Syracuse University
Melissa W. Wright, Pennsylvania State University
Brenda S. A. Yeoh, National University of Singapore

The Carpetbaggers of Kabul and Other American-Afghan Entanglements

INTIMATE DEVELOPMENT, GEOPOLITICS, AND THE CURRENCY OF GENDER AND GRIEF

JENNIFER L. FLURI

RACHEL LEHR

THE UNIVERSITY OF GEORGIA PRESS
Athens

© 2017 by the University of Georgia Press
Athens, Georgia 30602
www.ugapress.org
All rights reserved
Set in 10/12.5 Minion Pro by Graphic Composition, Inc., Bogart, Georgia

Most University of Georgia Press titles are
available from popular e-book vendors.

Printed digitally

Library of Congress Control Number: 2016955269

ISBN: 9780820350349 (hardcover: alk. paper)
ISBN: 9780820350356 (paperback: alk. paper)
ISBN: 9780820350332 (ebook)

*Dedicated to the memory of my foremothers
Sonia Tave Lehr, Luba Tave Hurwitz,
and Bertha Brod Kanare. (R. L.)*

*Dedicated in memory of my mother,
Mary Dinofrio Fluri. (J. L. F.)*

CONTENTS

Preface ix

Acknowledgments xiii

CHAPTER 1 Introduction 1

CHAPTER 2 The Carpetbaggers of Kabul 21

CHAPTER 3 Gender and Grief Currency 43

CHAPTER 4 "Conscientiously Chic"
*The Production and Consumption of
Afghan Women's Liberation* 53

CHAPTER 5 "We Should Be Eating the Grant,
but the Grant Eats Us" 65

CHAPTER 6 "Saving" Soraya 86

CHAPTER 7 "Our Hearts Break"
*9/11 Deaths, Afghan Lives,
and Intimate Intervention* 104

CHAPTER 8 Gender Currency and the
Development of Wealth 117

Notes 133

Glossary 141

Works Cited and Consulted 145

Index 161

PREFACE

The idea for writing this book began in 2007 when Jennifer was an assistant professor at Dartmouth College researching international assistance in Afghanistan. At that time Rachel was executive director of Rubia, Inc., a U.S.-based nonprofit organization. This organization worked in partnership with the Rubia Organization for the Development of Afghanistan, a local nongovernmental organization (NGO) in Afghanistan.

This partnership grew from a long-term personal relationship Rachel had established with Afghans in the early 1980s. In 2007 Rubia, Inc. began the registration process for becoming a 501C3 nonprofit with a board of directors. Jennifer became an active board member and met with and visited Rubia's programs and participants in Afghanistan. Over the course of these experiences we (Jennifer and Rachel) began to work together on a number of different academic projects. One of our collaborative efforts included developing and presenting a series of lectures about everyday life in Afghanistan and the geopolitics of conflict, aid, and development, titled *Rediscovering Afghanistan: Lessons from the Home*. We presented these lectures during 2007–12 throughout New Hampshire (NH), in partnership with the Arts Alliance of Northern New Hampshire and funded by the NH Humanities Council.[1]

We developed these lectures from Rachel's ethnographic research and experiences living and working with Afghans, and Jennifer's research on geopolitics and international aid and development in Afghanistan (Fluri 2006, 2008a, 2008b, 2009a, 2009b, 2009c, 2011a, 2011b, 2012). Jennifer's research included questionnaires and interviews with Afghans and international workers primarily living and working in Kabul, Afghanistan. Rachel's research was gathered while she was completing her doctoral dissertation in linguistics on Pashai, a language spoken by a minority population in Afghanistan. Pashai was the language spoken by the founders of Rubia. Our lectures attempted to provide a complex and complicated view of both international geopolitics and daily life in Afghanistan, which included presenting images, short videos, and stories not seen in the mainstream media. This multifaceted portrait of Afghan life was significantly different from mainstream media portrayals at that time. Many of our audience members were surprised by our presentations about everyday life; others found that our critiques of international geopolitics challenged their own views about U.S. interventions in Afghanistan.

In an effort to systematically gauge audience responses, we began conducting postlecture surveys.[2] These surveys revealed an interesting array of responses, with most expressing shock or dismay at our candid and critical representations of Afghanistan and U.S. geopolitics. By opening an intimate window into the everyday lives of Afghans (in rural and urban settings)—from swaddling babies, to sharing meals, to weddings and family celebrations—our lectures exposed an aspect of Afghanistan these audiences had not seen: intimate, domestic, and ordinary daily life.

In this way we were able to portray what Katz (2004) refers to as the "strange familiar." Our audiences recognized daily activities and family celebrations presented through video clips and still photography as familiar, while the specific arrangements and configurations of these activities remained strange or different. Presenting the places and activities of everyday life induced surprising comments; some of the most poignant and haunting were statements such as, "I never thought of *them* [Afghans] as human before." Although these comments were shocking, we realized that these audience members could not imagine Afghans as individual people, because the prevailing media representations about Afghanistan did not *render* them as such. With media attention largely centered on violence and suffering, there was little room for the consideration of everyday life in a war zone. The reactions from our audience members resonated with the political philosophies on grievability by Judith Butler, which we draw on throughout this book.

Our audiences struggled with the obvious contradiction between what we were presenting and the dominant representation or "grand narratives" offered in the media (Shabir, Ali, and Iqbal 2011). These grand narratives had situated Afghan men into narrow categories as terrorists, abusive patriarchs, or cautious allies. Women had been more narrowly defined as victims of localized oppression in need of foreign saving. These categorizations illustrate much of what Said (1979) discussed in his seminal book *Orientalism*, where he critiqued the ways in which people were represented visually and discursively. Said identified the ways in which Europeans "othered" people in the colonies, thereby creating a belief in "European superiority" through media, literature, and art. This often led to an eroticized and limited representation of people and places in spaces outside of Europe, particularly Asia and Africa.

Through our presentations we offered a counternarrative to the mediated ways in which Afghan people have been imagined, simply by illustrating Afghan men as fathers, brothers, uncles, and husbands caring for their families. Similarly, Afghan women were portrayed within the framework of the family as mothers, sisters, daughters, aunts, and wives—not as victims but as active members of extensive family networks. We sought to elucidate facets of daily life as it intersected with geopolitics—attempting to provide as complex a portrait as possible in forty-five minutes. If the audience left the lecture with a profound sense that the connection between the everyday and the geopolitical was much more entangled, complicated, and disparate compared with mainstream media portrayals, then in some small way we had met our objectives. This book was born from these lectures and our collective research and experiences in Afghanistan and the United States.

We seek to present the complexities, complications, and contradictions of U.S.-Afghanistan relations and unravel them through analyses at the intersection of the personal and the geopolitical. In order to effectively disentangle these multifaceted stories and view them clearly and critically, we center our analyses of American-Afghan entanglements at an intimate scale. The case studies and stories included in this book best exemplify the interlocking relationship between international geopolitics and everyday lives. We incorporate the use of narrative form as a method for presenting and examining the everyday as it intersects with geopolitical processes (Pratt and Rosner 2012; Wiles, Rosenberg, and Kearns 2005).

The narrative form allows us to discuss different programs with descriptive detail within the context of theory and analysis. The use of narration throughout this book fosters reflection and prevents us from thinking or speaking for individual actors. The case studies were chosen from our collective research in order to illustrate, unpack, and critically analyze these American-Afghan entanglements. We include our own interactions and interventions as part of this critique. As an entry point for our critical examinations, we identify and discuss the geopolitical discourses, which have become grand narratives. Although we recognize that organizations from over fifty countries have been operating in different capacities (i.e., military, aid, development, and private corporations) throughout Afghanistan, we primarily focus on the relationship between U.S. citizens and Afghan citizens.

We examine the ways in which geopolitically driven grand narratives translate into different forms of currency, circulating as a medium of exchange. Individuals with varying degrees of influence, privilege, and ability have shaped these grand narratives in order to exchange them for personal or professional gain (McKittrick 2006).[3] Our analysis looks at the ways in which geopolitical discourses have manifested as material practices of aid and development. We bring into focus the everyday actions of people whose lives in one way or another have been deeply affected by violence, assistance, and development associated with U.S.-led geopolitical intervention in Afghanistan.

These entanglements are fraught with challenges and mistakes; and we stand firm in our belief that Afghans must direct the contours of their own lives, rather than international donors. Afghan capabilities have continually stood in stark contrast to common development discourses that focus on their "lack of capacity." Dominant development programs have fixated on changing the culture to liberate women and meet the demands of capitalistic and market-driven development paradigms. This book seeks to demonstrate the geopolitics and messiness of assistance and development by examining the ordinary untidiness of American-Afghan entanglements.

Note on the Book Cover

The term "carpetbagger" originates from the American Civil War, when it was used to identify northerners who went to the southern United States to capitalize on post–Civil War Reconstruction in the late 1800s. We use this term (specifically in chapter 2) to refer to war and postconflict profiteers in Afghanistan. When we were in Kabul, Afghanistan, in November 2014, we saw "Yankee Go Home" spray-painted on one of the many graffiti-covered walls. It immediately struck us as both poignant and telling about the U.S.-led occupation. "Yankee Go Home" is also a common slogan used by many throughout the globe to express resentment toward the American presence in their countries. We stopped to take photographs of this wall and later chose to include it on the cover of our book. When the publisher asked us to provide a professional photograph of this image, we hired Afghan photographer Qais Najibi to make the image. In the year between when we first photographed this image and Najibi's photograph, the newly constructed wall had begun to crumble. Therefore, this wall is not simply an identification of local sentiments against the U.S.-led occupation but also an allegory for the already crumbling reconstruction of Afghanistan.

ACKNOWLEDGMENTS

Without the encouragement, curiosity, and support of our colleagues, friends, and families this book would never have seen the light of day. Jumping into this book project as coauthors took a measure of mutual trust and respect we knew we could count on. What we did not know was how it would strengthen our friendship and enhance our intersecting academic pursuits. Both together and individually we met scores of people in an array of contexts, from Washington, D.C., to Darrai Nur. We conducted interviews and gathered observations at both formal and informal settings, from the U.S. embassy to donor offices, restaurants, private homes, and gardens. We would like to acknowledge everyone—the many confidential informants and those who cannot be disclosed—who took the time to talk, examine, analyze, brag, bluster, dissimulate, and deflect as we gathered our data.

Specifically, we would like to thank the following: Margaret Mills for always being willing to talk and listen about Afghanistan; Ruth Mandel for her encouragement and support; Gay-LeClerc Lyons, who generously shared her depth of Afghan experience; Najibullah Sedeqe for impeccable guidance; Lina Abirafeh, who suggested we examine the international community; Rosemary Stasek, who lived and died her dream in Kabul; Sayed Naqibullah and Karima for their continued research assistance; Afghans for Tomorrow for providing a place for us in Kabul; and David Edwards for his research support and guidance. We also thank Amy Trauger, Sharlene Mollet, Tanalis Padilla, Caroline Faria, Mona Domosh, Frank Magilligan, Annabel Martin, Amy Allen, Annelise Orleck, Ivy Schweitzer, Faith Beasley, Rebecca Biron, Mary Coffey, Irene Kacandes, Roberta Stewart, Mark Williams, and Chris Sneddon for being remarkable colleagues and friends who were generous with their time, thoughtfulness, ideas, and understanding. Azita Ranjbar provided incredible and invaluable research assistance; she read an earlier version of the book and provided exceptional feedback. Haley Bolin served as a resourceful research assistant; and Alicia Lucksted, a great friend, read a much too early draft and encouraged us to go in new directions. We would like to express our gratitude to Mary MacMakin, Rangina Hamidi, Zala Ahmad, Jeanne Freeze, Jennie Wood, Catherine Rielly, Mohammad Nasib, and WADAN. Sharon Forrence and Steve Verrecchia generously contributed to our wartime kitsch collection. Valerie Begley and Tim Hollifield freely shared their Afghan experience and expertise. To the Rubia team and extended family, Sakhi Sharay, Hafiza and Zalmay, Roshanara, Sima, Sahiba, and Basri, we owe an incalculable debt.

The anonymous reviewers and editors at the University of Georgia (UGA) Press pushed us to expand in some areas and contract in others, helping to craft this book into a clearer statement of our ideas than it was at its inception. The New Hampshire Humanities Council, the Arts Alliance of Northern New Hampshire, and Frumie Selchen launched the lectures that led to this book. We would like to extend our special thanks to UGA Press editor-in-chief Mick Gusinde-Duffy and managing editor Jon Davies for their assistance and to Kay Kodner for her meticulous copyediting. All remaining errors and interpretations of data are of course our own.

Thank you to the Geography Department and Women's and Gender Studies Program faculty at Dartmouth College for providing encouragement, resources, and support for this research; the Rockefeller Center at Dartmouth College, for funding several trips to Afghanistan; and the Gender Research Institute at Dartmouth for providing seminars and forums for discussions. Many thanks to the following departments, programs, and institutes at Dartmouth College for funding the 2007 conference, "New England and Afghanistan: Building Paths of Understanding and Collaboration across Borders," which expanded our network of individuals who live in and care about Afghanistan: the Dickey Center for International Understanding, Rockefeller Center, the Leslie Center for the Humanities, the Geography Department, the Women's and Gender Studies Program, and the Asian and Middle Eastern Studies Program.

Thank you to the University of Chicago Committee on South Asian Studies for funding part of Rachel's research in Afghanistan, and to the Division of Humanities and Dean Tom Thuerer who was instrumental in making things happen. We gratefully acknowledge the American Association of University Women dissertation fellowship for supporting Rachel's research as well. We extend our appreciation to Amy Dahlstrom and Elena Bashir not only for mentoring Rachel's research, but also for their interest in the extralinguistic data of life in Darrai Nur and the lives of women in the Rubia community.

Early versions of several chapters in this book were presented at the University of Washington, Florida International University, the University of Georgia, and Brown University. Much thanks to the feedback received from graduate students and faculty at these speaking events. Thanks also to Katie Gillespie and Tish Lopez for their comments, review, and suggestions on chapter 7, a version of which is included in the book they edited, *Economies of Death: Economic Logics of Killable Life and Grievable Death*.

Last and most importantly we would like to thank our children, Jessica and Samantha (J. L. F.) and Jake, Zhenya, Anna, and Ben (R. L.); Jeff Symanski for his love and support; the Rubia board and volunteers; and all the Afghans and Americans who braved the messy entanglements in pursuit of something better.

**The Carpetbaggers of Kabul and
Other American-Afghan Entanglements**

CHAPTER 1

Introduction

"Afghanistan is one of those places in the world in which people who know the least make the most definitive statements about it," wrote Thomas J. Barfield in his history of Afghanistan (2010, 274).

If definitive statements are a measure of knowing the least about Afghanistan, this book humbly presents various complicated stories and analyses that are anything but definitive. Rather, we present complex, intricate aspects of everyday life in a geopolitical maelstrom. Each chapter offers empirically based and theoretically grounded examinations and analyses of geopolitics and development as seen through several examples of American-Afghan entanglements. These entanglements suggest the power and influence of the United States while illustrating the ways in which individuals and groups have charted alternative paths of interaction, intervention, and interpretation.

In order to situate these complexities, this chapter offers an overview of Afghanistan's geopolitical history and gender politics, followed by a discussion of various attempts to improve the lives of Afghan women by international activists, governments, and aid and development organizations. The geopolitical representations of Afghan women both before and after 9/11 are highlighted to explain how these "grand narratives" were formed through U.S. government leadership and mainstream media portrayals. Challenging these grand narratives serves as a central theme of this book.

Historical Overview of Gender Politics and Geopolitics in Afghanistan

Afghanistan's history as told by many Anglophone scholars regularly identifies this country as a small player, a buffer, or a rentier state—situating Afghanistan's position in international geopolitics as part of the larger plans of competing superpowers or empires (Maley 2009). Afghanistan's geographic location is often described as a place "in-between" other geopolitical pursuits, in the midst of or on the way to imperial conquest. Rory Stewart's popular nonfiction book *The Places in Between* (2006) uses quasi-historical accounts and personal travel narratives to discursively situate Afghanistan as sandwiched by empires. Afghanistan has also been represented as the "graveyard of empires," because successive imperial powers went into decline after failing to conquer it (Jones 2010).

These imperial histories of Afghanistan identify its internal politics as a result of tension between localized autonomous regions and the central government (Rubin 2002). The central government is considered the predominant negotiator between domestic and international politics, maintaining a weak hold on provinces outside the capital. British colonialists commonly used orientalist and racist phrases to describe people in the path of imperial conquest. Although the British Empire was unsuccessful in colonizing Afghanistan, it fought three wars there (1839–42, 1878–80, and 1919) and annexed a significant amount of land through various negotiations with Pashtun-Afghan leaders in the late nineteenth century (Barfield 2010; Fremont-Barnes 2009; Rubin 2002, 2015).[1] Afghanistan's physical landscape became part of a narrative fashioned by colonizers and imperialists, often described as a brutal and unrelenting geography.[2] Therefore, both people and location were imagined through the lens of conquest, which positioned Afghans as an unconquerable and unreliable "other" (Marsden and Hopkins 2011).

Colonial descriptions of Afghan people in the nineteenth century focused predominantly on men, while twentieth-century imperial geopolitics embraced another set of imaginary tales about Afghanistan's geography. This time, these tales included women. Successive Afghan governments and international interlopers have exploited particular *ideas of women* to forward various political agendas or to solidify governmental legitimacy (Zulfacar 2006). The patriarchal structures of Afghanistan's diverse societies place authority over women and mandate protection of them within families. These structures limit women's access to public space and separate them from the political affairs of men. Efforts to incorporate women as national subjects, subsequently under the authority and protection of the state, have often been perceived as challenging the authority and control of the patriarchal family. Throughout Afghanistan's contemporary history (1919–present), successive efforts to nationalize Afghan women have been met with suspicion and resistance from organized groups across Afghanistan. As such, there has been a distinct geographic component to governmental attempts to incorporate women into public and political life (Billaud 2015).

Many of the historical efforts to "liberate" Afghan women from patriarchal family structures have been experienced solely by urban and elite women. Afghan women's history across disparate socioeconomic, ethnic, linguistic, political, and geographic contexts underscores the diversity of women's experiences and how their access to changing social and political norms differs. As such, it is impossible to place Afghan women into a distinct and identifiable category (Mohanty 2004). As Maliha Zulfacar (2006, 27) states, "The term 'Afghan women' covers a multitude of traditions, ethnicities, tribal allegiances, regions, etc. The term as a socioeconomic entity is so broad as to be almost meaningless" (also see Ahmed-Ghosh 2013). Similar to many other countries, Afghanistan's citizenry encompasses not only a variety of ethnicities and languages but also a diverse system of thought, belief structures, socioeconomic classes, education levels, and experiences. Despite this diversity of Afghan women (and men), narrow representations of Afghan women as a distinct category—of suffering subjects in need of foreign saving—endure.

Over time many organizations and governments have used the idea of "protecting" or "saving" Afghan women in attempts to solidify political control. Over the last forty years, as Afghans have experienced various phases of political conflict, government overthrow, and international interventions, Afghan women have regularly been categorically positioned to articulate reform efforts or resist them. For example, when Afghan communists initiated a successful coup against the Afghan government in 1978, their reform platform addressed women by initiating compulsory education and raising the age of marriage. When the Soviet Union subsequently invaded Afghanistan in 1979, helping women was also part of its discursive representation of assistance (Centlivres-Demont 1994). The mujahedin rebels, fighting against the Soviet occupation, also sought to protect women—this time, from foreign and outside influences—claiming to preserve family and national honor. These U.S.-sponsored resistance fighters burned girls' schools and directly challenged the provisions toward women's rights and participation in public, political, and economic life outside the home (O. Roy 1990).[3]

Afghan women's bodies have been a continually shifting battleground. National and international interventions have attempted to disrupt the power of local patriarchal structures by nationalizing women (Edwards 2002). After the fall of the Soviet Union and subsequent fall of the Soviet-backed Afghan government, mujahedin groups fought each other in a bloody civil war from 1992 to 1996. During this era, women's bodies were both discursively and physically used as a war weapon that found expression in forced marriage, kidnapping, rape, and murder (Edwards 2002). In 1994 the Taliban, which had been organized in Afghan refugee camps in Pakistan, began to make political inroads into southern Afghanistan. Saving and preserving the honor of Afghan women would resonate as one of the most popular stories about how the Taliban gained support during their military surge in the mid-1990s. The most credible story told and retold about the Taliban's efforts to preserve the dignity and honor of Afghan women focused on the rescue of two girls who had been kidnapped and raped by local warlords, helping the Taliban to garner support and recruit soldiers (Rashid 2001, 25).[4] The Taliban's subsequent "protective" treatment of women (and girls) included barring them from work and school and prevent-

FIGURE 1.1. Woman wearing chadri/burqa. (Photo courtesy Rachel Lehr)

ing them from easily accessing public spaces. For example, women could only traverse public space accompanied by a close male relative, called a *mahram*, while wearing a *chadri*, a full-body veil with a mesh screen over the eyes known more often in the United States as a *burqa* (see figure 1.1). While Afghan women in some communities had worn the burqa/chadri earlier, it was not common for all women; the Taliban required all women to wear the garment in public.

The most recent attempt to nationalize Afghan women occurred in tandem with the October 7, 2001, U.S.-led invasion and occupation of Afghanistan. The U.S. geopolitical focus on Afghan women identified the burqa as an emblem of their oppression. This use of the chadri as a symbol of oppression was not new. Western European colonizers in the nineteenth and early twentieth centuries had already identified veiling practices in much of North Africa, the Middle East, and South Asia as a signifier of cultural difference and of women's localized subjugation. By focusing on cultural differences and identifying local forms of patriarchy as oppressive, colonizers were able to "other" the colonized.

Othering uses palatable symbols of difference and stereotypes focused on the strange rather than the familiar to represent people in foreign places (Said 1979). The veil thus became a symbol of tradition and religion, and colonizers sought removal of the veil as part of their colonizing efforts.

The objectified representation of Muslim veiling practices discounted its history and utility in various societies. El Guindi (1999), in her ethnographic review of the veil, explains the relationship between the veil, architecture, and privacy. "The *Mashrabiyya* (lattice woodwork screens and windows) in urban Arabesque architecture serve to guard families' and women's right to privacy—that is the right 'to see' but not 'be seen.' ... The *Mashrabiyya* embodies the essence of traditional notions of Arab privacy—who has the '*right to see whom*,' who has '*the right not to be seen by whom*,' and 'who chooses not to see whom.' ... In many ways veiling resembles a *mashrabiyya*; but whereas *mashrabiyya* is stationary, veiling is mobile, carrying women's privacy to public spaces. A woman carries 'her' privacy and sanctity with her, much the same way as when a Muslim worships in any space, converting it to sacred and private" (94–95; italics in original).

Several postcolonial modernist movements and regimes in the twentieth century continued to marginalize veiled women. Unveiling campaigns, forced and unforced, often in the name of modernization, occurred in Iran, under the Pahlavi regime (Kandiyoti 1991; Mabro 1991); in Turkey, under Mustafa Kemal, known as Ataturk, who also banned the fez (worn by men) (Mandel 2008); in tsarist Russia and later as part of the Soviet Union, under the Muslim modernist reformers Jadids (Khalid 2006); in Uzbekistan (Kamp 2008); and in Egypt (Kandiyoti 1991).

In Afghanistan, veiling and unveiling intersected with other aspects of modernization efforts and gender geopolitics in the early twentieth century. For example, a 1920s photograph of Afghanistan's Queen Soraya, unveiled and wearing a European-style dress, was used by conservative opposition leaders to discredit the authority of her husband, Afghan modernist monarch Amir Amanullah (Zulfacar 2006). In the 1950s and 1960s in Kabul, unveiled women were seen as a symbol of Afghanistan's burgeoning modernity. Local modernizers in a number of countries represented veiled women as a symbol of backwardness and oppression. Consequently, women's reveiling was integral to the transnational rise of countermodernity and pan-Islamic movements in South Asia, the Middle East, and North Africa in the 1970s and 1980s (Kandiyoti 1991).

Contemporary veiling remains a contentious issue for women living in some European states, as in the case of banning the veil from certain public places in France (Scott 2009). In 2004, when the French government banned religious symbols in public schools (including the headscarf or Muslim veil), women protested by attaching French flags to their headscarves and occupying public spaces (Silverstein 2004). By combining the headscarf and the national flag, they visually disrupted the assumed binary between French citizenship and religious identity (Lim and Fanghanel 2013).

In other places where veiling remains contentious, such as Turkey, veiling fashion challenges the association of veiling with women's oppression or seclusion. Veiling fashion combines corporeal piety with public displays of the body and consumer capitalism. Gökariksel and Secor (2009) argue that veiling fashion reveals a "sliding gap between the signifier (the veil) and its desired signification (Islamic womanhood)" (15). In other words, veiling fashion represents a physical, tangible, and palpable identifier of Muslim womanhood, while simultaneously countering inherent Islamic ideologies associated with veiling practices such as piety and concealment.

Other examples of the political economy of veiling include chador manufacturers in Iran. Several companies that manufacture the black cloth used to make chadors have lobbied the Iranian government to maintain compulsory dress codes for women since repeal of the law would undercut their businesses (Shaheed 2009). In this case there is an economic, rather than religious, incentive to ensure the enforcement of compulsory veiling.

In other instances, the veil has been used for various geopolitical and geoeconomic processes. For example, states' legislating of veiling/unveiling practices has been a method to control women's corporeal expression. Furthermore, the veil has become a site for capital production and consumption. Therefore, it is not the *veil* in and of itself that is problematic but rather how states and other power brokers use it for different political and economic purposes. Veiling choices should not be seen as a bodily marker of liberation or oppression (Moghadam 2002a). Rather, the enforcement of unveiling and veiling constitutes sociopolitical control over women's bodies. As Moghadam (2002a) argues, it is imperative to address and understand the more complicated aspects of culture, society, and politics that mitigate these decisions. Abu-Lughod (2013) views the concept of choice more critically, noting that for some "choice may not be the only litmus test for a worthy life" (18). Despite the diversity of experiences and choices associated with veiling practices, in many western spaces the Muslim veil endures as a symbol of oppression rather than liberation or choice. Various groups, organizations, and governments politically used the negative symbol of the chadri/burqa to garner support and assistance for Afghan women during the Taliban regime and after the U.S.-led invasion in 2001.

The Geopolitics of "Assisting" Afghan Women

Aspirations to help or assist women in Afghanistan during the Taliban era inspired extensive feminist activism globally. The Taliban regime restricted women's access to public space. Women were not allowed to work outside or leave their homes without the chadri/burqa and accompaniment by a mahram. Women were forbidden from seeing a male doctor and were barred from schools or any other form of education. Television, music, and other types of entertainment were also banned. Men were required to wear modest Afghan-style dress and grow long beards.

Yet, some Afghan individuals and organizations actively resisted the Taliban. The Revolutionary Association of the Women of Afghanistan (RAWA) was one such organization, which received significant notoriety in the United States prior to and immediately after 9/11.[5] RAWA, a radical political Afghan feminist organization founded in 1977, sought to connect to activists globally through use of the Internet in the late 1990s (Fluri 2006). The Internet was relatively new in Pakistan in the late 1990s, and RAWA members living in Pakistan seized on the opportunity to use this technology to seek financial and political assistance from individuals and groups living outside their geographic location. They eventually established a large, multinational support network (Fluri 2006). This network raised funds for RAWA and offered emotional and political support for the group's members.

RAWA's website and print publications highlighted the physical, political, and economic suffering experienced by Afghans in hopes of drawing international attention toward their cause and against the Taliban. The organization's website and extensive documentation of Taliban, mujahedin, and Soviet atrocities provided a complex portrait of oppression and political violence. Several supporters of RAWA and other U.S.-based feminist organizations demonstrated and lobbied the U.S. government in order to call attention to the plight of Afghan women and to end U.S. support of the Taliban. Supporters also put pressure on the U.S. oil company Unocal to abandon its negotiations with the Taliban to build a pipeline through Afghanistan.[6]

Celebrities and famous women's rights advocates in the United States, such as Jane Fonda, Mavis Leno, and Eve Ensler, also advocated on behalf of Afghan women. Celebrity involvement included public performances of unveiling. For example, Oprah Winfrey dramatically lifted the burqa off an Afghan woman during an event at Madison Square Garden in New York City to raise money and awareness for RAWA (Whitlock 2005).[7] The public unveiling of an Afghan woman by a U.S. female celebrity reinforced bias about the burqa as a symbol of oppression.

Several members of the U.S. Congress, such as Barbara Boxer (D-Calif.), Sam Brownback (R-Kans.), and Dana Rohrabacher (R-Calif.), enlisted the burqa-as-oppression symbolism to rally public support against the Taliban prior to 9/11 (Fluri 2008b). For example, in July 2000 at a congressional meeting on human rights abuses and the Taliban, Boxer, in response to a presentation about the Taliban, stated:

> I am a little disappointed in the testimony. When I see that you mentioned women and girls very rarely in these seven pages of testimony ... When a regime clamps

down on the majority of its population like it clamps down on women and girls, *and we can see from the Burqa*, the intent is to essentially make these people invisible, give them no recognition as human beings, I have to believe that our country should be very outspoken on this. Because *I think it helps us to rally public opinion against the Taliban, even more than all the things you talk about.*" (U.S. Senate Foreign Relations Committee 2000, emphasis ours; also quoted in Fluri 2008b, 147)[8]

As this quote suggests, the burqa was politically poised as a symbol of Afghan women's oppression and a method for rallying public opinion against the Taliban (Fluri 2008b). The burqa was identified as more oppressive than a headscarf, because by covering the face with a mesh screen over the eyes the wearer appeared depersonalized.

Although RAWA members saw the burqa/chadri as problematic, they used it as a practical tool of resistance in Afghanistan. For example, they concealed cameras and other forms of contraband (such as schoolbooks) under their burqas during the Taliban era. RAWA's utilization of the burqa/chadri offers a much more nuanced and complicated understanding of veiling and its utility in Afghanistan. For many Afghan women veiling was indeed an imposition, but not the only or primary component of the marginalization and abuse they experienced under the Taliban regime. In many other cases, women did not view or experience the chadri, in and of itself, as oppressive. Rather, it functioned as a banal, everyday practice for traversing public spaces. The use of the chadri as a symbol of oppression assumes that the experience of wearing the burqa is the same for *all* women. The symbolism of the burqa as oppressive is problematic because it collapses the complexities of Afghan women's experiences into this single, often misunderstood icon.[9]

RAWA's belief in democracy and secularism as a prerequisite for achieving women's rights helped them to secure connections with individuals outside the region. These international contacts offered political and financial support. As refugees in Pakistan, RAWA members had few opportunities to seek political redress. During the 1980s, RAWA's politics aligned with neither the Soviet-backed government nor the fundamentalist mujahedin resistance, relegating the group to an extrapolitical space without much popular support. After 9/11, RAWA was thrust briefly into the spotlight with the assistance of its network of international supporters.

Various international media outlets initially hailed RAWA's outspokenness and represented the group as a flagship feminist-political organization that actively resisted the Taliban. RAWA also received considerable attention from print media, in the form of four books published about the organization (Benard 2002; Brodsky 2003; Chavis 2004; Follain and Cristofari 2003). However, once RAWA members began to speak out against U.S. airstrikes, military occupation, and the misuse of international assistance and development funds, they were marginalized for their outspokenness. In Afghanistan, RAWA remains controversial and is often identified as having a "bad reputation" due to its political beliefs and radical feminist politics. This has prompted the organization to clandestinely focus on its sociopolitical work, such as running orphanages, schools, and literacy and income-generating projects for women.

In some respects RAWA's connection to its international supporters resonated with conventional liberal-feminist and activist expectations, while locally the organization's social and political ideas remain radical and marginalized. Despite being hailed for activism and resistance to the Taliban, RAWA's criticisms of the U.S.-led invasion and occupation of Afghanistan made it less geopolitically attractive in the United States. Popular support for RAWA waned because its criticisms did not fit into geopolitical expectations of the group's docility and willingness to accept international rescue. The construction of a "grand narrative" about Afghanistan and Afghan women grew out of post-9/11 geopolitics, which had been framed through political and mainstream media representations of Afghan women.

Developing a Post-9/11 Grand Narrative

Although there are multiple interpretations of Afghanistan post-9/11, a grand narrative has emerged as part of U.S. geopolitics. The following provides an overview of how the grand narrative of women's localized oppression and foreign saving/liberation was framed. The Bush administration co-opted Afghan and transnational feminist activism in order to strategically position "women" as part of the U.S. military and aid/development response (Hawthorne and Winter 2002; Hirschkind and Mahmood 2002; Hunt 2002). Because the burqa was effectively represented in U.S. media and politics as a symbol of Afghan women's oppression, women are seldom seen as making a legitimate choice when they wear the chadri/burqa. The simplistic binary representations of oppression and liberation in terms of being veiled or unveiled became solidified post-9/11. After the October 7, 2001 U.S.-led invasion of Afghanistan, Afghan women were subsumed into the United States' geopolitical discourse and linked to its military and political interventions in Afghanistan.

The Feminist Majority Foundation (FMF) took up the burqa's mesh screen as an emblem of solidarity by encouraging American women to wear a "swatch of mesh" as a symbol of the lost freedoms of Afghan women (Russo 2006, 571). These token gestures further institutionalized the burqa as an insignia of Afghan patriarchal oppression. The FMF had been working on the "Stop Gender Apartheid in Afghanistan" campaign since the late 1990s, and the group seized upon the post-9/11 "war on terror" as a political opportunity. FMF's post-9/11 focus on Afghanistan reaffirmed U.S. imperialism by positioning the organization within the geopolitical trope of "saving" Afghan women (Russo 2006). FMF incorporated orientalist and racist descriptions of Afghanistan and its people to further their cause. The FMF's president, Eleanor Smeal, helped to solidify the symbol of the burqa as oppressive by calling it a "shroud" during a presentation to the U.S. Congress (Fluri 2008b). As Ann Russo (2006) argues, "Afghan 'women and children' are made into spectacle by hypervisualizing their victimization by the Taliban; their plight serves as a justification for the heroic invasion, rescue and liberation by the U.S. military" (561).

Highlighting Afghan women's treatment under the Taliban helped to strategically position the United States as liberator rather than occupier. Several U.S. politicians supported this approach and sought to legislate for women's rights and to support development efforts focused on women. For example, on October 16, 2001, Congresswoman Caroline Maloney (D-N.Y.) wore a blue burqa on the House floor as a prop of political theater to request funds for Afghan women and to ensure that the U.S. military incorporate women into its protocols (House Session 2001). She was one of several women of the Congressional Women's Caucus to present on the behalf of Afghan women. Maloney's identification of the burqa as a shroud (similar to Smeal), combined with wearing the burqa on the House floor, reinforced its symbolic connection to Afghan women's oppression.

Identifying the burqa as a shroud suggests that the woman beneath it is a walking corpse. This form of discourse-laden necropolitics (Mbembé 2003) geographically positions women as non-living beings under the burqa. By contrast, suggesting liberation from the burqa is seen as necessary for an "actual" or "real" life. The link between the burqa and the living dead is exemplified in journalist Carlotta Gall's recent book, *The Wrong Enemy*, where she labels the burqa as turning women "into soulless beings" (Gall 2014, xi–xii). Associating the burqa with a shroud and the women wearing it as non-living beings provides a simplified political discourse. This simplification erases the complexities of its historical and contemporary uses to a narrow representation of despotism, misogyny, and death.

This framing of Afghan women further positioned the U.S. and coalition forces as their liberators, which became a discursive lightning rod against critiques of U.S. military strategy. For example, on October 31, 2001, U.S. Representative Cynthia A. McKinney (D-Ga.) critiqued the use of cluster bombs by the U.S. military in Afghanistan because these bombs were indistinguishable from food packages (the same color), which were being dropped simultaneously. In response, Representative Dana Rohrabacher (R-Calif.) stated:

> I think it is wonderful that we are dropping food packages.... The fact that we go out of our way to warn people that watch out, because there are some other things that are part of war machine that might be mistaken, it says something

good about us ... I would hope that the cluster bombs kills [sic] many Taliban leaders and Taliban soldiers as they possibly can. There is nothing we could do better for the people of Afghanistan than to kill as many Taliban soldiers who have been repressing them and murdering them as they have been. So let us—if it takes cluster bombs, that is fine. If it takes, you know, Samari [sic] swords, or pistols, I do not care what it is, let us get rid of these Taliban, *because they are Nazis, they are the Muslim Nazis, and all good Muslims of the world understand that.* . . . *Now, we have made a lot about women's rights today, and rightfully so, because obviously, the Taliban are to women what the Nazis were to Jews, but let us also recognize that the Taliban have been murderous and oppressive to everyone in Afghanistan.* (U.S. Congress 2001, emphasis ours)

Rohrabacher's remarks seem to suggest that aerial bombing, particularly cluster bombs, can distinguish between women and men, only bombing the Taliban. Rohrabacher's response to McKinney's critique further illustrates the ways in which invoking the "saving women" trope has been used to refute criticisms of U.S.-led military actions in Afghanistan.

Afghan women's liberation by way of U.S.-led interventions was further expressed through the Bush administration's incorporation of Afghan women's rights into its military, aid, and economic development interventions (Hunt 2002). U.S. President George W. Bush also attempted to offset anti-Muslim sentiments in various ways, including addressing women directly. For example, in an October 11, 2001 press conference, he stated: "I was struck by this, that in many cities, when Christian and Jewish women learned that Muslim women, *women of cover,* were afraid of going out of their homes alone, that they went shopping with them, that they showed true friendship and support, an act that shows the world the true nature of America" (Bush 2001b; emphasis ours). In this speech, Bush attempts to suggest a post-9/11 coming together of America through religious pluralism and descriptions of women. By identifying Muslim women as "women of cover," he assumes that all veiled women are Muslim and that all Muslim women veil—both of which are false representations. In this public speech he positions "friendship and support" as American values, and discursively reinforces the gendered stereotype that associates women with shopping. Later in the speech he urges the country to continue to reclaim daily life: "Now, the American people have got to go about their business. We cannot let the terrorists achieve the objective of frightening our Nation to the point where we don't—where we don't conduct business, where people don't shop. That's their intention" (Bush 2001b). This part of the speech is largely attributed to the popular belief that Bush told the country to "go shopping" in response to 9/11. The Bush administration's direct focus on Afghan women was further solidified in First Lady Laura Bush's radio address on November 17, 2001 (Bush 2001a). Laura Bush was the first first lady to give a presidential radio address, and in this address she identified U.S. military gains as liberating women. "Because of our recent military gains in much of Afghanistan, women are no longer imprisoned in their homes" (Bush 2001a). As stated in George Bush's document *The Global War on Terrorism, the First 100 Days*, "The First Lady led a worldwide initiative to highlight the Taliban's oppression of women which helped lead to the representation of women in the new interim government" (Bush 2001c).

Other examples of post-9/11 representations of Afghan women in U.S. media outlets included *National Geographic*'s search for the subject behind its ubiquitous image of the "Afghan Girl." The June 1985 cover of *National Geographic* illustrated the face of an Afghan girl whose bright green eyes stared directly into the camera lens. This image quickly became emblematic of U.S. efforts to support the mujahedin resistance against the Soviet Union, representing a "clean" and "bloodless"(Gallagher 2012, 71) framing of the war (Schwartz-DuPre 2010; Zeiger 2008). The "Afghan girl" image has been one of the most iconic *National Geographic* images, which has been reprinted regularly. The girl was anonymous because the white male photographer, Steve McCurry, who took her picture, asked neither her name nor her permission. However, this image catapulted McCurry from anonymity to notoriety and launched his successful career as a photographer. After 9/11, *National Geographic* sought to capitalize on the "newfound" U.S. attention directed toward Afghanistan by searching for and ultimately finding its "Afghan Girl" (Fluri 2014).

Another framing of Afghan women's liberation can be seen in the participation of Vida Samadzai as Miss Afghanistan in the 2003 Miss Earth Pageant. Samadzai was born in Afghanistan but raised in California. She participated in the international division of the Miss America Pageant in order to qualify as Miss Afghanistan for the Miss Earth Pageant. Although she did not win the Miss Earth Pageant, she received a special "Beauty for a Cause" award for "symbolizing the new found confidence, courage and spirit of today's women and representing victory of women's rights and various social, personal and religious struggles" (Armitage 2003). In this way the pageantry of the uncovered body represents corporeal modernity. This form of corporeal modernity is associated with national representation and corporate-driven ideals of femininity in order to market and sell beauty products (Cohen, Wilk, and Stoeltje 1996; Munshi 2001). While the participation in the pageant is presented as freedom, strict corporeal standards for inclusion are required. For example, contestants must be between the ages of eighteen and twenty-six, must never have married or have given birth, must be a minimum of 5 feet 8 inches tall, and must possess a proportionate body structure and facial beauty (Fluri 2009c, 250). This example reinforces the problematic assumption that the uncovered body is by definition a liberated one. The complexities of corporeal control and expectation associated with pageant participation (or one's "choice" to wear or not wear certain forms of clothing) should be critically examined alongside questions of choice associated with veiling.

In addition to pageantry, other corporeal alterations associated with "beauty" were transferred from the United States to Afghanistan. The "Beauty without Borders" program launched the Kabul Beauty School, which was sponsored by several beauty industry companies in the United States. The school taught Afghan female hairstylists how to perform modernity through hair, dress, and makeup. This project received significant media attention, including a documentary about its founding, articles in major newspapers and women's magazines, and a bestselling memoir by one of the U.S. hairstylists, which will be discussed more in chapter 4 (also see Fluri 2009c).

In 2003, rapper Lil' Kim appeared on the cover of *One World* magazine, wearing a sexualized burqa.[10] In this image her face is covered except for her eyes, which are digitally manipulated, reminiscent of the green color of *National Geographic*'s "Afghan girl." Her right arm secures the red burqa fabric that drapes over her left shoulder, revealing her body in a bikini-like garment that covers only half of her breasts. Her midsection is bare, while her left hand rests on her upper thigh in front of her genitalia. The use of the red burqa (the same color as the Afghan girl's scarf in *National Geographic*), colored eyes, and airbrushed sleek skin presents a re-representation of the burqa. Similarly, the veil was sexualized through postcards and other imagery during the height of western European colonialism in the Middle East and North Africa (Mabro 1991).

Other images of Afghan women have been used to reinforce the need for U.S.-led military and aid/development interventions in Afghanistan. This includes the 2010 cover of *Time* magazine, which displayed the face of Aesha, whose husband had abused her by cutting off part of her nose and ears. This cover image is accompanied by the caption, "What Happens If We Leave Afghanistan." The photographer, Jodi Bieber, won a 2010 World Press photo award for this image. Aesha's disfiguration and the violence perpetrated against her exemplify a horrific form of domestic violence, which was politically rescaled as a representation of Taliban justice and "tribal culture." Aesha was treated at a U.S. military hospital in Afghanistan, and eventually brought to the United States for reconstructive surgery. Aesha's story resonates as an emotional way to manipulate an intimate representation of violence against women in order to secure the need for continued military intervention.

Conversely, women in the United States who are severely injured as a result of domestic abuse, including fatalities, generally do not become cover-girl stories. The U.S. media outlets rarely, if ever, illustrate an image or story about a female U.S. citizen's beaten or mutilated body by her husband or boyfriend, especially if she is a woman of color (Tyner 2011). The abuse of women by their husbands or families in countries outside the United States thereby helps to reinforce domestic abuse as a crime that happens *there* rather than *here*, despite overwhelming evidence to the contrary (Butler 2006; Narayan 1997).[11] As these examples illustrate, the representations of Afghan women in the United States through mainstream media exemplify the veiled/unveiled and oppressed/liberated dichotomies. In an effort to challenge these binaries, this book seeks to interrogate the ways in which various international interlocutors have represented Afghan women.

During the Soviet occupation, civil war, and Taliban regime, Afghan women and men negotiated their lives under difficult circumstances and continued conflict. It is important to note that, prior to 9/11, Afghan activists and leaders sought assistance outside Afghanistan by appealing to the United States and other countries. In testimonies before the U.S. Congress in 2000, numerous appeals called for an arms embargo and diplomacy. These appeals identified bombings as exacerbating rather than halting extremist and militant activities in Afghanistan. Activists also highlighted the human rights abuses being committed by the Taliban as representative of neither Islam nor Afghan culture (U.S. Senate Foreign Relations Committee 2000). In addition to presidential and congressional framings of Afghan women and post-9/11 media representations, there was a plethora of popular books and novels about Afghanistan. Some of these books reinforced the grand narrative of localized oppression and foreign saving, while others attempted to provide a more complicated view of Afghanistan (Whitlock 2007).

Afghan men are often absent from these numerous representations of gendered suffering in Afghanistan. Afghan men have most often been represented as either abusive patriarchs or cautious allies (Mamdani 2004), while their victimhood is neither acknowledged nor given recognition. Afghan men have experienced abuse and public forms of corporal punishment including amputations, flogging, and executions. For example, RAWA's extensive documentation of Taliban atrocities included the now-infamous video of a burqa-clad woman, Zarmeena (who was accused of killing her husband), being executed by gunshot in a Kabul football stadium.[12] This video is part of a more extensive documentation project, which includes many videos and stills that portray the Taliban publicly executing men or amputating their limbs. A content analysis of RAWA's entire documentation archive revealed that the victims of corporeal abuses were predominantly men, with a ratio of five men to one woman.[13] Despite RAWA's attempts to publish their extensive documentation of Taliban atrocities, international media were not interested until after 9/11. Despite RAWA's extensive documentation of Taliban punishments, the most repeatedly screened video of Taliban abuse on international media outlets was the execution of Zarmeena. The video of Zarmeena's execution was repeated over and over again on several media outlets and in subsequent documentaries and fictional dramas about Afghanistan (also see Fahmy 2004; Stabile and Kumar 2005).

The repetition of this image helped to solidify it as typical rather than an inimitable representation of Taliban abuses. Most of the repetitive screenings of this video (such as being used as the opening scene in the film *Beyond Belief*, discussed in chapter 7) neither credit nor mention RAWA as the organization that filmed this execution. In addition, showing only a portion of this footage—

that of a woman being killed—renders absent and invisible the abundance of images and video footage of the vast numbers of Afghan men who were publicly executed or mutilated by the Taliban, also recorded by RAWA. RAWA used the footage of Zarmeena's execution to call attention to both Taliban atrocities and the illegitimacy of Taliban justice with regard to customary law and punishment in Afghanistan. According to Pashtunwali (Pashtun customary law), Zarmeena would not have been executed for killing her husband, because his family had already forgiven her. Thus, RAWA's political objective for circulating this documentation differed significantly from that of various international media outlets. While RAWA acknowledged and documented men as victims of Taliban violence, this was not included in the international framing of Taliban abuses.

Many Afghans celebrated the fall of the Taliban regime. However, situating the United States as liberator remains problematic due to U.S. contemporary and historical involvement in the country. The United States financially supported the mujahedin as a proxy to halt Soviet territorial expansion, which subsequently funded and perpetuated religious extremism in the region (Mamdani 2004). At the end of the cold war and fall of the Soviet-backed government, the mujahedin groups devolved into a bloody civil war (1992–96). The Taliban's rise to power included the support of the United States, which viewed them as a viable response to the "war-weary" people of Afghanistan. The United States also helped to bring back the civil war–era leaders after its 2001 invasion/occupation (Crews and Tarzi 2009). These leaders were known for using rape as a weapon of war and other human rights violations. They were also entangled in extensive translocal networks mitigated by divergent political influences, which positioned them at the intersection of modernization, military technologies, and international conflicts (Billaud 2015; Edwards 1996, 2002).

The many configurations of Afghanistan's diverse societies continue to be organized through patriarchal structures. However, U.S. representations of Afghan women's experiences of patriarchy do not situate them within the sociocultural and political contexts in which they live. Afghan women's oppression provided a geopolitical opportunity: it could be used to divert public attention away from historical interventions by the United States and the negative actions of Afghanistan's civil war–era leaders.

The poor, suffering, burqa-clad Afghan woman resonated as a predominant image/symbol of gender-based oppression in the early intervention period (Ayotte and Husain 2005; Fahmy 2004; Stabile and Kumar 2005). U.S.-led military, aid, and development interventions took up the mantra to "save" Afghan women both from the Taliban and "tribal culture." Therefore, the assumptions made about Afghan culture situate it as fixed and immutable rather than as diverse, fluid, and continually changing.

Effective methods for understanding the problems for women (and men) associated with the structures of patriarchy must incorporate a complex understanding of local communities in numerous diverse sites and situations.

Changes to existing systems and social structures are the prerogative of Afghans rather than internationals. Recognizing the multiplicity of experiences for men and women across various Afghan societies is vital in order to avoid reducing the experiences of *some* women as representative of *all* women in Afghanistan. The repeated images of burqa-clad women being abused in public, executed in the Kabul football stadium, or begging on the street illustrate specific portraits of some women in Afghanistan. They do not represent *all women* nor do they represent the entirety of women's experiences in Afghanistan.

Saba Mahmood's (2005) research on the women's mosque movement in Egypt offers an important empirical and theoretical critique of liberal ideals upon which much of Euro-American scholarship has been based. She critiques the prevailing definition of docility—"the abandonment of agency"—as argued by philosopher Michel Foucault. She invokes an alternative definition of docility, "the malleability required of someone in order for her to be instructed in a particular skill or knowledge" (Mahmood 2005, 29). She suggests that this form of docility, through Islamic instruction and learning, offers a place from which women articulate influence and authority. She argues that we must take pause and remain steadfastly critical when women's oppression in Muslim societies functions as a symbolic representation or threat to liberal and rights-based modes of thought and ideology.

Similarly, Abu-Lughod (2013) critiques the ways in which "saving Muslim women" has been taken up as a political mantra. Through several detailed ethnographies, she illustrates the complications of Muslim women's oppression, identifying its links to global economic inequalities. She asks why public discourses after 9/11 have focused on culture and religion in Afghanistan and other Muslim-majority countries as a reason for women's oppression rather than on history, politics, and economic policies.

The range of Afghan women's experiences, their knowledge, and their own ideas about change have rarely been taken into consideration; nor have these experiences become a starting point for social or political programs intended to assist women. The use of the term *gender* in aid/development often operates as a euphemism for *women*. Consequently, the role of men is unaccounted for, as are the interconnections between men and women in Afghanistan. Placing women into a singular category does not fully address the intersectional and integrated gender roles and relations within Afghanistan's diverse communities (also see Mohanty 2004; Narayan 1997). Zulfacar (2006) illustrates the counterbalances of gender politics over time in Afghanistan. Governments and organizations operating in Afghanistan have politicized the category of Afghan women to meet their own geopolitical goals (Billaud 2015).

The critique of geopolitical "saving" discourses does not refute that some Afghan women experience different forms of suffering and abuse. It is imperative to critically examine and challenge the ways in which the narrowly defined category of Afghan women has been projected. These projections do not reflect the ways in which Afghan women choose to identify or classify their own experiences, including experiences of abuse. For example, an Afghan woman may indeed object to several aspects of her life that cause her pain or suffering, while in other cases victimhood can be a form of agency for women (Grima 1992; Mills 2012). In some contexts the ability of women to brave suffering is seen as a form of power through social status. This power comes from enduring suffering and evoking the admiration of other women and men (Mills 2012). Therefore, there are many reasons for an Afghan woman to distance herself from certain social engineering projects associated with some development initiatives. Mainstream western sociocultural gender norms are not viewed by all as liberation. The ways in which Afghan society and personal lives are organized and experienced differ essentially from general sociocultural norms in the United States.

Although there are competing counternarratives by and about Afghan women, the "grand narrative" of local oppression and foreign saving predominated particularly in the immediate years following the October 7, 2001, U.S.-led invasion of Afghanistan. These discourses shaped not only a discursive geopolitics in the United States but also the provisioning of aid/development in Afghanistan through policy and program initiatives. The grand narratives about Afghan women have not remained solely within the realm of discourse but have manifested into the material practices of geo-economic development in Afghanistan.

Material Manifestations of Geopolitical Discourses

Many scholars attribute the post-9/11 missteps of aid and development in Afghanistan to the donor-driven approach, lack of coordination and collaboration among organizations, misunderstandings about gender roles and relations, and not recognizing the centrality of Islam to everyday life (Abirafeh 2005, 2009; Azarbaijani-Moghaddam 2004, 2007, 2009; Johnson and Leslie 2002; Kandiyoti 2007a, 2007b). When development programs are designed in Washington, D.C., or other foreign capitals with little or no local/recipient input, they often result in failed programs and neocolonial policies. Research on aid and development professionals has underscored the marginalization of ethnographic or anthropologic understandings of people and places within large development organizations, which are dominated by economists and economic ideologies producing flawed development programs (Mosse 2013). Development is often what happens *to* a community rather than *with* a community. Programs are designed to meet the needs of foreign investors or agendas set by donor governments or organizations. The patrons make decisions for their clients, as if to say—*we* know what you need, *we* know what is best for you (Lawson 2014; Peet and Hartwick 2015).

Development by design disempowers, naming the recipients as passive beneficiaries of assistance toward a "better life." However, empirical research has shown the development promise as often increasing poverty, disparities, and socioeconomic inequalities rather than alleviating them (Escobar 2011). So-called foreign experts regularly blame failures on locals' lack of capacity, rather than on the design and implementation of the project (Mitchell 2002). Recipients are expected to accept and be grateful for the aid while performing work designed by the donor. The skills and expertise of local populations, when they do not fit the development model, are either rendered invisible or identified as failures due to local inadequacies. What is often labeled "lack of capacity" does not take into consideration the vast forms of capacity inherent in local communities. Aid/development structures often miss local populations' various ways of making do (De Certeau 1984).

Assistance and development as extensions of geopolitics have become tools for demarcating the "ethically superior" from those associated with the dispossession of human rights (Abu-Lughod 2013). Humanitarian aid operates to theoretically reinforce rights-based claims while remaining constrained by the limited ability of organizations to actually orchestrate justice (Petchesky and Laurie 2007). Human rights concepts are often represented as undeniable and universal. However, careful study of human rights histories and discourses by several scholars reveals that these so-called universal claims are attentive to western European enlightenment, which favors individualism and autonomy—fitting neatly within capitalist economic structures (De Waal 1997; Forsythe 2005; Hancock 1989; Hunt 2007). These concepts often stand in contrast to the organization and functionality of family-based networks and relational community configurations that predominate in Afghanistan.

Overview of Chapters

This book examines the material effects of the geopolitical and mediated representations of U.S.-led geopolitics in Afghanistan during the period 2001–14. Through intimate portrayals of American-Afghan entanglements, this book details the ways in which the geopolitical "saving women" trope manifested into different forms of currency. Chapter 2, "The Carpetbaggers of Kabul," provides an overview of the international "scene" in Kabul, Afghanistan. This chapter explicates the extensive spatial and economic divisions between Afghans and the international assistance community. Specifically, chapter 2 highlights how security frames the ways in which aid and development have been provisioned and used to mitigate the interactions (or lack thereof) between international workers and Afghans. The extensive amount of funds circulating in Kabul from international donors included the creation of a temporally limited auxiliary economy that catered to the needs and desires of privileged international workers. This auxiliary economy is examined as part of the spatial milieu of the post–October 7, 2001, multibillion-dollar multinational mission in Afghanistan. The concept of gender currency is introduced in this chapter and more fully theorized in chapter 3.

Chapter 3, "Gender and Grief Currency," outlines the theoretical foundations for critically analyzing the corporeally contingent currency of gender and grief. This chapter engages with the philosophical concepts of bare life, legal exception, and potentiality (Agamben 1998, 1999, 2005), precarious life and grievability (Butler 2006, 2009), and societal spectacles (Debord 2009). These theories are put into conversation to illustrate how discursive representations of gendered corporeal vulnerability have manifested into different forms of currency for divergent geopolitical and economic opportunities. This chapter explicates the concept of gendered grief currency as a framework for the American-Afghan entanglements discussed in subsequent chapters.

Empirical examples of gender currency are provided in chapter 4, "'Conscientiously Chic': The Production and Consumption of Afghan Women's Liberation." Chapter 4 examines two case studies to illustrate how gender currency became embedded into material products for sale. This chapter highlights the ways in which women's bodies have become a site of both production and consumption by different organizations and individuals capitalizing on the geopolitics of saving Afghan women.

Chapter 5, "We Should Be Eating the Grant, but the Grant Eats Us," details the attempts by a small Afghan-run NGO in collaboration with U.S. volunteers (including Rachel) to form a community-based enterprise. The successes and failures of this project highlight the difficulties associated with privileging community and workers over markets and donors. The intimate entanglements and lack of professionalized development expertise in this venture offered opportunities to counter conventional development and capitalist modes of production, while simultaneously contending with continual economic challenges. By focusing on rural and nonelite Afghans, chapter 5 portrays how spatial and situational boundaries stymied the organization's attempts to seek and receive donor funding.

Chapter 6, "'Saving' Soraya," examines a project that sought to assist educated elite Afghan women through foreign exchange programs in the United States. This chapter offers Jennifer and Rachel's critical self-reflections and the challenges associated with gender currency and international assistance programs. Donna Haraway's (1988) concept of situated knowledges is discussed in this chapter by examining how conflicting knowledges can signal hierarchal relationships among transnational feminist activists on an intimate scale. Situated knowledges open up a space for understanding divergent forms of producing knowledge. The theater concept of the "fourth wall" is used to examine the invisible but often fiercely guarded border between differentiated knowledge claims, gender performativity, and disparate expectations for performing liberation.

Chapter 7, "'Our Hearts Break': 9/11 Deaths, Afghan Lives, and Intimate Intervention," examines two case studies to demonstrate the currency of 9/11 grief exchanged to raise funds toward assistance projects in Afghanistan. This chapter challenges Butler's (2006, 2009) discussion of the grievability of death by illustrating the ways in which Afghan aliveness represented by women and children's living-suffering became a grievable object in need of rescue. In other words, the representations and discussions of Afghan women and children's lives as worthy of "our" grief helped to situate them not as agents but rather as victims in need of rescue. This chapter analyzes assistance projects that sought personal interactions and connections with Afghans, based on common experiences of grief along with public representations of these projects through websites and documentary films. Although these projects challenged conventional forms of intervention, they were subsumed by geopolitical discourses and development agendas. This inquiry further elucidates the ways in which gender and grief manifested into currency, and how individual grief (for the loss of loved ones who died on 9/11) was framed as a form of U.S. nationalism.

The book concludes with chapter 8, "Gender Currency and the Development of Wealth," which provides critical reflections on the currency of gender and grief through the American-Afghan entanglements discussed throughout this book.

This book includes a glossary of Dari and Pashto words and academic terminology and acronyms. The transliteration convention in this book follows that used in the *Historical Dictionary of Afghanistan* (Adamec 2012).

CHAPTER 2

The Carpetbaggers of Kabul

> When there's blood on the streets, buy property.
>
> **MADELINE WHITE, PLAYED BY JODIE FOSTER, *INSIDE MAN***

> **Carpetbagger** An outsider; *especially*: a nonresident or new resident who seeks private gain from an area often by meddling in its business or politics.
>
> **MERRIAM-WEBSTER ONLINE DICTIONARY**

"When there's blood on the streets, buy property," is an infamous saying by the Baron de Rothschild, and stated by Jodie Foster's character in the film *Inside Man*, which details a successful bank robbery. In this robbery the only items stolen are the contents of an unmarked safety deposit box, which are the possession of the bank owner. In the film Jodie Foster's character, Madeline White, is recruited by the bank's owner to ensure that items in his safety deposit box will not be stolen during the enactment of the crime. The safety deposit box contains evidence of the bank owner's collusion with the Nazis during World War II in order to gain wealth and purchase the bank. Over the years since his war profiteering he tried to bury his secret through numerous philanthropic acts. In many respects this film offers an allegory for contemporary land grabbing and war profiteering masked as philanthropic-type assistance in Afghanistan. After the bombs stopped dropping in Afghanistan in October 2001, the CIA provided cash payments to former mujahedin to support the U.S.-led occupation. Many of these mujahedin leaders used that money to buy property in central Kabul. War profiteering in Afghanistan has included large contracting companies and private militaries, such as Halliburton and DynCorp, as well as smaller-scale individual entities that profit through real estate ventures, corruption, and development donor waste. Others used the geopolitical focus on Afghan women as a method for securing private profits or professional gain. This chapter provides an overview of both large- and small-scale carpetbagging in "postconflict" Kabul, Afghanistan.

After the dust settled from the October 7, 2001, U.S.-led invasion of Afghanistan, funds began to flow into the country from many different state-based and nongovernmental organizations (NGOs) tasked with providing humanitarian assistance, reconstruction, and economic development programs. The U.S. government has contributed $110 billion for aid and reconstruction (2002–15), along with funds from the other forty-nine nations involved in the NATO-led International Security Assistance Force (ISAF).[1] The intense flow of money to reconstruct the country was accompanied by the development of an auxiliary geo-economy that provided goods and services to international workers ("geo-economy" in the context discussed here refers to the spatial, temporal, and political study of economic resources). An outgrowth of well-funded international aid and development organizations led to the creation of businesses catering to their employees' needs, wants, and desires (Fluri 2009a; also see De Waal 1997). The auxiliary geo-economy includes many businesses seeking private gain under the guise of Afghanistan reconstruction.

This chapter describes the process of reconstructing the capital city, Kabul, and its spatial reorganization by international agencies and organizations. The disparate ways in which international workers and local-Afghans experienced aid and development economies in Kabul are central to this overview. International workers in Kabul encompass a diversity of individuals from various countries, working for foreign embassies, aid and development organizations, private businesses, contractors, private security firms, service sectors, and volunteer groups.

In an effort to signal the situational differences among international workers, the following terminology is used. "Privileged international workers" represents individuals working for international organizations earning salaries (approximately $15,000 to $35,000 per month), and/or individuals working in Afghanistan in an effort to secure future career opportunities in aid/development organizations or related fields such as security and logistics. "Regional-international workers" refers to individuals from neighboring countries working in positions related to the predominantly service-based sectors of the auxiliary aid/development economy. The term "expatriate Afghans" is used to designate those who emigrated to and became permanent residents (or citizens) of countries outside the region and have returned as part of the international aid and development effort. The term "local-Afghans" is used to represent Afghans who remained in Afghanistan or as temporary refugees in neighboring countries (such as Pakistan or Iran) during various phases of war and related conflicts. This terminology is admittedly an imprecise method to describe those who live and work in the conflict-development space of Kabul. Thus, more contextualization and diversity within these groups is provided throughout this chapter.

Overview of Reconstruction and Infrastructural Changes in Kabul

Since early 2002, Kabul has experienced massive amounts of building reconstruction, ranging from homes and businesses to large shopping malls. Many aspects of the city have improved; most schools have reopened, and many new schools have been founded. The population of Kabul has grown significantly with the increase of economic opportunities for Afghans. Returnees and internal migrants have established residences in the capital in hope of securing a better income. Privileged international workers occupy most of the expensive housing structures in central city areas, such as Wazir Akbar Khan and Shahr-e Naw, pejoratively referred to by some local-Afghans as *khorejiestan* (foreigner land) (see Dittman 2007; Suhrke 2007). Typical of other postconflict situations, international organizations pay much higher rents for prime real estate and therefore have created inflated prices for housing and office space. As one development worker casually observed, "The warlords own many of these properties, and they rent to the peace lords" (Fluri 2009a, 989; also see World Bank 2005). As identified above, the CIA offered cash payments to former mujahedin to assist with U.S. military operations against the Taliban. Some of this cash was used to purchase property when the market was at its lowest point in Kabul and other cities, and these properties are now rented at exorbitant rates to international organizations. Many Afghans formerly living in these areas of the city have relocated to less expensive outlying districts as a result. Local-Afghan-built and occupied housing increases each year on the mountainsides throughout Kabul. This land has not been demarcated or owned, and it remains outside the regulation of property rights that applies in the remainder of the city. These squatter settlements on the mountains are characterized by infrastructural difficulties, including a lack of potable water and inadequate sanitation. Raw sewage from latrines is emptied into the streets for lack of other options.[2] In some areas, these issues have improved under the purview of capitalist development. For example, water trucks regularly provide paid water services to residents of these communities.

Infrastructural changes to the capital city remain slow, marginal, and incomplete. The roads are a mix of paved, semipaved, and crumbling. During a research trip to Afghanistan in December 2012, an Afghan man aptly observed, as we passed a monument being constructed at one of the many traffic circles in Kabul, "They are spending about $35,000 on this monument. It is nice, but we really don't need monuments. The road to my house has been in the process of reconstruction for five years and it is still dirt and stone." Since our last field research trip (summer 2015) there were numerous nonworking traffic lights throughout the city, and staggering gridlocked traffic.[3] One bypass has been constructed, but it does little to offset congestion. Several major roads are closed to local traffic in response to car bombings, further exacerbating the traffic on major arteries in and out of the city center. Parts of the city, particularly near the U.S. embassy, can only be accessed by vehicles with permits to travel through the warrens of concrete barriers and multiple gates. Some passageways require repeated security checkpoints, with bomb-sniffing dogs and vehicle inspection mirrors. This inadequate infrastructure can be attributed to Afghan government corruption, ineffective coordination among donors, and extensive subcontracting from donor countries to for-profit private contractors.

Several of the so-called peace lords in Afghanistan have gained financially from economic structures associated with the continuation of conflict (Dittman 2007; Issa and Sardar 2007; JICA 2006). The use of international construction companies to build schools, offices, and other buildings has been marked by extensive subcontracting in Kabul and throughout Afghanistan, and this practice has not yielded positive results. Some of the funds allocated for reconstruction have been skimmed off the top, and this continues down the economic chain through different types of subcontracting.[4] Security concerns, whether real or manufactured, demand costly logistics and provisions and also curtail construction budgets. Funds are used for these expenses well before the purchase of materials and labor. Buildings have been constructed with intentionally diluted cement mix or without rebar, and roads have been paved with substandard materials that quickly deteriorate (Lister and Karaev 2004; Suhrke 2007).

By contrast, most privileged international workers enjoy more technological availability and relatively comfortable living conditions through the importation of material goods. These workers enjoy various creature comforts, along with regular access to clean and potable water, food, heat and air conditioning, and other conveniences.[5] The provision of municipal electricity in Kabul has increased in recent years, while the use of generators remains common within international offices and homes. Generators provide regular electricity, while their diesel engines have exponentially intensified air pollution in the city (Sediqi 2012; UNEP 2008). Privileged international workers enjoy the use of generators, private cars and drivers, and convenient residences at or near their places of employment, exemplifying their ability to live in Kabul without the same everyday difficulties experienced by most local-Afghans. These difficulties include limited or lack of potable water, intermittent or nonexistent electricity, extensively long commutes in gridlocked traffic on poorly reconstructed (or unreconstructed) roads, and rising prices for housing and other resources. A variety of governmental and nongovernmental organizations, as well as private-sector investment, have driven the priorities for construction in Afghanistan. Much of this process has not been coordinated and did not effectively include the local government, which has been fraught with corruption, low salaries, and high turnover (Sopko 2013).

Cosmo-Kabul

The international scene in Kabul is as diverse as the various individuals working within the city. Privileged international workers' salaries, combined with entrepreneurs seeking their disposable incomes, have developed a conflict-zone cosmopolitanism, which has shaped parts of Kabul into sites of globalized consumption.[6] For example, one can buy brand-name packaged goods at upscale markets catering to internationals, including Betty Crocker cake mix, Jif Peanut Butter, and Kraft Macaroni and Cheese.[7] An example of cosmopolitan consumption is exemplified in the following quote from a woman in 2008, who at the time operated a clothing store catering to privileged international workers: "It is much harder to meet the market demands here than in Paris or New York. The international community is filled with young people with too much money and time on their hands. They are bored and shop as an activity. We have to move inventory quickly and must always have new and emerging designs or they won't sell. Fashion gets stale quickly here."

Kabul's economic growth remains significantly dependent upon international donors. Aid and development includes reconstruction efforts and programs that seek to bolster the local-Afghan economy. Simultaneously, the auxiliary economy dependent on disposable incomes of international workers flourishes, providing avenues for consumptive forms of entertainment for internationals. This economy consists of temporally limited markets to meet the shopping wishes of privileged international workers. The businesses associated with the auxiliary geo-economy, in addition to logistics and security companies, include services, brothels, restaurants, hair and nail salons, gyms, spas, malls, shops, and food delivery. The auxiliary geo-economy is temporally limited because of its dependence on the excess incomes of privileged international workers. This temporary economy often undercuts the local economy and creates businesses and work opportunities for local-Afghans that are inextricably contingent on the livelihoods of international aid/development workers.

The economic benefits provided to many international workers aim to counterbalance the challenges of working in a conflict zone under security restrictions. Some organizations provide international employees with danger pay and/or post-differential (hardship) entitlements, which are based on perceived levels of danger and the presence of nonessential personnel. The U.S. government officials based in Afghanistan are eligible for both danger pay (35%) and post-differential entitlements (35%), as determined by the U.S. Department of State.[8] For example, a U.S. government employee or contractor who earns approximately $20,000 per month, with a 35 percent danger pay rate and a 35 percent post-differential entitlement, would receive an estimated additional

$14,000 per month. The value of work, time, and risk is quantified through these and other income structures. This system of quantification monetizes workers, placing a price tag on the value of their lives. Income incentives are one of the ways of rewarding "in country" employment.[9] Income disparity further highlights the economic divisions between privileged international workers and local-Afghans. Conflict-zone capitalism favors income and other economic incentives to entice internationals to work in places of relative insecurity, such as Kabul.

Local-Afghans working for international organizations earn a fractional amount when compared with their privileged international coworkers, while they receive much higher salaries than their contemporaries in government or NGOs (Dittman 2007). This difference in salaries is staggering, as exemplified by an aid worker from the United States who stated in frustration: "If the priority is local reconstruction and capacity building, why do they pay a local such low rates, $50–$100 per month, when an international comes in to do the same job and is paid $200 per hour?"[10]

Service workers from neighboring countries, such as India, Nepal, Pakistan, Tajikistan, and Uzbekistan, also come to Kabul for job opportunities. These regional workers obtain much different forms of work and salaries than other international workers in the auxiliary geo-economy. Entrepreneurs from regional countries open businesses that cater to or attempt to attract privileged internationals to spend their disposable income. For example, hairdressers have migrated from Tajikistan and Uzbekistan to Kabul on limited three-to-six-month visas to work in the service sector of the auxiliary geo-economy. They can make and save more money in Kabul than within their own respective countries.[11] Working in Kabul, an internationally mitigated and well-funded conflict zone, offers more economic opportunities. This signals a form of migration from the structural violence of economic inequalities at home to the economic "opportunities" associated with war-zone employment.

Not all international aid/development employees in Afghanistan receive high salaries. Income is largely dependent on the size and funding structure of respective organizations (see figure 2.1). Despite salary differences, workers (particularly from economically strong donor countries) retain various forms of social and economic currency within international spaces. Their facility with English, assumed capabilities, and access to the "international scene" ensure their value within this temporary geo-economy.

One example that encapsulates much of this international scene is the English-language magazine, *Afghan Scene*, founded in 2003 by two privileged international workers. The following is a description of the magazine from its 2014 Facebook page:

Afghan Scene Magazine is a monthly magazine focusing on culture, people and daily life in Afghanistan.

DESCRIPTION

An eclectic mix of commentary, gossip, excerpts, people, profiles, photos, history and reviews, Scene covers the diverse life of Afghanistan's growing expatriate, returnee and Afghan community.

Published monthly in full colour, it is the most popular English language magazine in Afghanistan, distributed widely across major NGO offices, guest houses, restaurants and businesses.

ASM provides essential information about what is going on in Afghanistan and in particular in the capital, Kabul.

info@afghanscene.com | editor@afghanscene.com[12]

This magazine presents tourist-style photographs and shorthand overviews of different communities in Afghanistan. There are also many articles by and about international civilian and military staff. The "Be Scene" section includes snapshots of privileged international workers' parties and images and vignettes about Afghan people or landscapes. Each issue advertises a plethora of restaurants, logistics and security companies, adventure tourism, and shops catering to internationals. The online version of the magazine includes suggestions

Population		
Privileged international workers (professional) Expatriate Afghans	Local-Afghans	International workers associated with the auxiliary economy in Kabul
Employment Options		
Aid/development organizations and NGOs (both faith- and non-faith-based) Embassies Private-sector organizations: private security, contractors, logistics, property management, war entrepreneurs	Property owner Driver Security guard Small business owner Office worker Service-sector employee Deminer Domestic laborer Day laborer	Security guard Small business owner Service-sector employee Sex worker
Type of Aid/Development Organization Based on Level of Financial Input		
Tier 1: Multimillion- to billion-dollar budgets with core and continuous funding		
Tier 2: Multithousand- to million-dollar projects/year without core funding		
Tier 3: Small-scale projects without core funding and with a significant use of international volunteers		

FIGURE 2.1. Overview of workers living in Kabul (2006–12).

for hotels, places to eat, and shops that accommodate privileged international workers and other expatriates.

Speaking English

The ability to speak English offers another opportunity for international privilege and economic access. Knowledge of the procedures for obtaining funding from or working within international organizations has become a necessity for many local-Afghans. The skills required to access the international donor community for a job or to attain funding often includes speaking, reading, and writing in English; computer and related office skills; and the ability to write proposals and project reports. With over fifty countries operating within military or civilian cohorts in Afghanistan, English dominates as the lingua franca of internationals. Local-Afghans who were educated in places where English was the language of instruction (such as refugees who attended English-language schools in Pakistan) have had an advantage due to their ability to communicate with international workers.[13] A command of English has become imperative for Afghans who wish to garner funds from international organizations. Individuals with English skills have more easily won various job opportunities, ranging from drivers to office workers and directors. Expatriate Afghans who had previously immigrated to English-speaking countries (such as the United States) have also seized opportunities requiring English-language skills. Many expatriate Afghans who have returned to Afghanistan earn international rather than local-Afghan salaries. In some cases this has exacerbated divisions between expatriate and local-Afghans.[14] Due to the demand placed on English skills, some local-Afghans focus on learning English rather than improving literacy in either their mother tongue and/or one of the two national languages, Dari and Pashto.

Many Afghans have also developed extensive family and nonfamilial networks that help them secure employment in various organizations (Monsutti 2006; Stigter and Monsutti 2005). In addition to networking and English-language skills, office and computer skills help to procure well-paid positions within international offices. Interviews with local-Afghan NGO employees revealed frustrations over the loss of good, well-trained staff. Once an employee gained skills, his/her employment opportunities increased, and he/she would often seek employment in international offices. This was generally met with a mix of understanding and frustration from local-Afghan organizations (Fluri 2012). On the one hand, local organizations did not blame individuals for wanting a higher salary; on the other hand, they could not compete with international organizations financially and had to deal with continual staff turnover. High turnover has limited the ability of local-Afghan-run and operated NGOs to improve the overall functioning of their organizations. This cycle created an internal brain drain of qualified workers in Afghan NGOs. From interview data it became clear that many local-Afghan NGOs expressed feeling like a de facto training center for international organizations without being compensated for this service.

Likewise, international organizations' institutional memory has mostly been vested in local staff. Most international workers are employed on temporally limited contracts. For many, spending a year or two working in Afghanistan conferred upward mobility in their careers. Working in a conflict zone was seen as a meaningful line item on their résumés, thus improving job prospects in the aid/development world. The following quotes from several international aid/development workers were obtained as part of research conducted in Afghanistan between 2006 and 2012 and illustrate how these sentiments were articulated.

> You have your standard UN types who do not engage with the country and society. They go to work, go to the guesthouse, and that is it. Maybe they are out occasionally in the international life but not with locals. But then there are the real hardcore workers. I was away for fifteen months and came back and saw some of the same people. They may be working for a different organization but they are still here. A lot of people who are committed to the country rather than to the job will jump from project to project because they like it here and/or are committed to seeing change happen here. The standard UN types are just here to put it on their résumé and build their career within the UN rather than make any kind of commitment to this place. For example, if you are here on a six-month contract, it takes the first three to get used to the place and then the next three you are preparing to leave. You can't count on people doing that kind of time here to get anything done. (Male Development Worker)

> You know, there are these gun bunnies that come here and see this as the "Wild West" because they can walk around with a gun and then they assume that this place is lawless and they can do whatever they want. This place [Kabul] draws an interesting array of people here. Those that really care, those trying to pad their resumes in the development game, and those that are here to be in the "Wild West." Many of these people know nothing about Afghan culture and don't want to know, and they don't want to rock the boat so they can get reassigned to their next development position. When I first got here, a person at USAID told me if I brought her a million-dollar proposal then we could talk, which is to say that they wanted quick impact. There is a lot of political pressure here and . . . lack of real understanding. Most of the development workers here care about their job, most don't care about Afghanistan. (Female Development Worker)

Many privileged international workers identified that "doing their time" in Afghanistan would help to ensure career mobility. They believed their willingness to work in an insecure place signaled a commitment and fortitude that would be rewarded by "better" aid or development posts in the future.

Security and Mobility

Life in privileged international compounds fosters a self-perpetuating sense of security inside the walls, and fears and limited experiences about what exists outside (Fluri 2011b). Personal security for privileged international workers has been a continual concern, increasing the cost of doing development, particularly for large and well-funded donor organizations. Security provisions include fortification of housing and office compounds with a high perimeter wall, laced with razor wire and surveillance cameras. Most Tier 1 and Tier 2 organizations (see figure 2.1) employ a staff of logistics and security personnel including drivers and armed guards. This type of bounded security protects individuals inside the walls, while preventing them from accessing people living outside the walls—particularly Afghans who do not work with or for international organizations.

Strict security protocols limit the mobility of privileged international employees, requiring those who leave a secured compound to be accompanied by a full security detail (i.e., armored vehicle and armed guards).[15] This deters many internationals from visiting the homes of their Afghan coworkers. For many Afghans, inviting internationals to one's home remains an important aspect of expressing hospitality to foreigners. However, Afghan homes do not meet the security parameters, and an armored convoy would draw unwanted attention to a local home that could compromise their security (such as being targets of the Taliban, other insurgents, or criminal violence).[16]

Privileged international workers mostly travel by air between locations within Afghanistan to avoid improvised explosive devices (IEDs), roadside bombs, and kidnapping. Flights within Afghanistan include commercial and chartered planes by large international organizations such as the United Nations (UN) and U.S. Embassy Air. Sometimes Afghans will also have access to these flights, which has become a sign of status among their contemporaries.[17]

Many privileged international workers have limited mobility locally, while their incomes and "attractive passports" allow them to easily leave and return to Afghanistan.[18] When security concerns increase or become problematic, local-Afghans cannot easily leave the country, particularly to destinations beyond the region, such as Europe and the United States.[19] Security and mobility opportunities differ significantly among international workers, expatriate Afghans, and local-Afghans. Generally, local-Afghans have more on-the-ground mobility within the country, while privileged internationals' mobility is contingent upon their security protocols.

Some privileged international employees with strict security protocols creatively violate or "work around" these restrictions. For example, some workers will manufacture a meeting in a particular location for personal rather than professional reasons. For people who work for organizations without security restrictions, there are local taxis that have become known among internationals for providing safe transport with English-speaking drivers.[20]

The U.S. embassy is a striking example of structural security in the form of a fortified compound that occupies two square city blocks, boasting one of the largest U.S. embassy compounds worldwide. Up to nine hundred people have lived in apartments and "hooches" (prefab container housing) built by U.S. contractors. This compound includes a bar (called the "Duck and Cover"), cafes, restaurants, convenience stores, dining halls, a dry cleaner, Pizza Hut, and multiple athletic facilities. Known by some as "Ameristan" (America-Land), much of the design and activities within this area derive from or are associated with life in the United States, complete with campuswide Wi-Fi and 110-voltage outlets. Some U.S. government employees have no need to leave this compound until they board their flight home. International workers with access to this compound (and other U.S. bases) are able to purchase wartime kitsch and souvenirs. For example, one can purchase an "Operation Enduring Freedom" coffee mug (see figure 2.2); or "Duck and Cover" souvenirs, such as a "Duck 'n' Cover" plush doll that, when squeezed, emits a siren sound and recites the standard alarm, "duck and cover get away from the windows" (see figure 2.3). Souvenir T-shirts, shot glasses, and postcards are also sold in this and similar compounds (see figure 2.4). Other examples include products developed by Creative Concepts Afghanistan, a company that produced items such as a T-shirt featuring the words "Kabul, Afghanistan 2009"; and another with an image of a margarita

FIGURE 2.2. Operation Enduring Freedom mug "Been There Done That!" (Photo courtesy Sarah Dennehy, Lizzie Drago, Carina Furino, Katelynn Hawes, Kyle Holden, Chad Howard, Katie Jerge, Thomas Morse, Melissa Pierce)

FIGURE 2.3. Duck and Cover plush toy. (Photo courtesy of Sarah Dennehy, Lizzie Drago, Carina Furino, Katelynn Hawes, Kyle Holden, Chad Howard, Katie Jerge, Thomas Morse, Melissa Pierce)

FIGURE 2.4. "Afghanistan Open for Business" postcard, sold widely in shops in Afghanistan. (Purchased by authors, origin of image unknown)

glass, complete with cocktail umbrella (the "ice cube" in the glass is shaped like a military tank). This image signifies the "party" atmosphere among many cosmopolitan and privileged international workers in this conflict zone. Shopping has become an aspect of conflict-cosmopolitan entertainment and a way to spend the excess incomes of many privileged international workers. The production and purchase of these souvenirs exemplify what Potts (2012) identifies as the "kitschification" of disaster. Kitsch distracts consumers from witnessing catastrophe; "the power of the souvenir" prepackages patriotism, nationalism, and catharsis (Potts 2012, 239). The provisioning of exclusive and cyclical markets for internationals living in secured compounds provided shopping as an activity, with souvenirs as a caricatural representation of the U.S.-led occupation and intervention.

These examples illustrate the integration of cosmopolitan consumption and security concerns. Much of this wartime kitsch attempts to satirize life in Kabul for internationals, operating as both a coping mechanism and a crass, cartoonish form of conflict-zone cosmopolitanism.

Various organizations have different methods for corporeal security. For most well-funded organizations (Tier 1 and 2; see figure 2.1) and embassies, security manifests through armored cars, walls, razor wire, and gates. Private security personnel or soldiers provide corporeal accompaniment as a layer of protection for international workers. In most instances, these provisions provide physical protection and signal military or security power. However, many Afghans view these fortified compounds and armored convoys as an expression of *fear* rather than *power*, and these structures are often the subject of ridicule. Most Afghan homes by and large do not have the same security provisions. Security is achieved through strategic networks based on family relationships and other alliances. Thus, armored compounds prompted several Afghans to ask, "What are they so afraid of?" and joke that the Russians were not so fearful. These are just some of the many ways that Afghans satirized the international presence, using humor as a method for coping with insecurity and uncertainty (also see Routledge 2010).

Dress has been another method used to express gender-based forms of security, which varies by location and personal beliefs. For example, the chadri signals corporeal privacy and one's connection to a larger network of family-based protections. Accompaniment by a mahram (a close male relative) provides an added layer of security through his corporeal protections of women. While we can certainly debate the corporeal vulnerability of a woman in a chadri compared to someone in body armor or a flak jacket, they both convey the expectation of bodily protection.[21]

Both international and local conceptualizations of security position men as threatening based solely on the possibility of violence associated with their gender. The chadri disrupts the male gaze and therefore the threat associated with potentially harmful male behavior (such as sexual harassment or abuse). In other cases, women and children can offer men a form of corporeal protection. Men traveling with women and children signal a lack of violence or threat to other persons. These men are not viewed as threatening to other local-Afghan men because they are acting as accompaniers and therefore not believed to be aggressors. Thus they are not viewed as threatening to internationals because the presence of women and children signals a similar decrease in the possibility of male-initiated violence.

Neither the chadri and mahram for Afghan women, nor the Kevlar vest and convoy for international workers, provide complete protection against various types of violence. Rather, these corporeal covers and forms of accompaniment exemplify distinct conceptualizations of security for different bodies traversing similar spaces in Kabul and throughout Afghanistan. In contrast to Kevlar, fortified compounds, and convoys, some internationals, particularly faith-based and small-scale organizations, view their relationship with the Afghan communities they serve (or work with) as their primary form of security. Afghan communities' positive perception of these international workers and their projects is essential for this form of community-based security. Dress, behavior, and accompaniment are central aspects of corporeal security in Afghanistan. However, these security accoutrements have been represented, experienced, and understood differently by a variety of individuals, families, groups, and institutions inhabiting Kabul and other spaces within Afghanistan.[22]

Private security/military and logistics companies, as part of the auxiliary geo-economy, rely on both the perception and experiences of insecurity. Private security services are more readily tendered by international organizations when insecurity or risk of insecurity remains elevated or inconclusive. Conversely, other businesses such as shops and restaurants that cater to privileged international workers have relied on the relative security expected in Kabul and the ability of workers to frequent their establishments. Kabul, during the early intervention period (2002–8), exemplified a spatial-security paradox as a de facto green zone. Internationals experienced a relative amount of security within Kabul, while a simultaneous sense of insecurity perpetuated the "need" for and hiring of private security companies.

Corporeal Expectations

The sartorial expectations of internationals have attempted to discipline local-Afghans. In many respects, local-Afghans curtail their dress to meet international expectations, both actual and perceived. Local-Afghan men identified the "need" to wear U.S. or European styles rather than Afghan clothes when working in or attempting to enter spaces controlled by international workers in Kabul.[23] Local-Afghan men further highlighted the importance of western-style clothes to improve their job opportunities within international offices or to increase their upward mobility within the international job sector. When they wore western-style clothing, Afghan men were more likely to receive entry to places restricted against local-Afghans and reserved for individuals with foreign passports. This was corroborated by several interviews and discussions with Afghan men, and also based on observations of men being barred entry to internationally controlled locations when wearing Afghan clothes. Those same men were later allowed entry to the same international offices or restaurants when they wore western-style clothing or if they were accompanied by a privileged international worker, who would vouch for them.

The dress of local-Afghan women has often been used as a method for judging the "progress" or development of Afghanistan. These assessments are expressed more subtly for women who wear clothing that communicates a careful negotiation between international and local expectations. Afghan men and women dressed in western-looking clothing, or accompanied by an international who would "vouch" for them, exemplify colonial-era forms of racism in the spatial configurations of places catering to or reserved for international (mainly privileged) workers.

A particular form of international corporeality that was coded in some cases by white skin color and in other cases by dress, language, and behavior illustrates a method for trading on whiteness (Faria and Mollett 2014). In this way, race and racial privilege are not merely read on the body but produced through encounters, repeated actions, and mundane practices of spatial inclusion and exclusion (Nayak 2006; Saldahna 2007; Sibley 1995). Whiteness signals privileged access to internationally controlled spaces (such as donor or contractor offices) or spaces serving international workers (such as restaurants). Dress provides a method for Afghans to perform whiteness in order to access these spaces. "Whiteness" refers to economic dominance among international workers, marked both by skin color and cosmopolitan performance. Thus, both sartorial and behavioral performances of whiteness provide privileged access to international spaces.

By contrast most international workers in Kabul, especially men, make slight or no clothing accommodations to meet local mores. Beyond clothing, certain behaviors of international women and men can make working for international organizations more challenging for local-Afghan women (and men) who view their behaviors as socially or morally suspect (Fluri 2011a). For example, the consumption of alcohol and extramarital sex among international workers often translated as a form of foreign cultural practice and behavior associated with specific political ideologies. Subsequently, extramarital sex and alcohol consumption when associated with political ideologies (such as democracy) caused many Afghans to link "foreign" cultural practices with political ideologies and view them with suspicion.

War Zone Entertainment

Most privileged international workers (when interviewed for this study) discussed feelings of enjoyment and adventure associated with their work in Kabul. Those who had previously worked in other war-impacted locations (such as Bosnia, Rwanda, or Iraq) identified being "addicted" to conflict zones and feeling more at home in these places than in their home countries. Their "addiction" was associated with the thrill they experienced living in a space of heightened security and the lack of oversight or laws governing their behavior. Others enjoyed the party scene, which reminded them of college. Some described international spaces within Afghanistan as akin to frat parties they attended while at university. When asked to compare working in Afghanistan with work experiences in other locations, many privileged international workers focused on the cosmopolitan aspects or lack thereof in other places. The following quote exemplifies the spatial or place-based comparisons discussed by some aid/development workers.

> Working in Afghanistan is slightly harder [than in other places]. The restrictions on mobility and dressing conservatively . . . , I want to ride my bike and not to worry about Afghans staring at me when I am in the pool. Liberia was more fun . . . there was music, people out singing and dancing . . . there was a beach and fish. It had a different energy, it was still dangerous, and there were riots . . . and security risk on a day-to-day basis. I could walk from my hotel to the office. But not here, and I can't walk at all . . . and I would not want to. Too much attention. (Female Development Worker)

Restaurants in Kabul that cater to internationals and serve alcohol have restricted entry to local-Afghans, indicated by a "Foreign Passport Only" sign at the entrance and monitoring by armed guards (see figure 2.5). Individuals "performing whiteness" were allowed entrance, while actual passports were rarely if ever checked. Other establishments would post signs stating, "We do not serve alcohol to Afghan Nationals." Performing whiteness through dress and other corporeal markers (i.e., western-style clothes, clean-shaven men, loosely draped or no headscarves on women) became a barometer for measuring which persons would be allowed to enter. Other establishments, such as "Chinese restaurants," were known as fronts for brothels soliciting male international workers.

FIGURE 2.5. "Foreign Passport Only" sign from an international restaurant in Kabul, Afghanistan, 2006. (Photo courtesy Jennifer L. Fluri)

Sex Workers, Sexual Harassment, and Abuse

International male interest in transactional sex predominantly occurs with sex workers who have been either trafficked or legally brought into Afghanistan from other countries. The distinct separation of international sex workers (mainly from China and Thailand) from Afghan sex workers is largely associated with international taboos against sexual relations between international men and local-Afghan women. These restrictions are partly due to the "saving Afghan women" trope that manifested into social and sexual barriers between international men and Afghan women. Furthermore, these types of relationships are prohibited due to strict adherence to local mores and fear of local males' retaliation. The following quotes exemplify international workers' descriptions of international sex workers in Kabul.

> There are Afghan prostitutes. It is just too hot [too dangerous] to use an Afghan prostitute. You don't know if she is going to tell someone that he tried to rape me or touch me. There are women who are interested in the foreigners because they will pay more money, but it's too risky for us. There's no such thing as expat-Afghan dating; only maybe Afghans coming back from the U.S. The people who tried have had a lot of problems and eventually had to leave the country. I know a man who had an affair with an Afghan woman and he was killed by her brother. Another guy, this Jordanian guy, he had an affair with an Afghan girl. Not an affair that he slept

with her. But he didn't know that friendship was also a taboo thing. He was confronted by police and he admitted it and was put in jail. The girl was also arrested. She is still in jail and he got out after a year. I saw him at the Lebanese restaurant. He lost like 30 kilos. That tells you something, for expats here it's an absolute no-no. You will get in big trouble. (Male Contractor)

Yeah, well, brothels were popping up like mushrooms until last year [2005]. There are some but no new ones. They mainly cater to the international community, only men. The military? Not that much because of their restriction on going out at night, not allowed to leave their bases except for certain things like going out on patrol. Although, I know that people, like contractors, help them to get off the base. (Male Contractor)

The main clientele is private security firms and rich Afghans. Who are the women? They are all Chinese, they come here officially, everything is arranged. There is a flight to Kabul from western China. They are official with visas and everything. The going price is $50–$150 per night. They are run by Chinese men, they call him a "tour operator." He flies in with the women and out and gets new ones. Not the same women all the time. They come on three- or six-month visas, and then they [the men] get fresh meat, if you will. They range in age from 22 to 35. They are under the cover of a Chinese restaurant. So it's a joke here, we say, "There is food here as well?" Under the umbrella of a Chinese restaurant, the brothels are nowhere and everywhere. (Male Private Security Officer)

Sex work is seen as one of the various "services" offered as part of the auxiliary geo-economy. Incongruously, while much of the rhetoric surrounding international interventions in Afghanistan includes "liberating" or "empowering" local women, sex work and human trafficking of nonlocal women abounds. Exploitation and sexual harassment of international women by international men has also been ubiquitous among privileged and regional international workers (Innocent 2011).

In addition to male international workers who paid for sex, most female international workers complained of sexual harassment from international male coworkers. Sexual abuse and harassment has become an expected aspect of international work in Afghanistan and other locations (Kent 2007; Vandenberg 2005). The spatial-sexual separation of Afghan women from international men is due in part to local protections for women and partly as an extension of the "saving Afghan women" geopolitical discourse, which has placed Afghan women as sexually "off-limits." The "saving women" trope and local mores (both actual and perceived) offer some measure of protection for Afghan women against sexual harassment or abuse by international men. Paradoxically the increase in sex work, sex trafficking, and sexual abuse is perceived by many organizations as an unintended yet predictable aspect of wartime entanglements.

The expectation of sex work also positions these workers as corporeal proxies to protect other women (both Afghan and international) from sexual harassment and abuse from international men. Several respondents discussed the "need" for sex workers as a method for decreasing or preventing the sexual abuse of female privileged international workers (Fluri 2011a). Because sex workers are seen with less legitimacy as international workers, their bodies are conceptualized as protection proxies for international women whose work is perceived as more legitimate. These conceptualizations and configurations of female sexual proxies divert attention away from holding privileged international men accountable for their sexually aggressive and abusive behavior. Interestingly, at the geopolitical scale Afghan male behavior is often cited as patriarchal and abusive to women. However, privileged female international workers cited the abusive and harassing behavior of male international workers rather than that of Afghan men.

Location, Location, Location?

The ability of privileged international workers to engage in extralegal activities without repercussions illustrates the unique configurations of "postconflict" spaces such as Kabul, metaphorically identified by Billaud (2015) as a carnival. Additionally, international development workers' opportunities are mainly tied to their assumed status as privileged, competent, and skilled. When a project fails or is not executed according to plan, a plethora of excuses are proffered that predominantly blame local-Afghans or conditions associated with insecurity.

Many international organizations require visual proof as a method for evaluating project implementation. This is largely accomplished through photographs of projects, often using cameras equipped with GPS coordinates and time stamps. In some cases these images provide a façade portrait of success. Increased security concerns often prevent on-the-ground monitoring and evaluation. Community-based participation in evaluations remains rare. Many Tier 1 and some Tier 2 organizations determine the success or failure of projects based on the quality of report metrics and the visual documentation of projects. The ability to "successfully" spend one's budget becomes a marker for measuring effectiveness. This has been casually referred to by some U.S. organizations as a "burn rate." The quicker one can "burn through" his/her budget, the higher the rate. Higher burn rates translate into successfully completed projects and a quicker path to promotion for privileged international workers. Since the 2008 formation of the office of the Special Investigator General for Afghanistan Reconstruction (SIGAR), there have been significant attempts to more fully account for U.S. spending, which includes a reevaluation of burn rate "success."

The predictability of aid/development fieldwork and monitoring is satirized in the "Field Visit Bingo" game (see figure 2.6).[24] This game strikingly illustrates some of the assumptions made about the commonality of places based on a

School building with your logo	A meeting under a tree	Drip irrigation kit with treadle pump	Project activity that didn't work because it rained too much/didn't rain enough	Housing made from materials stamped with UN or USAID logos
Beneficiary with smart-phone (bonus point: with any Apple product)	Poor attempt at local language prompts good-natured laughter	Community member who sits at the back of the group, says nothing, and glowers	White Toyota Land Cruiser	Obligatory courtesy-call to local chief/headman/colonel/district commissioner that lasts at least 30 painful minutes longer than scheduled
Slum/village with more satellite dishes than barefoot children	Water tank with your logo	Given the seat of honour at least three times in one day (**bonus point:** *offered choicest entrails at lunch*)	Irregular bowel movements	More NGO signs than local shopfronts
Tea with condensed milk, from a thermos flask	Beneficiary who speaks more languages than you do	Project achievement testimony that can be entirely explained by broader contextual changes	Someone with the same name as your grandmother	Introduced as "the person who paid for the project"
Traditional Birth Attendant	Translation into English that doesn't seem to match what was just said. Not even close.	Health centre with your logo	Offered food/drink by field staff, in front of community members (**bonus point:** *in a refugee camp*)	Beneficiary taking pictures of you
An ingenious use of an everyday item you'd never have thought of by yourself. Ever.	Government administration building with your logo	Nearly run over goat/cow/chicken/beneficiary child	Coca-cola	'Self-sustaining' community group asking you to extend project support
Local police/militia commander with uncomfortably close relationship with your staff	Something you'd be mortified to show your donor	Presented with a list of things the community expects you to provide	Bore-hole installed three years ago by your organization and no longer working	Local staff member throws litter from Land Cruiser while driving between communities, can't understand your distress
Beneficiary dressed better than you	Farmer demonstration plot ruined by flock of hungry goats and lack of fence (**bonus point:** *for third season running*)	Pit latrine	The words 'empowerment', 'sustainability', 'participation' or 'capacity-building' (**bonus point:** *used by a beneficiary*)	Community group claiming their success is entirely due to your organization, despite considerable signage to the contrary
Community-based organization whose actual function you can't describe in less than 15 words	Impromptu awkward speech to expectant community group	Sunburn on just one arm	Abandoned building with NGO logo on it (**bonus point:** *your logo*)	Suspiciously empty seed-bank/warehouse
Project activity delayed by dysfunctional administrative systems	More time spent in 4x4 than visiting projects	Poster in community space showing a stick figure defecating (**bonus point:** *accurately depicts diarrhoea/worms*)	Community user group unable to afford spare parts	Offer of marriage (**bonus point:** *expressed in terms of cattle*)

FIGURE 2.6. Field Visit Bingo. This open source, noncopyrighted "game" has appeared on several websites and blogs, such as *WanderLust: Notes from a Global Nomad*, *Afghan Scene*, and *Stuff Expat Aid Workers Like*.

lack of mechanization or "modern" resources, along with the haphazardness of development project implementation. Despite the spatial dissimilarity of places, many development experts compare places based on need or problem similarity (Kothari 2005). Subsequently, various locations are often provided with similar development projects, despite the significant diversity between places based on a number of sociopolitical, economic, and contextual factors. The unique geographies and specificities of place and their distinctions are erased, rarely recognized, or incorporated into projects or programs. This cookie-cutter development approach has become the norm. Many organizations are not able or, in some cases, unwilling to see or understand the distinctive qualities and unique attributes of different places and people. Much of aid/development procedures and methodologies take a neocolonial approach, attempting to make *them* like *us* (Duffield 2007; Mosse 2005). Economically driven development projects seek to enroll places and people into the global capitalist economy, albeit at the bottom rungs of this hierarchy as cheap and, at times, dispensable labor.

As in other places experiencing development in the midst of continued conflict, Afghanistan has its own unique relationship to assistance and development practices. In 2001, Kabul was marked by extensive destruction and disrepair from the devastation of the civil war and Taliban rule. Humanitarian need in Afghanistan was high, and many Afghan organizations and leaders had been advocating for international attention and assistance prior to 9/11 and the U.S.-led invasion on October 7, 2001. However, the U.S.-led international mission did not effectively incorporate local-Afghans' knowledge, existing capabilities, the impacts of war trauma, or diverse beliefs as an integrated part of reconstruction and aid/development assistance. Additionally, large donors and government agencies such as USAID used for-profit implementing partners and contractors to carry out their work (Roberts 2014). A lack of coordination and collaboration among the nearly three thousand governmental and nongovernmental organizations operating in Kabul at the height of development interventions has further contributed to shortfalls in outcomes and massive perpetration of fraud.

The vast amount of funds directed toward Afghanistan helped to produce widespread forms of both international and local corruption. Government ministers and the judiciary engaged in regular forms of bribery and extortion partly in response to low salaries and increased living costs (Katzman 2009).

Conclusion

This chapter has shown some of the ways international salaries are allocated and spent as part of the war economy. The Kabul economy has been both ancillary to and dependent upon the geo-economies of internationally funded conflict aid and development. These geo-economies have developed temporally limited and internationally contingent auxiliary economies. Kabul's auxiliary geo-economies have included cosmopolitan lifestyles marked by consumption of processed foods, alcohol and drug use, and sex. Differentiated constructions of gender, corporeality, and security demonstrate the multiple layers of co-existence demarcated by spatial inclusion and exclusion. Such constructions are intersected by gender and racial performances and mitigated by violence and perceptions of insecurity. The currency associated with skills for both local-Afghans and international workers has been a method for exchanging one opportunity for another, securing mobility, and in some cases generating material wealth. The following chapter reviews several political philosophies often used to analyze U.S. geopolitics, gender politics, and geo-economics in Afghanistan.

CHAPTER 3

Gender and Grief Currency

This chapter considers Judith Butler's (2006, 2009) theories on precarious life and grievability, together with Agamben's (1998, 1999, 2005) theories on sovereign exception, bare life, and potentiality and Debord's (2009) analysis of social spectacle. This chapter links these theories and situates them within several empirically based examples in order to illustrate the ways in which the gendering of grief, precarity, suffering, and geopolitical rescue have translated into different forms of currency.

Butler (2006, 2009) defines "precarious life" as one that is (1) dependent on others, (2) part of social life, and (3) including obligations toward others. Butler's theoretical discussion of precariousness and grief connects these concepts to the ways in which they were framed, visualized, and represented as part of the United States' post-9/11 responses. This framing included legitimizing international aid and development's claim over geographic spaces and people in Afghanistan under a larger umbrella, defined as "alleviating Afghan suffering." Development organizations were further tasked with cultivating Afghan potentiality toward a "modern" country in an image more recognizable to the United States and its allies. To conceptualize precarious life, Butler (2009) defines "grievability [as] a presupposition for a life that matters" (14). She links the value of life with whether or not a life, when it is extinguished, is mourned. When a person's death is not grievable, his/her former life has not been politically valued or counted. A death that is viewed as absent of grief can be used as political fodder rather than politically valued. The ability to extinguish life is interlinked with the framing of grievability and political value, suggesting that a grievable life is one that retains political value upon death. Lives that are not grievable within the U.S. context have little or no political value and therefore can be extinguished without public outcry or concern.

The United States as a sovereign state with legitimate control over the means of violence strengthens its sovereignty through violence that kills. Butler (2009) further explores the ways in which grief is identified and incorporated into the political framing of 9/11 and its aftermath. Framing, she argues, represents not only the intention but also the nonintentionality of operational power that demarcates how something—such as grief—is represented as "reality" (Butler 2009, 74). Thus, those in power, such as the president and first lady of the United States, have privileged access to the media and a significant and at times overarching role in shaping "reality" to meet particular political ideologies (Bligh, Kohles, and Meindl 2004a, 2004b). In addition to direct access to the media, state leadership under the banner of sovereignty has privileged access to and power over the means of violence.

Agamben (1998) in his discussion of state sovereignty suggests that the ability to kill or be killed is foundational to political life: "the first foundation of political life is a life that may be killed, which is politicized through its very capacity to be killed" (89). Agamben's examination of sovereignty suggests a binary framing between political life—a full, complete, and meaningful life—and natural life, the most basic form of physical aliveness. Agamben (1998) uses a Greek term, *zoë*, to identify the basic biological aspects of a person as "common to all living species" (1). Thus *zoë* represents the biological state of physical aliveness. In contrast, Agamben uses the term *bios* to represent a method of living properly and politically. In this dichotomous representation, *zoë* is the state of biological aliveness separate from access to or participation in political life. Agamben views the distinction between *zoë* and *bios* as a fracturing caused by the machinations of western politics: "Western politics has not succeeded in constructing the link between zoë and bios, between voice and language, that would have healed the fracture. Bare life remains included in politics in the form of the exception" (Agamben 1998, 11). Agamben uses the term "zone of indistinction" to identify the ephemeral separation of "political" life from "natural" life. Western politics attempts to separate but often conflates biological life and political life in the realm of legal exception. Exception signals the suspension of law and legal protections. This occurs when a government claims a "state of emergency" in order to suspend the constitution or laws that afford citizens certain protections from abuse by the government. Agamben further argues that the state of exception often becomes the rule and method for eroding civil liberties. The USA PATRIOT Act, formed after the 9/11 "state of emergency," has been identified as an example of the suspension of citizen rights through legal exception, which, until it is repealed, remains the political "norm" (Collins 2002; Evans 2001; Munster 2004).

When life is bare in Agamben's terms, and not grievable in Butler's terms, it rests in a precarious place of expendability, which can be argued to be a politically expendable life. Sovereignty for Agamben (1998) is the power to take life, thus determining which lives are worth living, expendable, or ancillary. Sovereignty can "untie" a person from political life. Agamben implies that the "untying" of political life produces *bare life*, "which dwells in a no man's land"—

the zone (or space) of indistinction (between life and death) (90). This method of political theorizing links sovereignty with the ability to legitimately express power through violent means. The ability to untie one from political life without extinguishing that life produces bare life as an ontological condition of modern politics. To untie or separate someone from the ability to control his/her own life suggests bare life, or the condition of biological life, controlled by others and without access to political recourse.

Contemporary political structures control individuals' biological needs, such as access to food, water, and shelter. People in spaces marked by extensive precarity, such as conflict zones, have been identified by scholars as examples of bare life. Bare life has been associated with conflict zones, particularly when modern political violence and development simultaneously mitigate death and limit access to the biological conditions for sustaining life. Critiques of the theory of bare life in conflict zones address how people survive outside of the structures of modern politics and development through multiple ways of being and accessing resources.

Gregory (2004) takes up Agamben's theories on sovereignty in his analysis of militarism in Afghanistan, Iraq, and Palestine. He defines Afghanistan within Agamben's *zone of indistinction*—where people (the Taliban, Al-Qaeda, refugees, and civilians) can be killed with impunity. Other political geographers have incorporated similar theoretical frameworks, which aggregate bodies into a macroscale analysis of geographic spaces (Elden 2013; Graham 2004). These analyses remain devoid of nuanced or qualitative understandings of space at an intimate scale. Therefore, microscale examinations of places embroiled in conflict, along with theories of violence, are necessary to challenge the suppositions made at a macroscale level. When civilian lives in places such as Afghanistan are discursively reduced to bare life, this signals a lack of recognition of these deaths, suggesting their deaths are not grievable (Butler 2006, 2009) and without political meaning or value (Hyndman 2007).

Deaths may be recognized as collateral by virtue of their otherness within the localized Afghan context of the U.S.-led occupation and receive no recognition as lives "worthy" of grief in the United States. However, those same deaths clearly matter and have been accounted for within the contexts, communities, and families who survive the intensity of these losses. Many critical scholars push against macroscale representations in an effort to question the state's legitimacy in deciding which deaths count as grievable and which are relegated to collateral (Fluri 2012; Hyndman 2007; Hyndman and De Alwis 2004; A. Roy 2002). Minca (2007) argues for new theorizing that does not accept bare life as the ontological condition of modernity.

Macroscale analyses of state-sponsored violence fall significantly short of a critical and embodied analysis that challenges the spatial confinement of bare life solely within a zone of indistinction. As Ong (2006) argues, "bare life does not dwell in a zone of indistinction, but it becomes, through the *interventions* of local communities, NGOs, and even corporations, shifted and recognized as various categories of *morally deserving humanity*" (24, emphasis ours). In this way she illustrates how the categorical placement of bare life is not fixed but rather a fluid and continual process that includes multiple actors. Dunn and Cons (2014) critique the concept of bare life by identifying refugee camps not as indistinct zones but rather as "sensitive spaces" (2). They demonstrate that concepts such as sovereign control, citizenship, territorial integrity, and identity are "untenable and unstable" in such spaces and subsequently undermine conventional "ideas of security and belonging" (Dunn and Cons 2014, 5). They refocus critical attention toward "aleatory sovereignty" as "rule by chance" to offer a more nuanced understanding of sensitive spaces, authority, power, and control. Thus, experiences of life in a conflict zone are far more complex, rich, full, and layered than macroscale geopolitics and analyses at this scale suggest.

Afghan deaths that do not resonate as grievable in the United States have been represented as expendable (by U.S. military strategists), while simultaneously operating as political currency. The use of civilian deaths as currency signals a shift in U.S. military strategy in Afghanistan from carpet bombing to counterinsurgency (COIN) (Qazi 2010). COIN was implemented in Afghanistan under the tutelage of General David Petraeus.[1] The COIN strategy was initiated in an effort to "win hearts and minds" based on similar strategies used in Vietnam, despite their well-documented failures (Qazi 2010). The COIN doctrine seeks to minimize civilian casualties to ensure military advantage. For example, the U.S. military's *Counterinsurgency Manual* identifies the concept of proportionality in reference to civilian injuries or death: "The principle of proportionality requires that the anticipated loss of life and damage to property incidental to attacks must not be excessive in relation to the concrete and direct military advantage expected to be gained . . . proportionality requires that the advantage gained by a military operation not be exceeded by the collateral harm" (Petraeus and Amos 2006, 7–6). Civilian deaths are therefore valued in relation to their ability to ensure military advantage; the political value of civilian deaths can be exchanged because it has geopolitical currency rather than recognition or grievability. The currency of civilian lives has also been incorporated into discursive attempts to discredit violence when it causes civilian causalties. The U.S.-led international forces, the Afghan government, and insurgents all point to civilian deaths when caused by their respective enemies in efforts to delegitimize these acts of violence.[2]

Civilian deaths, particularly those of women and children, have a geopolitical currency or exchange value, discursively invoked to invalidate certain acts of violence. In this way bare life ontologies are formed through geopolitical discourse rather than exemplifying the material conditions of everyday life. Afghans do not experience their lives as bare—even in the midst of conflict, uncertainty, and displacement. The ontological condition of their daily lives refuses to be categorized as "bare." This refusal is not a dramatic example of organized resistance but rather a banal expression of living under everyday conditions of protracted political violence. The dynamism of the everyday produces and reproduces political subjects despite biopolitical attempts to separate, exclude, and eliminate them through processes of legal exception and spatial indistinction.

Afghan deaths may remain anonymous and unrecognized within nationalized forms of grief and remembrance in the United States. In Afghanistan these deaths are integral to the processes of social reproduction that are "the fleshy, messy indeterminate stuff of everyday life" (Katz 2001, 710). The expected anonymity of Afghan civilian deaths in the United States, when qualified by invoking the gender and age of victims, extracts a modicum of grief for the purposes of geopolitical currency. Identifying women and children among the civilian dead (particularly when the enemy causes these deaths) presents the currency of these deaths through the assumed political innocence of the subjects, signaling grief. This grief is not meant for the actual loss of these particular lives but rather serves as geopolitical currency exchanged in an effort to contest the perpetrators of violence. Thus, a modicum of grief extracts political currency—in order to frame the enemy as *other* and their violence as illegitimate (also see Enloe 2000a, 2000b, 2004).

Mbembé (2003) argues that contemporary forms of colonial occupation occur through a "concatenation of multiple powers: disciplinary, biopolitical, and necropolitical" (29). His theorization of contemporary necropolitics critiques the maximum destruction brought forth by modern warfare and precarious forms of social existence. He argues that necropower operates as a platform for territorial and corporeal control, which blurs the lines "between resistance and suicide, sacrifice and redemption, martyrdom and freedom" (Mbembé 2003, 39). This blurring is indeed a condition of modern political conflict. Conflict development exemplifies an intersectional link between the living biopolitics of social engineering and the necropolitics of controlling death. The discursive reduction of Afghan civilians to bare life situates them as collateral damage at the macroscale of aerial bombings. In contrast, the COIN doctrine mitigates civilian deaths for military advantage. Within a development framework, civilians are placed in a state of gendered, grievable living-suffering and potentiality toward rescue. In other words, the objectified suffering of Afghan women and children intends to emotively stimulate sorrow for them. This catharsis has developed into various assistance programs. The humane response to alleviate suffering may be commendable, while the path of alleviation is fraught with the expectations of those "in charge" of alleviating suffering rather than of those victims who experience suffering. In this way, precariousness and vulnerability are the conditions upon which aid and development are enacted. Therefore, it is imperative to question the ways in which development structures privilege those enacting assistance rather than individuals (or groups) experiencing suffering.

Agamben's (1999) analysis of potentiality offers an instructive method for investigating how the material practices of rescue have been derived from contemporary aid/development discourses in Afghanistan. Agamben (1999) discusses Aristotle's definition of potentiality in two ways: (1) as a child whose potentiality requires him/her to "suffer an alteration (a becoming other) through learning" in order to gain knowledge; and (2) as an adult who possesses knowledge while remaining in a state of potentiality until he/she brings his/her knowledge into actuality (179). International development frameworks have discursively positioned their target populations in the child/learner state of potentiality. This framework requires a transformation in order for Afghan potentiality to be actualized. The international development worker's potentiality is subsequently actualized through his/her provision of knowledge and "expertise" (Kothari 2005).

Development programs attempt international interventions as both necessary and essential for actualizing the potentiality of Afghans. Correspondingly, many international workers frequently described adult Afghans as "children." Common phrases included "this country is being run by teenagers," "Afghans are like children and should be treated as such," and "it is difficult to do work here because the country is basically run by 13-year-olds." These quotes are representative of the many casual comments made about Afghans by privileged international workers. These sentiments resemble colonial discourses and reflect larger aid and development policies that are framed by paternalistic assistance structures (Peet and Hartwick 2015; Sheppard et al. 2009).

An oft-repeated mantra among international development workers is the need to build "Afghan capacity." "Capacity" is defined within a particular framework; therefore, most development workers have been unable or unwilling to see the existing capacities and capabilities of Afghans. Aid and subsequent development efforts seek to alleviate suffering and improve lives through the actualization of potentiality. By suggesting that Afghans lack capacity, sequestering them into a learner "childlike" status, these development workers discursively defined their own position as "expert."

When the state of learner potentiality is combined with precariousness, the gendered living-suffering of Afghans becomes objectified. Development potentiality, when situated within Butler's conceptualization of grievability, suggests multiple scales and sites of grief, which are put to work as part of U.S.-led geopolitical framings. In U.S. public discourse, grievable deaths are represented by those who died on 9/11 and Americans lost in the line of duty (both military and civilian). Engle (2007) argues that Afghan lives lost as a result of the U.S. response to 9/11 did not receive significant reporting at the individual scale because they were not recognized as "mournable losses" (70). There is a clear spatial and situational distinction in Afghan civilian casualties based on the gender and age of victims. These deaths when caused by U.S.-led coalition forces are not represented (in the United States) as mournable. However, Afghan civilian deaths when caused by the Taliban, Al-Qaeda, and other insurgent violence offer a form of political currency if "women and children" are among the dead.

Although Afghan deaths (particularly those caused by U.S.-led international forces) are not necessarily identified in the U.S. media lexicon as "grievable," Afghan *aliveness*—in a state of suffering or oppression, particularly those of women and children—remains grievable. Situating gendered living-suffering as grievable discursively reduces the subjects' full lives to a theoretical conception of bare life in need of rescue. This gendered qualification of the suffering subject manipulates an emotional response to rescue bare life. The framing of Afghan women and children's *aliveness as grievable* situates them as targets for rescue and development potentiality. Conversely, neither dead Afghan men nor their live bodies signal grievability or rescue but rather elimination, control, and sociopolitical engineering. This epistemologically frames development as a transformative process from Afghan precariousness and livable grief toward a life "worth living," which is also recognizable within a western-defined international development framework. Gendering the grievable as apolitical women and children morally situates them in the representative space upon which assistance and development are enacted.

Butler (2009) argues "there can be no sustained life without . . . sustaining conditions, and those conditions are both our political responsibility and the matter of our most vexed ethical decisions" (23). In Afghanistan, vulnerability and need are conditions that have been manipulated and capitalized upon by individuals and organizations for personal wealth and professional gain. Gregory (2004) suggests that "without sustained reconstruction of the Afghan economy, and without a concerted effort to establish the institutions of a genuinely civil society, the same matrix that supported the growth of al-Qaeda will reassert itself" (73). Gregory falls into the development as security trap critiqued by Duffield (2001). Duffield's research is of particular note because he details the overt ways in which USAID associates international development with strategic conflict prevention.

Development's promise and disciplinary framework manipulates precarious vulnerability as both a form of rescue and a preemptive strike against terrorism. It accomplishes this through reconstruction as well as by creating the conditions for future allies rather than adversaries (Duffield 2001, 2007; Essex 2013). Poverty, illiteracy, and underdevelopment are also framed as some of the underlying causes of terroristic violence. However, privilege and capital are rarely examined in relation to military, paramilitary, or terrorist violence. It is imperative to recognize that Al-Qaeda has been a well-funded organization and that Osama bin Laden was a privileged, wealthy individual among the Saudi elite.

The actions of Al-Qaeda and the United States target poor, disenfranchised, and uneducated individuals in ideological struggles to develop soldiers and "win hearts and minds." Thus, poverty itself is a currency that fuels the coffers of development and insurgency toward divergent forms of sociopolitical control. By examining the more intimate aid/development interactions associated with American-Afghan entanglements, a calculated representation of precariousness, grief, and suffering emerges.

This is not to suggest that reconstruction and relief efforts in Afghanistan are unnecessary or unimportant. Rather, this chapter underscores the need to critique the false link between aid and development as a military strategy. The line between providing aid/development and mitigating or preventing conflict is not clearly demarcated. Many organizations associated with peace and stability in Afghanistan have been integral to the perpetuation of militarized assistance and related violence (Fishstein and Wilder 2012; Wilder and Gordon 2009). There are multiple intersecting matrices between the institutions that promote peace building through aid and development and those that produce and profit from both state-driven and privately hired military violence (Goodhand 2006). The policies associated with "winning hearts and minds" and COIN view civilian lives and deaths as valuable currency for strategic operations. The concepts of value and the valuation of life at the macroscale of military, aid, and development geopolitics manipulate precarity and grievability through the machinations of violence and assistance.

Liberal political beliefs and theories on morality and the universality of human rights are replete with paradoxes of militarized aid/development (Slaughter 2007). Universal rights claims often miss out on the specificities of daily life in places that value relational rather than individual social configurations (Abu-Lughod 2013). Human rights discourses do not represent the "universal" but rather are based on a classification of individualism according to western ideologies that fit within rather than critique the inequities inherent in global capitalism (De Waal 1997; Forsythe 2005; Hancock 1989; Hunt 2007). In many respects, the geopolitical manipulation of human rights to secure militarized humanitarian intervention has become a currency—that can be exchanged—to produce new forms of wealth and power inequities through continued violence. As Joseph Slaughter (2007) argues: "We knew that the Taliban were a violent and repressive regime, especially toward women, but we did not acknowledge that fact until we needed a humanitarian rationale for prosecuting the so-called War on Terror in Afghanistan. More perversely, we Americans somehow manage collectively *not to know* that we are torturing (or outsourcing the torture of) 'enemy combatants'—a pseudo-legal designation that places the individual outside the realm of legal personality and rights—at Guantanamo Bay and elsewhere" (12). Efforts to alleviate humanitarian suffering have been complicated by the geopolitical representations of Afghan women's and children's aliveness as a grievable-object of suffering. The manipulation of this objectified framing exemplifies the crux of neocolonialism and humanitarian imperialism (Bricmont 2007).

The intimate grief-based entanglements discussed in chapter 7 demonstrate how personal emotion/affect has been scaled to meet nationalized remembrances of 9/11. Institutionalized remembrances helped to position the United States as a moral leader with the right to seek retributive justice. Similarly, the "saving women" trope has been used to support military action and militarized forms of aid and development. In order to contend with the representation of the Taliban and by extension Afghanistan as a site of terror, women and children were disaggregated from the population as innocent victims in need of saving and protection. The material practices of aid and development infused with geopolitical rescue discourses and myths required a spectacle that transferred Afghan women into a particular form of geopolitical and geo-economic currency. Because the United States discursively positioned itself as Afghan women's liberator, tales of freedom and opportunity had to follow and be framed accordingly.

The representational drama of Afghan women's transition from saved to liberated was illustrated through various mediated spectacles (see chapter 1). Debord's (2009) analysis in his *Society of the Spectacle* identifies the link between spectacle and commodity. He considers spectacle as "a social relationship between people that is mediated by images" (12). He continues: "The spectacle corresponds to the historical moment at which the commodity completes its colonization of social life . . . that world we see is the world of the commodity" (29). In this way Afghan women's liberation became commercialized through the material practices of assistance and development. As discussed in the next chapter, some elements of the auxiliary aid/development economy in Kabul capitalized on the currency associated with Afghan women's "foreign liberation" to market products made by Afghan women or sell stories about these women. Thus, the *representational value* associated with the appearance of assistance became a currency that could be exchanged.

Conclusion

Afghan women's objectified oppression and liberation, through the fetishization of foreign rescue, rendered their political and economic subjectivity into a commodity. Grewal (2003) argues that "consumer culture has a hand in producing political subjects and identities" (559). In this case, the manipulative reduction of political subjectivities to bare life and grievable aliveness produced Afghan women's living-suffering into a currency that has been both exchanged and consumed. The exchange value of this currency has also produced signifi-

FIGURE 3.1. U.S. geopolitical framings of gender and grief currency.

	Grievable	Not Grievable	Potentiality	Currency
United States	Deaths—victims of 9/11	Deaths—non–U.S. citizen victims of 9/11	*Learned-Potentiality* International development workers	Grief—9/11 surviving family members
Afghanistan	Aliveness: Afghan women and children's living-suffering	Afghan deaths	*Learner-Potentiality* Afghans	Afghan women and children Afghan civilian deaths caused by the "enemy"

cant material wealth for some privileged international workers, illustrating how the dramatic retelling of gendered suffering, saving, and salvation became embedded into commodities. These commodities have been exchanged by way of Afghan women's suffering/saving/salvation, which is sold to produce wealth for the foreign few on the backs of the impoverished many.

Figure 3.1 provides a visual matrix for illustrating how the taxonomies of grievability, potentiality, and currency are discursively framed through various representative lenses of U.S. geopolitics in Afghanistan. In the United States, 9/11 deaths were grievable, while Afghan civilian deaths were not grievable. However, Afghan civilian deaths caused by the Taliban or other insurgents retained geopolitical currency. The grievability of living-suffering as represented by Afghan women and children has been emotively manipulated toward geopolitical military saving and reduced to bare life in need of rescue. Development workers have been situated in a state of learned potentiality, while Afghan potentiality is positioned in the learner (childlike) state of potentiality. The combination of development potentiality and grievable living-suffering materializes into forms of gender currencies that have been exchanged in various ways. The following chapter provides examples of gender currency exchanged through the sale of commodities and representations of American-Afghan entanglements.

CHAPTER 4

"Conscientiously Chic"

The Production and Consumption of Afghan Women's Liberation

Chapter 3 discussed different political philosophies to illustrate how gender and grief have become a form of geopolitical and development currency. This chapter extends the concept of gender currency by examining different representations of Afghan women's suffering and "rescue" as a unit of social, political, or economic exchange. For example, hiring Afghan women has become a form of gender currency for many international organizations, who hire Afghan women or represent themselves as "assisting" Afghan women in order to secure grants and contracts from larger donor organizations. Special grants for aid/development programs that have focused on gender opened up opportunities for Afghan women and international gender specialists. Several organizations hired gender specialists to work on gender mainstreaming (Abirafeh 2009). Gender mainstreaming has become a development strategy for promoting gender equality and bringing gender issues into the mainstream of society (Jain 2005). The title of "gender specialist" identifies privileged international workers tasked with improving women's rights and gender relations in Afghanistan. However, most of these "gender specialists" had little or no background knowledge or understanding of Afghanistan's multivarious societies, cultures, gender norms, and relations.[1] Therefore, the contextual, spatial, and social aspects of gender were not properly or fully integrated into various programs (Abirafeh 2009).

Funds for Afghan women have remained minimal relative to the overall budgets and allocations for aid/development projects generally. The competition for limited funds has created conditions for both rivalries and collaboration among women's groups (Azarbaijani-Moghaddam 2006). Gender-specific funding also led to a backlash from men, which was exacerbated by a lack of jobs and educational opportunities, both actual and perceived (Abirafeh 2009). Social changes to existing gender roles, rooted in outside influences, have been easily targeted as foreign and consequently negative. Simultaneously, jobs for Afghan women within international offices have been coveted because of the substantially higher salaries these jobs offered compared to similar positions within local-

Afghan-run organizations. In 2014 questions were raised about the effectiveness of women-focused programs from the office of the U.S. Special Investigator General for Afghanistan Reconstruction (SIGAR). The 2014 SIGAR report questioned the ability of programming to achieve its stated goals in Afghanistan.

> State and USAID contend that their existing planning, budgeting, monitoring, and reporting mechanisms provide sufficient information for tracking the number and funding of projects, programs, and initiatives that, either wholly or in part, support Afghan women. However, over the course of the audit, State and USAID could not identify the full extent of their programming and funding for women. As we note in the report, USAID could not determine how much of the $849 million it reported spending on the 15 programs that specifically supported Afghan women in fiscal year 2011 through fiscal year 2013. USAID subsequently reported that it disbursed $1.3 billion to 30 programs that specifically supported, or had a component that specifically supported, Afghan women in fiscal year 2011 through fiscal year 2013. These reporting discrepancies suggest that existing mechanisms for tracking spending on women's initiatives in Afghanistan are insufficient to show whether initiatives funded by State and USAID are responsible for improvements in the lives of Afghan women. (Sopko 2014, 14–15)

This example underscores the differences between the discourses of saving or assisting Afghan women and the material practices of development distributions, which have been mired in wasteful spending and undocumented resource allocations. Much of the international assistance for Afghan women attempted to incorporate laborers within a global capitalist and neoliberal economic framework. Subsequently, local-Afghan feminisms or methods that local-Afghan women use to influence and create spaces for authority within existing social structures have received less funding from international donors (Kandiyoti 2005). The majority of international aid and development funding has focused on transforming Afghan women into "liberated" economic subjects, despite the limited and often low-wage labor experienced by nonelite women workers.

For example, widows often occupy the lower end of the socioeconomic strata, while international aid/development workers frequently glorify their work as "resistance" and highlight their unaccompanied mobility in public space as "liberation." While widows may have more mobility in public space, this often comes in tandem with a loss of protections and resources expected of a husband. The attention to widows' mobility and their work in paid employment outside the home exemplify what Abu-Lughod (1990) has identified as "romancing resistance." This romanticizing obscures the social difficulties experienced by these widows and the vulnerabilities associated with mobility, low-wage employment, and the reduction or loss of familial protections or safety nets. As Anila Daulatzai's (2006) ethnographic research on widow-run bakeries in Kabul argues:

> The celebration of the alleged feminist resistance of the widows at the bakery implies that the most salient forces which women in Afghanistan would want to oppose are Afghan men, and traditional social structures and institutions. In maintaining such perceptions, international aid institutions are pitting widows against Afghan men or a misogynistic, patriarchal cultural environment, and are thus glossing over the possibility that their own presence in the lives of Afghan widows (as well as women in general, and men and society at large, for that matter) could be experienced as that of a force that needs to be negotiated, and might be opposed. (302)

International representations of Afghan women's labor as resistance (or liberation) camouflage the precariousness of low-wage labor, and Afghan women's own interpretations of their experiences as widows and workers. Daulatzai's research identifies that the widows in the bakeries do not view themselves as trailblazing resisters to patriarchy. They identify their work as necessary for survival rather than as a liberal-feminist affront to local patriarchy. In fact, the widows were upset and concerned about the ways in which they were being represented by internationals. These widows asked: If they were so-called heroines of Afghanistan, why were they not given higher wages and better work conditions from the organizations that lauded them? In addition to the misrepresentations of Afghan women workers in the widows' bakery, other privileged international workers have sought to capitalize on the currency of saving/liberating Afghan women.

Women's Liberation and Labor Currency

Various private and for-profit businesses as part of the auxiliary aid/development economy sought to capitalize on the currency of Afghan women. For example, a flurry of boutique clothing design companies initiated activities in Kabul in the early international intervention period (2002–6). These companies hired Afghan women to produce clothing and materials, which were marketed first to privileged international workers in Afghanistan and then to niche markets in the United States and Europe. As discussed in chapter 2, the term "privileged international workers" refers to individuals working for international organizations and earning salaries (approximately $15,000 to $35,000 per month) and/or individuals working in Afghanistan in an effort to secure future career opportunities in aid/development organizations or related fields such as security and logistics.

Some of the boutique clothing businesses claimed to offer basic education to seamstresses and pay what they identified as a fair wage, fashioning themselves as socially responsible enterprises. Much of the discourse surrounding these forms of social enterprise resonates with similar ideas that champion low-wage factory work as acceptable when unemployment or subsistence poverty is the alternative. For example, *New York Times* columnist Nicholas Kristof (2009) has expressed his belief that sweatshops, although not ideal, provide opportunities and help to lift people out of subsistence poverty. This mode of thinking is dangerous because it situates sweatshops and similar forms of low-wage labor within a hierarchal struggle, suggesting that poverty can be alleviated rather than perpetuated by market-driven capitalism. This method of analysis glosses over (or actively renders invisible) the structural violence inherent in capitalism. The capitalist structural violence refers to the ways in which low-wage labor is extracted from people living in places of endemic poverty and desperation, in order to keep costs low and profits high.

Desperation becomes the fertile ground upon which less egregious forms of exploitation or cyclical low-wage employment are made. This type of logic fuels exploitative practices, which can be easily retooled as both "better than what exists" or a path to "liberation" (for additional critiques see Alcoff 1991; Oyěwùmí 1997; and Wilson 2011). In situations of economic deprivation, a low-wage job may indeed seem like an attractive or better option than other types of labor or unemployment. The danger of this mode of thinking is that it helps to perpetuate the myth that low-wage, long-hour, and unregulated factory work increases opportunities for laborers who are "lucky" to have this job. This assumption ignores the historical economic factors that have led to poverty in these locations. It also sidelines the role of low-wage labor within neoliberal capitalist economic structures, which demand and rely on poverty to produce new forms of wealth.

Conflict-zone aid/development projects in Afghanistan enter into locations of extreme need or deprivation in order to provide assistance, which also: (1) produces new forms of wealth for internationals and a small number of Afghans; (2) provides assistance to individuals who are in situations of humanitarian privation because of geopolitical violence; and (3) creates conflict development, which re-enrolls Afghans into a new system of economic inequality and insecurity. Because the products of Afghan women's labor (such as textiles) cannot compete internationally with the cost and quality of goods produced in mechanized factories in other countries (such as China), many organizations rely on donor subsidies to keep sale prices artificially low; the products then are often sold in niche "fair trade" markets. Alternatively, better-quality products are sold in limited luxury markets.

Additionally, the gendering of desperation, as discussed in books such as *Half the Sky* by Nicholas Kristof and Sheryl WuDunn (2009), geographically situates suffering and oppression as something that happens elsewhere in places outside of the United States and Europe. Abu-Lughod (2013) provides a poignant critique of geographic stereotyping in Kristof and WuDunn's book. She points out that while this book catalogues the abuses experienced by women and girls across the globe, it does not include extensive coverage of gender-based violence in the United States or Europe.

As discussed in chapter 2, the "saving women" trope has positioned Afghan women in a protected category by way of geopolitical discourse, while various forms of gender-based harassment, exploitation, and abuse among international workers abound. Much of the poverty that exists in Afghanistan is a direct result of multiple decades of international intervention, geopolitics, and conflict. This has been further buttressed by corruption, warlordism, and despotism among the Afghanistan governmental leadership (Rashid 2008; Rubin 2015). Entrenched poverty and political conflict combined with the geopolitical attention focused on women translates Afghan women's low-wage labor into liberation and opportunity rather than exploitation.

Individuals in situations of economic need may take jobs for low wages, particularly when faced with limited or no alternative options. The belief that this is a reasonable alternative discursively produces conditions for continued and cyclical poverty. Roy (2010) identifies how the contemporary concept of "ethical economics" has become foundational for reconceptualizing poverty as a site of potential entrepreneurship. Her research shows how waged labor has manifested into a form of servitude that positions wages as charity. Roy (2010) argues, "Wage-earning labor is presented as servitude and wages as charity. It is in this way that the poor are folded into the structure of microfinance—not as laboring bodies but rather as moral subjects, as either bootstrapping entrepreneurs or as lazy encroachers" (Roy 2010, 193). Global capital economic systems rely on low-wage labor in places of economic need, in order to enable consumption in places of relative wealth. In the case of Afghanistan, conventional forms of low-wage labor have been refashioned as "opportunity, liberation, and freedom" for Afghan women.

In addition to the re-representation of work as liberation, grievable living-suffering combined with geopolitical rescue has manifested into Afghan women's labor packaged as liberation and a currency that is exchanged by way of effective marketing. Organizations have used the geopolitically driven currency of Afghan women's labor-liberation as a marketing tool to draw consumers toward the product of women's labor as a form of liberation that can be purchased. This avoids the conundrum of assistance by way of enrolling women into low-wage labor. In these marketing scenarios one does not merely purchase a handbag, scarf, or shirt made in Afghanistan; one buys the tale of a woman in the process of being liberated. Through the act of consumption, customers enjoy a "feel good" moment associated with their virtual participation in the alleviation of an Afghan woman's suffering toward economic liberation (see Richey and Ponte 2011). Low-wage labor is veiled by the currency of assisting/liberating Afghan women, and this "liberation" is discursively embedded into the product for sale.

There is a corresponding and manipulative use of geographic scale (Herod and Wright 2002) in this and other scenarios that link consumption with assistance. The currency of Afghan women is connected to the international scale and to the strong and unrelenting discourses associated with the U.S.-led military/aid/development mission. Much of this discourse was borrowed or stolen from Afghan and international feminist attempts prior to 9/11 to draw attention to the plight of Afghan women under the Taliban regime (Hawthorne and Winter 2002; Hirschkind and Mahmood 2002; Hunt 2002). It also borrows from liberal capitalist/feminist attempts to secure gender equality through gender parity, which assumes that economic opportunity is the best (or only) path to progress. These economic frameworks rely on capitalist belief structures and ignore the specificities and complexities of place, people, and belief. The international intervener becomes the primary voice and authority on local suffering and its alleviation (Kothari 2005). Marketing campaigns present a neat, clean, and camera-ready portrait of the privileged international worker's benevolent entanglements with Afghan women. This positions the privileged international worker as a spokesperson for Afghan women's suffering and rescue.

Conscientious Consumption and the Development of Privileged International Wealth

The company Tarsian and Blinkley (T&B) represents itself as a form of social entrepreneurship where "profit and social responsibility merge."[2] This organization's website defines the company as a "not very profitable, for profit" business, that creates "conscientiously chic" clothing. While the business model for this organization neither alters nor radically reconceptualizes existing income inequalities from labor-to-consumer, it discursively positions itself as a social enterprise by virtue of hiring Afghan women.[3]

In the case of T&B (and similar organizations), the currency of Afghan women's "liberation" becomes a particular form of branding and niche marketing. The various magazine articles and advertisements for the T&B clothing line identify it as both chic and ethically conscious, "the feel good purchase." Simultaneously highlighted is the "need" to design clothes to meet consumer demands in a highly competitive fashion industry, as exemplified in the following quotes:

1. "Fashion is brutal; no one is going to care about Afghans," she says. "The difficulty will be the marketing." Which is why her latest collection is intentionally "hip and young and sexy. 'It has little surprises,' she says, 'a

thin crocheted line of midnight blue, two fingers of sequins, and richer, stronger colors. I don't think my mother will be wearing it.' . . . She describes the designs as a mix of casual and feminine, 'East meets West,' 'girliness in a war zone.'" (Gall 2004)
2. "Earthily gorgeous, and the crochet on top is teasingly sexy. Plus, it's made by Afghan women for a company that pays them fair wages." (Lucky Life 2005)
3. "Sarah Takesh, Clothing Entrepreneur, Kabul, Afghanistan. Collaborating with Afghan Women to Produce Gorgeous Designs, Wages, and a Taste of Liberty." (Takesh 2005)
4. "Says Takesh, whose pieces have been featured in In Style and are sold on-line: 'The world doesn't need just another clothing label. Families are eating because I'm here.'" (Brooks 2006)

The first quote is from the *NY Times Magazine* style section article titled "Silk and Human Kindness"; the second quote is part of an advertisement in *Lucky Life* magazine; the third quote is from *Organic Style*; and the final quote is from a spread in *People Magazine*. As the quotes and subsequent advertisements and articles suggest, this clothing line attempts to merge fashion sense with social responsibility. Fashion and market/consumer demands are privileged in the quote, "no one is going to care about Afghans." Takesh is represented as an economic "hero" by way of her business model and "harnessing the women's exquisite embroidery skills and their eagerness to work" (Gall 2004). These articles and advertisements highlight that Afghan women's paid employment is by definition "liberating," and this currency adds value to the product for sale.

Consumers are rarely privy to information about the laborers who make the products they purchase or the chain of production of material goods. While Afghan women's labor is mentioned, women's *liberation rather than their labor* becomes embedded into the product and a key advertising tool for niche markets. This type of marketing required a privileged international worker to brand women's labor as liberation, act as the Afghan women's interlocutor, and define what indeed constituted "fair wages" (see Fridell 2007). The basic and often banal experience of labor for low wages becomes retooled as an act of freedom for the laborer, while both stressing and privileging the demands of the consumer market.

This type of marketing subtly reinforces the Euro-American assumptions that posit the covered body as oppressed and the uncovered "sexy" body as free/liberated.[4] The "sexy and stylish" designs associated with the end product advocate corporeal freedom with the added value of conscientious shopping. This suggests that by purchasing the garment the consumer is engaging in an act of sociopolitical "freedom" through dress while simultaneously supporting Afghan women's income "liberation." Economic opportunity can indeed be an important component for women to challenge patriarchal structures, particularly in capitalist societies; however, it is not the only method. Economic opportunity translates differently in societies with differentiated systems of what constitutes value. This is particularly significant in places such as Kabul, where many economic opportunities depend upon temporally limited projects.

The media attention received by small for-profit and often-struggling new businesses, like T&B, helps to market Afghan women's labor as "liberation" to sell products. This branding capitalizes on the currency offered by the geopolitically inspired desire to "save and assist" Afghan women and the ability of these organizations to capitalize on this currency.[5] This works by highlighting Afghan women's abject poverty and oppression and identifying their labor as a site of economic and social liberation. For example, T&B defines its business model as "conscientiously chic," as T&B founder Takesh expresses in the following quote.

> The rigor of capitalism is happily at work ... but it's a brand of capitalism that believes that one bottom line (profit) can serve the other (social objective) and together they can work in harmony to create a successful business that accomplishes a social agenda. I'd like to think of it as a conscientiously chic bridge between the haves and the have nots ... in a world where the ever-widening gap requires longer and bigger bridges than ever before. (quoted in Butchy 2006)

Although T&B's labor model is neither novel nor groundbreaking (i.e., low-wage labor to export goods for consumption in markets outside the spaces of production), they refashioned the geopolitical currency of Afghan women's labor-liberation as a model of social enterprise. Simultaneously, the market is privileged over both the liberation and the labor of Afghan women. Privileging the market over labor suggests acceptance of the disciplinary frameworks of global capitalism that favor the international interlocutor and consumers as economic heroes. Correspondingly, Afghan women's desperation is seemingly conquered through these tales of labor-liberation. Inadequate assistance through low-wage and temporally limited work in these scenarios becomes commendable rather than yet another example of economic desperation as fodder for low-cost capitalist production. The U.S. beauty industry was involved in supporting a project in Afghanistan that traded on the geopolitical currency of Afghan women's liberation.

Beauty-Liberation?

The Kabul Beauty School, also known as the Beauty Academy of Kabul, is another example of an Afghan women–focused project that received significant media attention and corporate funds in the early intervention period (Fluri 2009c). Mary MacMakin, a U.S. citizen, longtime resident of Kabul, and founder of Physiotherapy and Rehabilitation Support for Afghanistan (PARSA), first conceptualized the idea of creating a beauty school in Kabul after the fall of the Taliban. Her vision intended to encourage women's enterprise by providing venues for women to offer beauty services to other women for weddings and various special occasions. MacMakin joined forces with Terri Grauel, a New York–based hairstylist, to solicit financial support and product donations from several beauty industry corporations. The project also received support from the Afghanistan government's Ministry of Women's Affairs. This project, designed to help women, simultaneously traded on the currency of "saving" Afghan women to generate funds and support. As a result, one of the privileged international women involved in this project traded on the currency of Afghan women to generate her *own* personal wealth.

The Beauty Academy of Kabul received extensive media coverage in popular U.S. women's magazines such as *Vogue* (also a sponsor), and a documentary film was made about its founding (Mermin 2004). Similar to T&B, the Euro-American representations of this project through different press releases and feature stories linked the "beauty academy" to women's emancipation. Several articles in various magazines included headlines or descriptions of this project that associated it with liberty, freedom, or women's empowerment, such as "Lipstick Power," "Extreme Makeover," "The Power of Beauty," and "Life, Liberty and a Touch up" (Fluri 2009c, 242). For example one news article stated: "Hairdos and makeup help define a woman's persona, but at a beauty school in Kabul after the fall of the Taliban, each stroke of red lipstick and each snip of the scissors boldly punctuated a new found freedom for women in Afghanistan. . . . The Beauty Academy of Kabul, where perms and blush are metaphors for freedom" (quoted in Fluri 2009c, 242). Thus, this project was represented as a path to liberation and subsequently traded on the geopolitical currency of "saving" and liberating Afghan women.

When the funding for the school ended, Debbie Rodriguez transitioned the school into a salon that catered to privileged international workers. Thus, the academy-turned-salon became enrolled in the auxiliary aid/development economy in Kabul. This project, which was intended as a project to develop local-Afghan women-to-women sustainable enterprise, turned into an American-run business that catered to the temporally bounded incomes of well-paid internationals and wealthy Afghans. The most overt example of capitalizing on the currency of Afghan women can be found in Debbie Rodriguez's pseudomemoir, titled *The Kabul Beauty School: The Art of Friendship and Freedom*, or alternatively titled *Kabul Beauty School: An American Woman Goes behind the Veil*, which received a movie option with Columbia Pictures. Rodriguez details various acts of "saving" in the text as well as her own experiences living in Afghanistan. She identifies herself as the founder of the Beauty School, which is disputed by most of the women involved with the initial project (Ellin 2007).

Rodriguez exemplifies an extreme and highly popular method of capitalizing on the currency of Afghan women. For example, in the documentary film about the Beauty School, Rodriguez admonishes the students for coming to class without makeup and properly styled hair by stating: "There needs to be something special about you that makes you different than the woman who is the secretary or office worker ... you can't have fuzzy perms and bad hair color and bad hair cuts. It is your job as hairdressers to set the new trend for new hairstyles and hair color. It is your responsibility ... if you guys don't do it how can Afghanistan change and get into a more modern type look. How will Afghanistan change if you guys don't change?" Rodriguez associates hairstyles and makeup with the need for Afghanistan to modernize through stylized forms of corporeal modernity.

In her book, Rodriguez capitalizes on bare-life rescue dramas by describing Afghan women's living-suffering and herself as a foreign liberator. For example, in the text she details how she saved a woman from the patriarchal punishments of shame and dishonor by helping her to fake her virginity on her wedding night. Thus, the foreign interlocutor explicates stories of suffering/savior/salvation as an object to be purchased, securing Rodriguez's material wealth. Objectified suffering infused with geopolitical desire toward rescue has in this case become a currency exchanged for the personal wealth of a privileged international worker, while increasing the precarity of the women she had supposedly saved or assisted. The women featured in her book have protested that their lives are at risk in Afghanistan due to media attention and that they have not received the funds promised to them by Rodriguez. The salon closed soon after Rodriguez left Afghanistan.[6]

Beauty parlors may indeed be excellent spaces for women-to-women enterprise (Menon 2005); however, this example explicates how Afghan women's geopolitical currency was used to create an idea that met western notions of corporeality. Meeting western notions of liberation attracted donors such as Paul Mitchell, *Vogue*, and Estee Lauder. Similarly, western notions of liberation drove the donor interest in nontraditional livelihood programs for women, such as solar lantern builders, cell phone repair, sign painting, and pottery. These trendy projects failed in part because their design was not informed by local knowledge about gender roles, employment patterns, mobility, and social status.

In addition to wartime profiteering by Rodriguez, the Beauty School of Kabul exemplifies the subtle and seductive expectations of women's bodies through beauty regimens. Surprisingly, these regimens are represented as liberation, while simultaneously placing corporeal expectations on women's faces and bodies. In the United States, advertising corporeal expectations has become a "necessary" process to meet the profit-driven demands of the multibillion-dollar beauty industry (Bordo 2004; Walker 2004; Wolf 2002).

Conclusion

Many of the individuals and groups that rushed to Afghanistan after the fall of the Taliban government were interested in the U.S. national response and "rescue" mission in Afghanistan. Some of these individuals (who were interviewed by the authors) viewed their participation as either a duty or a way to assist Afghan women who were imagined as similar victims of 9/11-style terrorism. In other cases, individuals saw the economic opportunity afforded by trading on the geopolitical and geo-economic currency associated with Afghan women. The economic power of the international aid/development community further dictates the exchange of various gendered currencies. Language, skill, and capacity have been defined and determined by donors without much understanding of existing structures or significant input from local-Afghans. The examples included in this chapter illustrate a few of the many organizations that translated the grievable-object of Afghan women's living-suffering and international rescue into currency, which was then exchanged for personal profit or professional gain.

Nigel Thrift (2008) argues that objects are not passive, inanimate properties but are involved in various overlapping negotiations with humans. The representation of T&B's consumer products and Rodriguez's book illustrates the interlinkages between the currency of Afghan women and their commodification through products and stories. In this way consumption becomes enrolled into the processes of suffering alleviation through style. Thrift (2008) suggests that "style wants us to love it and we want to be charmed by it" (14). The "saving women" trope refashioned for style and trendiness invites the consumer to engage through a manipulative act of care that charms the consumer into a corporeal process of benevolence. Wearing the product associated with Afghan women's labor-liberation, or purchasing the mythology of beauty-liberation, captivates the consumer by suggesting this purchase and product are an expression of "doing good." The material objects produced by T&B and Rodriguez have become imbued with meaning through the ways in which Afghan women's currency was marketed and capitalized upon. The discourse of "conscientiously chic" provides the consumer with the opportunity to be charmed by both style and assistance through the machinations of market-driven capitalism.

This chapter delineated the development of the post-9/11 and post–October 7, 2001 Afghanistan, and the various forms of currency generated by the manipulation of geopolitical discourses. The structures of conflict aid and development operate to produce the disposable incomes of well-paid workers, which result in auxiliary and temporally limited economies. The labor- and beauty-liberation discussed in this chapter exemplifies a form of carpetbagging (see chapter 2) that capitalizes on the currency associated with helping Afghan women. Correspondingly, the low-wage labor of many Afghan women is being promoted as an "undeniable" act of charity/assistance rather than opportunistic exploitation of war survivors. The following chapter provides an ethnographic overview of an American-Afghan entanglement that also attempted to sell products made by Afghan women. Chapter 5 examines the opportunities, challenges, and pitfalls associated with privileging workers over markets.

CHAPTER 5

"We Should Be Eating the Grant, but the Grant Eats Us"

This chapter takes an analytic approach to how Rubia was designed and how donors attempted to discipline it. Out of respect for the privacy of various individuals, names have been changed. This chapter about Rubia speaks about a specific time in the organization's development and expansion. The data for the chapter was collected between 2000 and 2011, when the author, Rachel, was directly involved in the field. Rubia continues to work for women in Afghanistan and elsewhere, although the work after 2011 is beyond the scope of this chapter. Rachel's Afghanistan scholarship predates her involvement with the Rubia community by more than two decades, through her studies of Persian and Tajik language and literature in Iran, Afghanistan, and Tajikistan. The American-Afghan entanglements described in this chapter recount the efforts of rural, nonelite Afghans to improve the economic circumstances of their own community in the absence of development expertise.[1] The organization Rubia, founded in 2000, was intended to generate income for Afghan refugee communities through small-scale handwork production. Rubia's successes, failures, opportunities, challenges, and unexpected interventions are reviewed in this chapter as an example of a collective enterprise. The attempts by this organization to remain community driven, while operating within (or at the margins of) global capitalist structures, demonstrate the difficulties of privileging laborers over market demands and consumer desire.

Refugees and Work in Pakistan

Sakhi and Rachel were students together in Dushanbe, Tajikistan, in the early 1980s but lost contact in the intervening years. When Sakhi reconnected with Rachel eighteen years later, his family was living in Pakistan's Lahore slums with other Afghan refugees from their home region in Nangarhar Province. Sakhi sought Rachel's assistance in helping his family and community to secure economic opportunities. Sakhi and Rachel quickly realized that, without external sources of funding for equipment and infrastructure, they could not embark on a large-scale enterprise. In lieu of these material inputs, they chose to create a small-scale operation to generate income for the families from Nangarhar now living as refugees in Lahore.² Rachel suggested they focus on traditional textile techniques in order to incorporate the existing skills of men and women in this community. Cooperatively identifying possible solutions for generating income led to the formation of Rubia's embroidery project. This project relied on women's skills as embroiderers and integrated men as tailors, managers, and merchants.

Sakhi's community had chosen to live outside of the refugee camps in Pakistan, and as unregistered illegal residents they were ineligible for refugee services.³ Because of their informal and undocumented resident status, they were careful to avoid detection by Pakistani authorities. They chose to live clandestinely while attempting to improve their economic situation. For Sakhi, similar to many Afghans, the well-being of his family and community were his primary concern. As their life in Afghanistan was predominantly rural, family life and work were closely intertwined. Most of the members of this community had not experienced clear, distinct demarcations between work, play, and family socializing. Sakhi guided Rubia's programs in a way that fit within his family's and community's existing cultural norms, values, and social structures. Rachel, as an invited guest, was a visitor in this community. She was interested in assisting Sakhi and the others to reach their goals. Rachel did not have development or humanitarian aid experience. Partly due to her lack of expertise, she had neither the intention nor the desire to change the social dynamics of this community, despite how much it differed from her own sociocultural contexts. Over time she developed close personal relationships and friendships with several members of this community, while simultaneously remaining an outsider—both unwilling and unable to socially engineer the community's conservative patriarchal gender roles, relations, and social hierarchies. Nevertheless, despite this lack of overt influence, by virtue of her presence and extensive work with this community she both influenced and was influenced by them.

The Lahore neighborhood where Sakhi's community lived was a maze of narrow streets. As a place marked by low-cost housing, open ditches conveyed sewage, female sanitary products, and rubbish. The stench was palpable, and Afghan women often held their noses with a bit of cloth as they walked in the street. Many newly arrived refugee women were disoriented and saddened by their displacement (Kattak 2002). Although adaptable, they remained confounded by the unfamiliar surroundings, as many had never traveled before. The refugees in Sakhi's community were from the mountain villages in a region of Nangarhar Province in eastern Afghanistan, where they cooked over open fires, baked bread in tandoor ovens, relaxed beyond the *qala* (domestic compound) walls in the shade of mulberry trees, and walked through fields to visit relatives. The foreshortened horizon of the crowded, urban Lahore neighborhood was oppressive. The refugees were accustomed to the dusty floors of their mud-brick *hawli* (inner courtyard) at home. Therefore, the cramped brick quarters of the city slum were difficult for them by comparison.

As Sakhi's community sought to explore the kind of handwork business women could engage in at home, Rubia's directors considered several locally produced handicrafts. In the Afghan refugee population, there were already a myriad of carpet producers in and around Pakistan; Rachel knew they would not be able to compete with those businesses. More importantly, this was not a carpet-weaving community.[4] Most women had some embroidery skills, as it was customary to embroider household decorations, ornaments, and wedding and infant gifts. Home-based handwork fit within existing gender-based expectations that limited women's mobility. Embroidery offered a convenient form of work because it was easily incorporated into the fluidity of daily chores and required limited capital investment. Women and teenage girls, homebound by *purdah*[5] and practicing the craft of Afghan embroidery, were an available and invaluable resource for this enterprise. Handmade embroidery is an exclusively women's craft in Afghanistan; these skills have been historically passed from the fingertips of mothers to daughters.

The women working for Rubia were not part of existing handicraft and sales networks in Afghanistan (see Wilson, Everdene, and Klijn 2012). Rachel and Sakhi sought to bring Rubia's embroidery to an international marketplace. Rubia's business plan focused on developing hand-embroidered, tailored products in Afghanistan and selling them in the United States, and then reinvesting the funds generated from those U.S. sales in Sakhi's community. The plan intended to develop a community-driven and self-sustaining business that incorporated the skills of both women and men in the community, with Rachel as the primary arbiter for international sales.[6]

Rubia implemented this business model based on market awareness and the ability to generate economic returns that could be reinvested into the project and community. Rubia was conceptualized as a self-supporting organization rather than dependent upon aid or development subsidies. Small-scale, localized handicraft projects that focus on women's skills are found all over the world. Often designed by aid or development specialists, these programs are intended to "empower or liberate" women through paid employment. Such programs have been subsidized and supported by larger development organizations intending to meet "gender-mainstreaming" initiatives, which seek to incorporate women into various aspects of paid labor and entrepreneurialism. Other models include for-profit businesses that are market- and bottom-line-driven, rather than designed to accommodate a community's needs.

Rubia, from its inception, was set apart from most other NGOs and businesses because, although there were pressing economic needs, the community would not privilege the business over other aspects of community, particularly coveted sociocultural mores. The community as a whole was always at the forefront of every decision made by Rubia. Both Sakhi and Rachel were vested in the community rather than in the market or development matrices. This, however, proved to be a significant challenge when they were faced with compounded funding needs or attempted to sell Rubia products in the United States. The representation and marketing of Rubia products was regularly subsumed into the grand narratives of saving/assisting Afghan women, particularly after 9/11, which will be discussed in more detail in a later section of this chapter.

Sakhi had asked fellow community members, Zahra and her husband Habibullah, to assist with the early planning of Rubia. Zahra was a master embroiderer and the only woman in the community who had graduated from high school. Rubia hired Zahra for her skills; her husband was hired to help with the community's gender relations. Hiring the husband of a talented female embroiderer occurred in several other cases. Husbands became an integral part of the business, assisting their wives in pattern transferring, collecting embroideries, recordkeeping, and ensuring accurate payments. The men served as a mahram providing necessary forms of accompaniment for their wives, which enabled women to meet with each other outside their respective homes.

Although Zahra had been reluctant to take on this work at first, concerned that it might not last, she later told Rachel the demands of the project helped to lift her mood and relieved some of her concerns about her family's economic problems. As Zahra's leadership role in Rubia increased, her prominence among the embroiderers grew. When she became Rubia's assistant director, she began training and overseeing all the distribution and production of embroidered goods.

In order to meet their families' economic needs, Rubia's embroiderers performed duties within the purview of their expected role in maintaining and reproducing the household (Mandel and Humphrey 2002). In their village in Afghanistan, some women had run small home-based businesses, such as dressmaking or selling cheese and baskets to their neighbors. Such businesses worked within existing social norms rather than challenging them. Earning supplemental income was not equated with increased empowerment or seen as a means of liberation. It was an extended aspect of their household responsibilities. Thus, many of the women working for Rubia welcomed the chance to earn income; however, they did not view this (or other forms of waged labor) as liberation from existing forms of patriarchy. While waged income was necessary and desired, it did not meet the emancipatory expectations associated with similar projects receiving development subsidies.

In this community the resources women earned from Rubia were pooled within their respective families. The money earned belonged to the embroiderer, and although she usually spent it on household needs—food, medicine, rent, or clothing—she might also spend it on a special piece of fabric for a dress to wear to a wedding. Rachel observed that women sometimes spent some of the money on gold jewelry. When there was surplus cash, women would buy gold as an investment, which they could sell when times were difficult. Therefore, even luxury items were purchased with thought of the family's collective needs and to offset the potential of future financial hardship.

Work/Home Space Continuum

Rubia never set up an office when operations were located in Pakistan. Organizing work within domestic spaces matched the resources and needs of the community. In Pakistan, all of Rubia's operations were home based. The "office" consisted of a few metal trunks where recordkeeping items and supplies were stored; the "conference room" was a pair of cots in the *hawli* courtyard. As an extension of household production, the business worked well within this setting.

Women worked at home, between their chores, following the rhythm of life in the neighborhood. Skills training and design instruction took place at different homes. Work was gathered and collected at home, and payment was made through home visits. Since many of the women spent most of their time in household-related chores—preparing dough, cooking, and washing laundry, in addition to childcare—the embroidery work occurred in-between these activities. Women were offered *only enough work* to accommodate their lifestyle, in consideration of their domestic responsibilities. Sakhi intentionally balanced the embroiderers' work structures in order to avoid exploitation, jealousy, and pressure that would lead to additional time-to-labor burdens. Paid and unpaid labor was shared among women, especially in extended and multigenerational households. For example, Nazia, Najiba, and Gulbanu, three unmarried sisters, explained to Rachel that since Nazia was the faster, finer embroiderer she would do most of the stitching, while Najiba and Gulbanu (ages 16–20) did most of the cleaning and cooking. That way they pooled their collective energies to meet their family's needs.

Some gender and development scholars have identified an increase (rather than decrease) in women's time-to-labor burdens. Gender and development scholars define this as a double or triple burden, because women's paid labor does not necessarily alleviate their existing and expected unpaid domestic work (Momsen 2004). In many extended and multigenerational households, female family members will do less of the unpaid domestic work when they are also earning some form of paid income. Therefore, we cannot simply identify women's paid labor as always adding a double or triple time-to-labor burden within a multifamily and relational home/work domestic space. Similarly, it is much too simplistic to assume that women's paid labor, in and of itself, leads to "liberty" or autonomy as expected in late-consumer capitalist economies. In some cases, women gain authority or influence within their families associated with their paid labor, while in other situations women who predominantly engage in unpaid domestic responsibilities have more influence or authority. Paid labor (both male and female) generally contributes to the family as a collective whole, rather than the liberation or autonomy of individual members. There are, of course, exceptions and challenges to each of these scenarios. Inextricably linking human worth to a person's productive labor runs the risk of questioning one's personal or human value upon the loss of paid employment. Quantifying a person solely or predominantly based on economics can be problematic, because it limits or places conditions on a person's intrinsic value.

Women's participation in paid labor through traditional handwork—rug weaving, embroidery, tailoring—has been criticized because it constrains women's opportunities, keeping them bound to the domestic sphere (Kessler-Harris 2004). Home-based work was central to Rubia's embroiders, which simultaneously increased women's mobility. Because of the home-based work, they had more opportunities to meet collectively in the homes of other embroiderers. The lack of strict time demarcations between paid labor, unpaid labor, and leisure time allowed time and space for the female workers to interact socially through their work relations. Most homebound women have not had any hands-on training to improve their techniques or learn patterns and design innovation, color selection, or quality control. These skills distinguish poor- from high-quality products. Some studies have shown that women who are well trained and provided the materials for commission work produce higher quality, more marketable products that in turn provide better pay (Wilson, Everdene, and Klijn 2012).

In the case of Rubia, pattern and motif planning discussions took place on the floor of Zahra's house over bottomless cups of astringent green tea and sugar candies, her seven children hovering, one still nursing in her lap. Much of her work with other women occurred with babies on knees and at breasts. Instruction was individualized, slow paced, and congenial. While any woman may have access to domestic spaces, only men with the most privileged relationship to the family can comingle there. In a community setting where women could receive income from work that occurred in the home, Rubia utilized domestic space as a site of income generation. Ensuring the privacy of women within the home also protected them from the scrutiny of outsiders.

Issues of comportment, politeness, moral behavior, civility, and humility infused conversations among women and men working for Rubia. For example,

Sakhi said, "Maryam goes wherever she wants, but her husband is as honest as they come, so we work with her, for his sake." Those present understood these vague allusions to mean that because of her unaccompanied mobility, Maryam had "loose morals." This aligns with Sana Haroon's discussion of comportment and peer pressure where "women seen in public were exposed to rumination about their sexuality ... which put them and other women within their families in a great deal of danger" (Haroon 2013, 197). The notion of *izzat* (honor) associates women's sexual propriety with male honor in ways that pose a risk of violence, shunning, or worse for women who are seen as less than virtuous. Women embody family honor by way of their virginity before marriage and virtue after marriage; men are tasked with ensuring the sanctity of women and home by protecting this honor (Kakar 2004; Kandiyoti 2007a). As a result, women protect themselves and their family members through strict observance of *purdah* (see Papanek 1973).

Embroidery classes held in Zahra's home were scheduled six mornings a week, but women came throughout the day to seek embroidery advice or to review lessons. Often a younger brother or sister was sent to Zahra with a question. Lifting the textile out of a plastic bag, they asked, "Does this color go here?" "Should this area be filled with chain stitch or couching?" Because the embroiderer could not leave home without prior arrangement—permission from her husband or a suitable mahram accompanier—the young boys and girls played an instrumental role. Children were able to retrieve anything their elders wanted or needed: a pack of cigarettes, a needle and thread, or salt for cooking. Children could be seen skipping along with plastic bags of embroidery dangling from their fingers as they moved between other household errands.[7]

The pace of embroidering and the setting for work stand as counterexamples to business models where a commodification of time dictates an often rigid separation between work and play (see Katz 2004). Other handwork businesses have faced a similar issue—how to economically account for embroidery time. Some organizations unsuccessfully tried to bring these embroiderers out of the home and into the studio or factory.[8] Because Rubia's embroiderers worked intermittently, between other household chores, they were paid by item, known as "piecework," which helped maintain the fluidity of time, rather than requiring a strict demarcation between paid and unpaid work. This avoided the commodification of time, and pressures placed on women, as seen in many clothing factories (Brooks 2007).

The structures of the labor, which operated outside of conventional capitalist frameworks, allowed for a method of income generation within the rhythms of daily family life. For example, Rachel once observed three women at an engagement party sitting together, embroidering portions of a Rubia shawl they were eager to finish. The fluidity of work/living space, as well as the integration of paid and unpaid labor, allowed the embroiderer to incorporate her labor within the demands of daily life. As feminist scholars have identified, the patriarchal structures that bound women into certain expected behavioral practices have been difficult to destabilize. Rachel as an economic collaborator had neither authority nor influence to enact gender-based social change in this community. For Rachel, many of the gender roles and relations within this community were challenging. However, viewing problematic gender roles through western eyes did not justify attempts at social engineering, despite the urging and expectations of donors.

Returning to Afghanistan

By August 2001, Rubia had a manageable number of female embroiderers, living close enough to one another to make working together easy, with a ready supply of fine materials, convenient shipping from Pakistan, relative security, electricity, and running water. Rubia's location in Pakistan was significantly altered by the October 7, 2001, U.S.-led invasion and occupation of Afghanistan and subsequent fall of the Taliban government. In early 2002, several community members involved with Rubia began sending emissaries back to Afghanistan to investigate a return. After much discussion and debate, the community decided to establish Rubia in Afghanistan, as part of the community's return to their village in Nangarhar Province. Rumors proliferated about the amount of international aid flowing into Kabul. By early 2003, enough community members had returned to Afghanistan for Rubia to move its operations and become an official NGO in Afghanistan.[9]

As villagers from a rural area in an eastern province, Rubia's workers did not have the social or political capital in Kabul to register their small business as an NGO, which was the first step necessary toward accessing international donor funds. Afghan ministers and ministries continually changed their responsibilities, jurisdictions, and requirements. New application forms, identical to the previous ones, had to be completed again and again.[10] The frustration that workers experienced in dealing with their own government's capricious policies was mirrored in their attempts to gain access to development funding held by international donors (Gupta 2012). Most donors did not speak either of Afghanistan's two national languages, Dari and Pashto. Zahra, Habibullah, and Sakhi all spoke multiple languages, none of which were English. They could run their own business, overseeing the production of embroidery for more than a hundred women, but they were locked out of pursuing additional funding for business expansion in their own country.[11] Rubia also lacked the funds necessary to hire local-Afghans with English skills who could help them gain access to international subsidies. As discussed in chapter 2, English-language skills enabled local-Afghans to more easily secure work in international organizations, which paid them much higher salaries than local-Afghan-run organizations.

Rachel became Rubia's intermediary with the international community. However, she did not live in Afghanistan and could only travel to the country periodically. Thus, her efforts to network on behalf of Rubia in Kabul were sporadic. When she was in Kabul, she visited one donor organization after another, trying to find funding and support for Rubia's income-generating projects and marketing initiatives, education, and management training for core staff. She bounced from the United Nations Development Fund for Women (UNIFEM) to the United States Agency for International Development (USAID) to the International Organization for Migration (IOM). Rachel, by virtue of her U.S. citizenship and facility with English, easily moved in and out of international offices. Simultaneously, her ability to speak Dari, along with her close and privileged relationship to Sakhi's family and community, enabled her to navigate between local-Afghan and international spaces. It became clear that having and maintaining an office in Kabul could prove beneficial for Rubia to secure funding from international organizations. The deep pockets of the international aid community caused a spike in rentals, which, as discussed in chapter 2, pushed many Afghans to the city's outlying districts. Rubia was caught between the need to have an office in Kabul while maintaining the bulk of its operations in the Nangarhar village, where most of the embroiderers now lived.[12]

Many Kabul offices were housed in residential-style compounds, obscuring the physical separation between home and office. The social demarcation was blurred as well since these compounds served as both housing and workspace for international and local-Afghan organizations. For privileged internationals, working and living in the same location was both convenient and cost effective. It reduced the need for extra rental properties and the high cost of secured transportation.

Rubia's first office was a small older residence in central Kabul. The office challenged expected gendered divisions of space for the Rubia community, because the office straddled both public-work and private-domestic spaces. The intersection of these spaces invited concerns about propriety and exposing women to uncomfortable public scrutiny, both actual and perceived. In Kabul the fit between Rubia's style of business and the professionalized environment proved untenable.

Home/Office Space in Kabul

In Kabul, Afghans were concerned about the watchful gaze of neighbors. Oppressive gossip could result in negative social sanctions due to perceptions of unacceptable behavior (Schütte 2013). Intense in-group surveillance of one another's behavior is used to maintain social equilibrium; gossip can be a powerful method for challenging one's virtue or honor. This posed a problem for various offices and businesses that doubled as residences in Kabul at that time. Many came up with inventive solutions. Some organizations had one entrance for women and a separate one, around the corner, for men. Some NGOs took pains to keep appointments for men and women on separate days. Many Afghan workers spoke about feeling as if they were being watched or talked about. It became necessary for businesses and NGOs to communicate with surrounding neighbors about the purpose of their organization and to provide reasons for why people were regularly coming and going. Over thirty years of political conflict, war, and uncertainty had perpetuated extensive speculation about individual mobility and mistrust of neighbors in various places in Afghanistan, especially in cosmopolitan, urbanized Kabul.

Zahra and Habibullah moved from Lahore to Kabul and went to the Rubia office every day to work. The male tailors met with staff at the office, and foreign visitors came to see Rubia's showroom. This configuration did not fit everyone's needs. The office disrupted the expected division between home and public workspaces. Many of the chores that were previously housekeeping tasks became the responsibility of the predominantly male office staff, including cooking, cleaning, and guarding. However, the fluidity of time and space that allowed women to work in between the domestic labor in their own homes was not possible for those in the office environment.

In Kabul, Zahra had to leave her home behind to work at the office. Although she took her youngest child with her, it did not allow her the same ability to manage her paid labor for Rubia and unpaid household work. Sometimes groups of women came to the office to turn in or receive work. Often they came in pairs, or accompanied by a close male relative (mahram). The office gave them a legitimate destination, both for business and pleasure. They brought picnics or stayed for tea and candy. Most women preferred to embroider at home, but those who paid regular social visits to the office also viewed this as an opportunity to secure more paid labor. Men came to the office seeking work for their wives, delivering goods, or picking up new orders.

Rubia's office soon became a hostel for the Nangarhar village community. Members of this community when visiting Kabul used the office as an overnight guesthouse. The office became a workspace by day and a dormitory at night. This increased Rubia's prestige among villagers and provided security. It also burdened the NGO's limited resources and made starting work in the morning troublesome. Sometimes overnight guests did not depart early enough in the morning, which made it difficult to ensure the expected gendered separation of spaces within the office.

Gendered spaces at home had been clearly established. In Lahore, Sakhi and Habibullah had shared their private spaces with each other's families. Being invited into each other's private family area displayed trust and mutual respect. This privilege is mostly reserved for closely related individuals. Men knew whose homes they could enter and which ones they could not. The Kabul office presented conflicts on many social levels. Soon the mixed-gender gatherings that took place there—including guards, cooks, tailors, and male visitors—evoked too much gossip or fear of gossip.

Zahra wanted to be a cosmopolitan Kabuli (a person from or identifying with Kabul's more modern urban lifestyles), although her husband's family was not. She struggled to hold onto her access to the office despite her sporadic attendance. With seven children, she found it difficult to meet her commitment to come to work and manage her household. She was able to go to the office to work, with her husband accompanying her as a mahram, but she was concerned that overnight male guests would compromise her mobility. Zahra exercised her power by remaining at home to guard her family's honor and maintain social equilibrium. Over time she worked more from home than within the Rubia office. It had become impossible for her and the other women to feel comfortable coming to the office with so many nonfamilial male visitors. The office dislocated the familiar framework of gendered space and could not provide a suitable work environment for the women. Zahra and the other women found their mobility currency was limited. Once the office space became more public and less like a domestic space, protection of their honor and integrity was no longer ensured.

The office had become a skewed version of "home." It provided the hospitality space as a *mehman khana* (guesthouse), without the protected privacy for women expected in a typical domestic setting. Guest space is clearly circumscribed in many Afghan homes. It is a room where men entertain male guests, often with a separate entrance, to distinguish this space from the larger, female-dominated domestic space. When the office simulated family space, it was welcoming and acceptable for women. The more the office emulated a *mehman khana*, the less suitable it became for women. Similar to other Afghan organizations, women experienced contextual difficulties when home and workspaces were strictly demarcated. A professional office met the donor expectations by separating home and work; it also helped to clearly commodify one's time. Similar to many other small organizations in Afghanistan, Rubia moved locations, opened and closed offices, and continued to struggle with donor expectations and how best to integrate personal, family, and community beliefs with donors' structural and social expectations of changing gender norms.

The Problem of Seeking Donors

Rubia's business model, which focused on the community and the needs of its workers, presented significant challenges for maintaining a business. The low cost of handmade goods in Pakistan, India, and China made it impossible for Rubia's products to compete in similar markets, while maintaining its payment structure and community-based focus. In an effort to expand Rubia and provide additional services to the community, Rachel as Rubia's primary international liaison began to seek other sources of funding for Rubia.

The donors Rubia was able to seek funding from were mainly interested in women's empowerment, health, and education. Although healthcare was a concern for this community, education (for either men or women) was not identified as an immediate need. Education, similar to work, was seen as acceptable for women but not a legitimate reason for traversing public spaces. Public spaces are sites of both uncertainty and possible disruption to one's reputation and family honor, therefore traversing public spaces can potentially lead to negative social sanctions. Although education and economics were bound together in the eyes of many donors, it was an uneasy alliance for this community. In a survey Rubia conducted, embroiderers identified improvements in personal and family security as the most pressing need, similar to other surveys conducted in Afghanistan (Rennie, Sharma, and Sen 2008).

In an effort to gain funding by way of meeting donor expectations, Rubia intended to link education with economic opportunity. Embroidery provided the economic incentive for integrating educational programs. When Rachel first discussed this nascent project with friends who worked in development, they identified statistics to argue that improving women's education was key to poverty reduction and better health outcomes. Rachel was convinced that she needed to integrate a literacy component into Rubia's business model. She quickly discovered that the "necessity" to incorporate education into Rubia was more important to donors than the community or workers employed by Rubia. Donors expected that women who embroidered would necessarily attend literacy classes. Some donors suggested that women who did not attend class should be banned from access to embroidery work. Donors have commonly used these types of coercive "incentives" in an effort to socially engineer communities (Goodhand 2002; Suhrke 2007). However, excluding women from embroidery in an effort to force education neither made sense to this community nor altered their beliefs and practices.

Sakhi explained that some of the embroiderers' families would not send their girls/women to class. "It might happen eventually," he said, "but not right away." The donors would have to be patient. However, donors operate on a much different time horizon than this or many other Afghan communities. Most international development projects have life cycles, endpoints, and expected outcomes to be achieved within a specific time frame. Most development workers are hired for one- to two-year cyclical contracts, where deliverables are couched in terms of metrics, commodified time, and professional work schedules.

The Rubia community rejected this commodification of time as well as repudiating forms of value that privileged paid over unpaid labor. The community's rejection of donor-driven attempts toward education does not mean that all members of this community were in agreement. There had always been overlapping interest by some women in both embroidery and education. Literacy classes were organized on a voluntary basis and took place in homes. Over the years, embroiderers came to literacy classes, as did girls and women beyond the embroidery community, due to the trust built up over time between the community leadership and Rubia's local-Afghan directors.[13] This was further reinforced by Rubia's extended presence in the community, as well as its unwillingness to require education as a precondition of work to meet donor expectations.[14]

Watches and Time

Mass public education in the United States following the industrial revolution was designed to transition farmers into efficient factory laborers. The discipline of attendance is prioritized as school bells ring and tardiness is recorded. That same regimen does not apply to many unschooled rural Afghan communities. They had not been restricted by the rhythm of work that strictly demarcates one's day between work and nonwork (see Katz 2004). They rise before the sun and proceed through the rigors of their day with little attention to an institutionalized punch clock or other commodifications of time. Recognizing Americans' approaches to time, Afghans often joked, "Americans have watches but Afghans have time." Whether embroideries were completed on Monday or Thursday was of little consequence to Rubia's Afghan workers and managers. Rachel, who was uninterested in disciplining the Rubia community to meet the time demands of the U.S. market, planned well in advance to receive materials "on time."

With the introduction of global capitalist market logics, new forms of discipline were required to meet consumer expectations and the expectation of commodified time and labor. While Afghan families and communities have been extensively disciplined around principles of honor, gender norms, and relational responsibilities, this form of discipline remained invisible to the market. Aid and development workers often lamented the "undisciplined behavior" of the Afghans with whom they worked, particularly when Afghan employees would take extended leaves for a wedding, funeral, or other family obligations. Aid/development workers, whose only purpose in Afghanistan was *to work*, were unable (or unwilling) to see that Afghan discipline focused on home and community, rather than the global market. Afghans *live* in Afghanistan while internationals *work* there. In other words, internationals were predominantly working in Afghanistan without their families; their lives revolved around work, further distancing them from understanding the importance and demands of family life and obligations for Afghans.

The joke about Americans having watches and Afghans having time underscores the ways in which development and military technologies (i.e., watches) are expected to discipline the spaces and social interactions of Afghans. Stating that Afghans "have time" illustrates two interrelated points. First, Afghans place importance on time and the way in which it is spent—that is, with family and community—because relational interactions have significant value. Second, time signals an understanding that international aid/development intervention and military occupation is temporally limited. Ultimately Afghans will remain in the spaces and places socially, politically, and economically engineered by internationals. Therefore, spatial and social understandings of and control over places, especially private domestic locations, is of paramount importance to many Afghans.

Scaling Up Grassroots Organizing

Rubia's first major grant in Afghanistan was from USAID. This grant offered an opportunity for more women to earn income in the Nangarhar village. Evenings at home were spent sitting on cots in the dark courtyard of the *qala*, backlit by *alekayn* (kerosene) lanterns. Men and women sat together discussing who would fill which positions. They considered which women had the most mobility due to age, marital status, and standing in the community; they also deliberated on which women could visit other women's homes within the context of familial networks. Lists of women were written and rewritten repeatedly as they tried to distribute two hundred positions fairly. Fairness was deemed necessary for ensuring community harmony and security in an effort to avoid rivalries or harmful gossip that may be caused from someone being excluded or slighted.

Men from throughout the valley approached Sakhi to insist he include their wives, daughters, and sisters in the program. Sakhi's most equitable solution sought the assistance of local elders/leaders—*maliks*—of each of the ten major clan networks.[15] The maliks chose twenty women each from their respective clans to work with Rubia. This solution brought more men into the process and showed genuine respect for local leaders, strengthening Rubia's position within the larger community. Selection took a significant amount of time due to the input of many individuals and the attention placed on building consensus in order to avoid future conflicts.

In order to keep the work at the village level and involve as many people in planning and implementation as possible, Rubia constructed a scaffold-like network of mentors, dispensers, and recordkeepers. Zahra trained women to become mentors in colors and stitch techniques and placed them in charge of a group of women. These mentors were often older or widowed women, with more mobility, authority, and respected standing within the community. Many women, whose diminished dexterity skills and eyesight made it difficult to embroider, were able to supervise other women, dispense materials, collect piecework, and distribute payments. Disbursements were made in group settings, so that everyone was aware of what the others received. This successful procedure was designed by the participants themselves to mitigate jealousy and prevent exploitation.

Privileging Workers over Markets

Many development projects that started in Afghanistan in 2002 trained large numbers of women in different skills. They did not create employment opportunities. After the training period ended, women (and men) were left on their own to develop individual businesses (Abirafeh 2009). For example, short-term projects were intended to spark entrepreneurialism. Unfortunately, without providing suitable resources for starting a business, many of these projects resulted in increased unemployment and debt. Rubia's model was not only to train but also to employ women and pay them equivalent to what their husbands, fathers, brothers, or sons could earn. The philosophy of Rubia was organized to accommodate the lives of rural Afghan women without significantly adding to their domestic-labor burdens.

Rubia strived to balance community needs and privilege them over the demands of a market-driven approach. For example, one product that sold well was being produced more slowly than the market demanded. Rubia conducted a survey of its embroiderers in an effort to understand how to improve the pace of production without increasing women's time-to-labor burdens. The survey revealed that stitching in the stiff wool fabric used to make the bags that sold well in the United States hurt the embroiderers' fingers. In response, Rubia discontinued using this fabric to protect the embroiderers, privileging these women over the market. This allowed for innovations in fabric choices and new marketing opportunities rather than the expected loss of market share formerly dominated by the wool-fabric handbags. However, economic difficulties were also associated with privileging workers over the market. Rubia's U.S. volunteers often struggled with how to sell enough products at a particular price-point in order to provide regular embroidery work for the women, while maintaining fluid time-work schedules in Afghanistan. This led Rubia to seek funds from donor organizations.

As Rubia sought additional funding, USAID and other donors began to layer the organization with meaning and purpose in an attempt to squeeze it into their image of a "typical" woman's business and empowerment-building NGO. Rubia's efforts to seek funding to strengthen its operations was at times foregrounded by initiatives and circumstances determined by donor organizations. The potential for international donor funding provided new opportunities for Rubia. However, these came at the cost of exchanging on the gender currency of assisting Afghan women. The more Rubia sought additional funding streams, the more donors tried to discipline Rubia into a particular model of development, which included highlighting the work of women and rendering invisible male workers and supporters. This led Sakhi to exclaim in frustration, "We should be eating the grant, but the grant eats us." In other words, the expected gains from donor funding were offset by the donors' increased demands and requirements.

Rachel often explained to donors that Rubia was a family enterprise, not only for women. One expert counseled Rachel to specify on grants that Rubia was *in the process* of becoming a women-run and owned NGO in order to become more attractive to donors. Rachel observed other groups gain access to funds when they stated they were women-owned or women-run, even when this was not the case. Rubia's Afghan directors were not ashamed of who or what they were and were unwilling to ascribe to insincere claims in order to receive funding. Sakhi would often say, "But we are helping people, we are giving women a chance to earn some income. Why wouldn't they support us?" Despite employing women, Rubia did not fit the preconceived model of women's "empowerment" designed by donors. Unable to compete with the cheap cost of goods from neighboring countries that flooded both Afghan and international markets, Rubia focused on niche markets in the United States.

Selling the Story

In an effort to effectively sell Rubia products in the United States, Rachel and other U.S.-based Rubia volunteers were charged with marketing these products in niche venues. As Rubia began to look for ways to sell its goods in the United States, the initial product selection and branding were designed in the United States. Rubia's U.S.-based volunteers consulted interior designers, development designers, and companies that specialized in fair trade. They were repeatedly told that "the story" would sell the product. Many of the niche markets available to Rubia included sales events, such as "Christmas presents that make a difference," "gifts that give," or "fair trade" expos and festivals, which encouraged the use of storytelling as a method for selling products. Some of the ideas suggested to Rubia included the type of "conscientious shopping" discussed in chapter 4. Rubia's U.S.-based volunteers had mixed feelings about using this method of marketing to sell products. Some viewed this as a "means to an end," because more sales translated into funds for the community in Afghanistan. Others found this to be a disingenuous method for selling products. Most importantly, Rubia's Afghan community did not see themselves as a story for sale, suitable for U.S. consumers.

Attempts to commodify their images and focus on female embroiderers met with suspicion and rejection from both male and female community members. One woman told Rachel, "You can take my photo as long as it doesn't end up on a museum wall." This woman, similar to other members in the community, did not view her life as an exotic story available for others to view and consume.[16] Their story was one of hard work, respectability, and personal integrity. Every time people tried to frame them as poor or needy, they rejected that characterization. The portrayal of them as "in need" diminished their own sense of dignity. Despite their limited personal resources, Rubia's Afghan directors were concerned about those less fortunate, extending additional assistance to more vulnerable members of their community such as widows and the war-wounded. Their story was not about lack of education, women's limited mobility, patriarchy, Islam, or poor health practices. To this community, Rubia products exemplified hard work and a relational commitment to the sustenance of their community. They were happy to share their *actual* story. However, this story did not neatly fit within existing expected representations of poor, suffering women emancipated from patriarchy by foreign development interventions. Rubia's community members (both men and women) explicitly asked Rachel not to include their personal stories as a marketing strategy.

Selling the Product, Not the Story

The small hangtag that accompanied Rubia's products was designed as an opportunity to *tell* rather than *sell* the community's own story. Initially, Rubia's hangtag had only the logo, an embroidered motif. Marketing experts pushed Rubia to include the image of a woman and something about "her story." Since none of the women in the Rubia community were willing to be depicted, it would be difficult to meet this request. Rachel suggested using the image of a woman in a burqa holding an embroidered pillow to solve this problem (figure 5.1). In the United States, many female customers identified the burqa as negative, viewing it as an emblem of Afghan women's oppression and suffering. Rachel attempted to explain to them that this garment was not a barrier for Afghan women but rather an agent for their mobility. For many U.S.-based customers with whom Rachel and other volunteers interacted, the burqa remained an oppressive wall, beyond which they could not see (also see Jay 1993; Mirzoeff 2002; Sturken and Cartwright 2009).

Rubia's U.S.-based sales occurred mainly through special sales events and niche markets, which provided volunteers the opportunity to directly interact with customers. Attempts to provide a more pluralistic or nuanced understanding of Afghan people (both men and women) often proved to be an ineffective marketing strategy. Many customers wanted to support Rubia, based on their own beliefs about "how best" to assist Afghan women. A survey conducted of customers in the United States indicated that they purchased products or supported Rubia because they believed they were helping women to get out from under the burqa. The removal of the burqa was neither the goal of Rubia's U.S.

FIGURE 5.1. Rubia hangtag. (Used with permission by Rubia, Inc.)

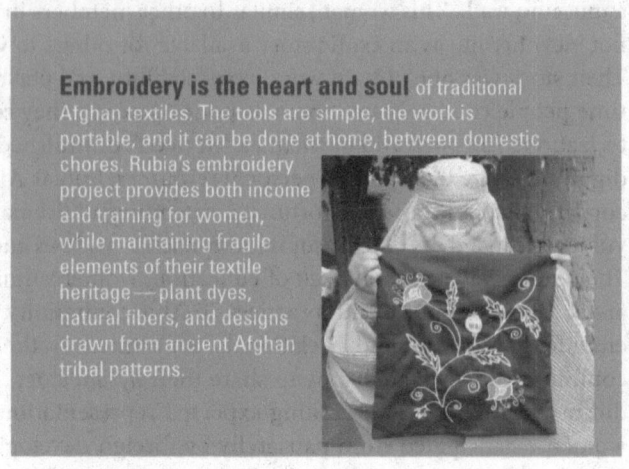

Embroidery is the heart and soul of traditional Afghan textiles. The tools are simple, the work is portable, and it can be done at home, between domestic chores. Rubia's embroidery project provides both income and training for women, while maintaining fragile elements of their textile heritage—plant dyes, natural fibers, and designs drawn from ancient Afghan tribal patterns.

volunteers nor that of the Afghan community, in contrast to the expectations of their U.S.-based consumers.

In many respects, the push to sell the product by selling the story illustrates how the living-suffering of Afghan women as a grievable object (as discussed in chapters 3 and 4) can be consumed through the purchase of goods made by Afghan women. This type of sales technique portrays Afghan women's living-suffering as alleviated by foreign rescue, which subsequently reinforces the "grand narratives" shaped by geopolitical and geo-economic discourses. Desperation and precarity are represented through the burqa-clad body as a corporeal representation of otherness. In order to consume *her story* of foreign liberation from localized suffering, her liberation must be embedded in the product of her labor. Therefore, showing a burqa-clad woman on Rubia's hangtags disrupted the liberation (burqa-lifting) moment expected by many U.S.-based consumers. Marketing materials presented Rubia's Afghan workers as a community rather than a compilation of individual stories. Rubia's website attempted to focus attention on the workmanship, tradition of embroidery, and history of the designs in an effort to rebrand Afghan women's handwork as high quality and aesthetically pleasing.

Signatures Viewed as Virtual Sisterhood

Rubia had embroiderers sign their work by stitching their name in Persian letters on the back of each piece they completed. The signatures allowed the managers to track each person's work and incorporate basic literacy training. Many of Rubia's customers viewed the signatures as akin to making a virtual connection with an embroiderer. Some customers fancied themselves as collectors, asking for more items by *Layla* or *Jahan*. They wanted pictures of these women, suggesting Rubia engage in programs similar to the virtual "Sponsor a Sister" program run by Women for Women International.[17] Some customers sent pictures of the pillows in their homes to Rubia in order for them to be shown to the embroiderers. Marketing experts advised Rubia to emphasize the person-to-person approach, and these signatures were seen as an important way to brand this virtual connection.

The numerous field visits to Afghanistan by Rubia's U.S.-based staff and volunteers provided information to customers at direct-sales venues. Rubia volunteers conveyed to customers, through their firsthand experience, details of the everyday lives of the women (and men) who made the products for sale. The stories met the consumers' desire for authenticity, while falling short of their expectations of women's liberty. Seeking a personal connection has become a technique of macroscale and multinational assistance organizations. Many organizations offer virtual person-to-person connections as a method for seeking individual donations from supporters (Strüver 2007). Organizations such as Heifer International, Mercy Corps, and Oxfam Unwrapped offer web-based shopping formats that provide items for purchase such as "empowering women," "comfort a child," or "purchase a cow for a village." Each website also includes disclaimers identifying these as "symbolic gifts" rather than an actual item sent to the individuals pictured (Wilson 2011). Therefore, many U.S.-based customers read the signature of Rubia's embroiderers as way to identify the women and provide a virtual connection between themselves and the laborer in an effort to personalize their consumer experience. For the Rubia community in Afghanistan, the signatures did not garner the same level of connection with consumers, nor were they viewed with much significance beyond serving as a method to track work and ensure payments. Most embroiderers did not link their own signatures with their individual identity; sometimes they signed the name of their husband or son, or used nicknames. Beyond receiving proper payment for work completed, the connection between their individually signed identity and the product of their work remained largely immaterial.[18]

While Rubia was limited in its ability to compete in the capitalist marketplace, its strengths challenged the existing structure of market-based capitalism. These strengths included Rubia's connection to and privileging of the community's and workers' ideas, needs, and concerns over the market or consumer demands. Rubia's volunteers attempted to educate its U.S. customers rather than allow them to engineer the functionality of Rubia in Afghanistan.

Conclusion

The socially responsible or "conscientious" for-profit business model reinvests some of its business profits toward a values-based economic venture by creating foundations and local community programs. The balance of profit and social good varies widely among ventures. Some are employee-owned and operated; others are socially responsible in name only. Marsden (2013, 97) identifies "market Islam" as a feature of the Afghan moral landscape. He points to multiple studies that show that Muslim entrepreneurs engage with "Islamic normative conventions" as part of their business practices. Rubia, as a small community-based organization, exemplified Islamic normative conventions. The demands of "entrepreneurship, material success, and moral connectedness" were clearly dictating the decision making of the Afghans who developed and ran this organization (Marsden 2013, 98).

The moral integrity of the Afghans' work had particular resonance and relevance. It operated in a familiar community where leaders were accountable to their family, friends, and neighbors. Accountability was more than financial responsibility; it extended to a code of conduct including protecting the privacy and respectability of people about whom they were concerned. It also meant behaving in socially acceptable ways that would enhance their local prestige and reputations rather than impinge upon them. Concerns about the watchful observation of others around them, and guarding against negative perceptions that might lead to accusations of un-Islamic behavior, were regularly discussed within the Rubia community. The pressure to be seen as treating everyone fairly and protecting the reputation of women was paramount to other decisions.

Rubia found itself at the intersection of a mismatched reading of realities. Rubia was created as a way to earn income through waged labor. Simultaneously, donors, supporters, and customers vested symbolic purpose—such as women's liberation and empowerment—into this work. The community, forging their own path to economic improvement, did not relinquish their agency in the process. However, agency in determining the direction of their business should not be mistaken for western-style liberation. Neither should their work be seen as charity. They were a community seeking work and income and expecting to be treated with dignity—not as symbols or tokens of geopolitical or geo-economic development.

Rubia in the United States chose the tagline, "Mending Afghanistan Stitch by Stitch," while this motto was never used in Afghanistan. For the men and women working with Rubia it was their business, a means for economic relief from poverty, not a symbol of national reconstruction. Providing women with economic opportunities does not in and of itself rescue them from patriarchal structures. Exchanging patriarchal power relations for the time-space discipline expected of low-wage workers at the most vulnerable end of the global-capitalist hierarchy does not by definition signal women's liberation or empowerment.

This chapter illustrates the difficulties for organizations like Rubia to both attend to community needs and privilege workers over market-driven capitalist production/consumption frameworks. Rubia's U.S.-based volunteers attempted to provide a more balanced view of this community and resist or challenge the grand narratives about Afghan women. Selling the story of victimized Afghan women in an effort to sell products offered a seductive, albeit unfitting, mode of advertising for Rubia.

As many have stated in response to critical analyses of consumer-based assistance, "So what if you sell the story of assisting and saving, if it helps women earn income isn't that a good thing?" Privileging workers and community conceptions of time and value over market-driven disciplinary frameworks pushed Rubia to sell in niche markets. These alternative sales venues expected emotive expression of the suffering-subject as exchange currency. While these ventures may indeed provide necessary income in the short term, they will not alleviate the economic problems in Afghanistan that are similar to other places beset by endemic poverty. Advertising female suffering as alleviated through work and foreign consumption does not provide a viable or long-term solution. Temporally limited heartstring-tugging marketing will not address the structural conditions of continual low-wage work and the growing spatial divisions between places of production and consumption (Richey and Ponte 2011). It allows "us" to continue to believe we only need to consume "better" or "more justly," while subtly diverting attention away from the physical and structural violence of cyclical poverty in Afghanistan and other places.

CHAPTER 6

"Saving" Soraya

The previous chapter examined Rubia's organizational effort to provide supplemental income for an Afghan community by selling Afghan-made products within niche markets in the United States. The American-Afghan entanglements between Rubia's community and its U.S.-based volunteers made this form of economic opportunity both possible and problematic. The messiness of these entanglements illustrates the potential for small-scale organizations to operate outside of existing development paradigms. These conflicts required a constant negotiation between the needs and desires of Rubia's worker community and the expectations and demands of development donors and niche-market consumers.

This chapter provides an equally messy but significantly different American-Afghan entanglement. The individuals and organizations discussed in this chapter were attempting to "save" and assist an Afghan woman by helping her leave Afghanistan and participate in a cultural exchange program. Soraya, unlike the women in the previous chapter, was an urban Kabuli from a relatively privileged family. She was educated, spoke English, and was able to work and move through public space without the accompaniment of a mahram. While a student at Kabul University, Soraya worked for a small international NGO run by an American woman. As part of this examination of "saving" Soraya, the authors incorporate critical self-reflexivity, based on their own involvement in this project in different capacities. Out of respect and protection for the individuals involved in this project, pseudonyms are used for all organizations and persons (except the authors) discussed in this chapter.

Background

The Women's Educational Leadership Organization (WELO) was formed by a group of American women who identified themselves as champions of women's education and leadership in the United States. After 9/11, WELO sought to extend their expertise by working with Afghan women through educational exchange programs. These one-way exchange programs brought female educators from Afghanistan to the United States to participate in six-week training programs, funded by the U.S. Department of State. To extend this project beyond the six weeks, they began to raise funds to initiate cultural exchange fellowships for young female Afghans. Participants in this program would audit college-level courses and speak at public events about their experiences in Afghanistan and hopes for the future. The conceptualization of the program was designed and developed in the United States. WELO reached out to Jennifer, asking her to participate in this project, which included helping to recruit Afghan women by working with WELO's primary Afghan contact, Nusha.[1]

Nusha lived in the capital city, Kabul. She was from an educated family; spoke English, Dari, and Pashto fluently; and held a master's degree in education from a U.S. university. Jennifer met with Nusha in Kabul to review WELO's program and offered to help her recruit and select candidates for the fellowship. Nusha asked three pertinent questions: (1) Would the program lead to a degree from a U.S. university? (2) Could the young women earn income while in the United States? and (3) Would the fellowship provide the young women with the opportunity to continue their education in the United States beyond the one-year program? "No" was the answer to each of her questions, because WELO's program was not designed to accommodate these provisions.

Nusha politely and emphatically stated that the program would not work and should be redesigned. For a young person to go to the United States for a year and return without a degree made little sense to Nusha. She also recognized that the income-earning restriction was an irreconcilable difficulty for potential candidates. Although she understood and appreciated the idea of a cultural exchange, she believed the program's parameters offered little benefit to young Afghans.

Nusha was concerned that it would be difficult to find suitable candidates. The candidates would need to possess advanced English proficiency and have permission from their families. This would be further complicated by the lack of a degree or income-earning opportunities. Nusha suggested WELO restructure the fellowship as a scholarship program that would allow a young woman with a bachelor's degree to receive a master's in the United States, because master's degrees in education were not offered in Afghanistan at that time.

Nusha's suggestions were based on her own experiences. She had previously participated in one of WELO's six-week exchange programs, while also earning a master's degree in the United States by way of another scholarship program. While she was appreciative of the organization's assistance and promotion of Afghan women's education and leadership, she was outspoken and critical of WELO. This conundrum is often experienced by Afghan women who receive opportunities from international organizations, under the auspices of "empowering" women. Such empowerment-focused organizations are in many cases unwilling to listen to or incorporate the ideas of the very women they seek to empower (Collaborative Learning Projects 2010; Kandiyoti 2007b; Sangtin Writers and Nagar 2006).

Nusha's concerns raised questions for Jennifer about the WELO program. However, Jennifer had just been introduced to Soraya, a young Afghan woman who was keen to be accepted into the program. Soraya's employer, Jane, a U.S. citizen, had moved to Kabul in 2003 where she had started a small NGO. Both Jennifer and Rachel had known Jane for several years. Jane and Rachel had met through mutual friends in Afghanistan, and Jane guest-lectured about her work in Afghanistan to students in Jennifer's development courses. Jane first traveled to Afghanistan from the United States after 9/11, as part of a delegation of concerned Americans and Afghan returnees. Jane explained to Jennifer and Rachel that after spending several weeks in Afghanistan, she "fell in love" with the country and decided to stay and exercise her entrepreneurial skills by starting a small nonprofit. Jane identified herself as a radical feminist and staunch advocate for women's rights in Afghanistan. She believed she could assist Afghan women by helping them to advance their educational opportunities outside the country.

Jane expressed the need to "get Soraya out" of the country for security reasons, and Jennifer suggested the WELO fellowship as a possible avenue for accomplishing this. Jane's interests in helping Soraya leave Afghanistan were based on her own negative perceptions of Afghan patriarchy and sociocultural mores combined with her experiences in the United States. Jane had pulled herself out of an economically depressed region in rural America. She was as smart as she was ambitious, and she succeeded in graduating from an Ivy League school. She was the first in her family to pursue higher education. Jane's feminist consciousness was raised through leaving home for college. Jane feared that Soraya would soon face a life like her own mother did—marrying young, having children young, and going "nowhere." Thus Jane was determined to protect Soraya. Jane believed she could "save" Soraya from the local patriarchy by helping her escape to the United States and further her educational aspirations. Jennifer was moved by Jane's assertions that Soraya's situation in Afghanistan was insecure and precarious. Jane had been Soraya's employer for over a year and was a frequent guest in Soraya's home. Jane as a DIY (do it yourself) rather than a typical aid/development worker had more intimate knowledge of Soraya's life and circumstances. Soraya expressed her interest in the fellowship to Jennifer without identifying her situation as dire; her method of communication was indirect and deferential. By contrast, Jane, in a more direct style of communication, expressed Soraya's situation as more perilous. Jane's urging combined with Soraya's eagerness led Jennifer to submit her name as a possible candidate. To Jane the precariousness of Soraya's security was obvious and required immediate action. While safety was also a concern for Soraya, her experiences of insecurity were much more everyday and banal. Her lack of urgency signaled the ways in which insecurity had remained a continual part of her daily life, not an exceptional or dramatic situation necessitating an urgent response.

Soraya's qualifications as an education major with college-level English-language skills made her a suitable candidate for the WELO fellowship. WELO had explained to Nusha that, despite her concerns, they were determined to move forward with their program idea. Soraya met with Jennifer and Nusha to discuss the fellowship. Nusha reiterated her apprehensions and hesitations about the viability of the program to both Jennifer and Soraya. Soraya continued to express her interests in the fellowship, despite Nusha's misgivings. Jennifer believed that submitting Soraya as a candidate would help to solve several interrelated difficulties: helping WELO to find a suitable candidate, assuaging Nusha's concerns with Soraya's enthusiasm, and supporting Jane's desire to help Soraya leave Afghanistan.

In hindsight, Jennifer should have either stepped away from this project or more ardently supported Nusha's objections. While WELO saw Nusha as a primary Afghan interlocutor, they did not regard her as an expert. Jennifer continued to suggest Soraya for the fellowship based on her stated commitment to act on WELO's behalf in Afghanistan and attend to Jane's concerns about Soraya's safety. At the time Jennifer believed that both WELO and Jane had much more experience with transnational feminist activism and therefore vested them with more authority. Subsequently she privileged their beliefs about the fellowship over her own doubts and Nusha's stated concerns.

Soraya quickly became the *only* suitable candidate for the fellowship as the other candidates lacked one or more qualifications. For example, some candidates lacked permission from their families. Other candidates were married and had children; the fellowship only provided funding for one person, not an entire family. The additional candidates did not have facility with English. The lack of viable candidates can be seen as Nusha's attempts to indirectly communicate the unviability of this fellowship program. Jennifer's intervention sidelined Nusha's attempts to derail the poorly designed program. Soraya ultimately received the fellowship.

Jennifer felt confident that Soraya understood the program's parameters and limitations. Privately, Jane assured Soraya and persuaded her that Nusha's concerns about the program's limitations (such as her inability to earn income) could be overcome. Jennifer and Jane both met with Soraya's family to review the program and help assuage Soraya's parents' concerns about her traveling abroad alone. Jane agreed to travel with Soraya to the United States, and Jennifer arranged to be her guardian in an effort to assist Soraya and ensure her safety. After Jennifer returned to the United States, Jane was instrumental in helping Soraya prepare for her trip. She chaperoned and funded Soraya's trip to Islamabad, Pakistan to interview for and obtain her visa.[2]

Soraya arrived in the United States just after the start of the Muslim holy month of Ramadan, which ends with the celebration of Eid.[3] She began fasting a couple days after her arrival, which she found difficult outside her Afghan context. Soraya's arrival to a place in the United States without an extensive Muslim population and no public recognition or celebrations of Eid (which is a major holiday in Afghanistan) contributed to her feelings of disorientation and loneliness. As an urban dweller, she found adjustment to rural life in the northeastern United States overwhelmingly fraught. Soraya experienced profound homesickness; this was the first time she lived away from her parents and siblings. She said that Jane had assured her that "everything would be better and easier in the United States," while she found this new location strange, incomprehensible, and cold.

Jennifer met daily and spoke often with Soraya about her experiences and concerns. Soraya also met regularly with Rachel. Within a few months, Soraya expressed concern that many of the individuals she encountered viewed her as a poor, suffering, or oppressed woman. She found this alarming, because she considered herself as part of the educated Kabul elite. For example, in an attempt to banter with others, her response to "how are you doing?" was "I am very cold." Soraya's response was an effort to engage people in conversation by talking about the weather because she had observed, "Americans like to discuss the weather." Several individuals became concerned about her response and subsequently contacted Jennifer in order to donate their used coats to Soraya. Jennifer discussed this with Soraya. She politely accepted these "gifts," but simultaneously conveyed how insulted she felt that people assumed she was a poor person who needed (and would accept) a used coat simply because she came from Afghanistan. The coats were secondhand and they conflicted with her urban-Kabul fashion sensibilities. More significantly, they represented an affront to her honor and status as a woman from a well-respected family.

This and other attempts to assist Soraya by providing her with used material goods became somewhat of a joke between Soraya and Jennifer. They found it humorous partly because it reminded them of the many "collect and send" projects they had witnessed in Afghanistan. Many individuals and organizations in the United States post-9/11 organized collection programs of old and used materials to be sent to Afghanistan. This was often based on assumptions about "what was needed." Afghanistan was often imagined as a barren place without access to material goods. Both assumptions fell short, as needs were often articulated by internationals rather than Afghans, and material goods could be purchased from local and regional markets. Most of these projects created more hassle and substantial costs to the recipient organizations than the value of the materials sent. These costs included sorting and transporting donated materials along with the difficulties of storing or disposing of goods that were broken, not useful, or inappropriate. In many respects these programs, similar to the pile of used coats for Soraya, exemplify imagining rather than asking about need. In most cases organizations that have managed "collect and send" gifts found it would have been much easier and certainly more cost effective to receive cash donations to purchase local goods rather than sort, distribute, and dispose of donated material goods from abroad. The cash donations would have supported markets in Afghanistan, a sorely needed boost for the local economy.

Soraya, similar to these recipient communities, had the ability to claim her own needs and preferences. Perceptions of her were fueled by western, liberal assumptions that view agency as independent of one's own body, society, or other sociopolitical contexts (Marsden 2009). Part of Soraya's agency in the United States included choosing her own clothing. Soraya wore a headscarf that tightly concealed her hair; she also wore loose-fitting clothing that fully covered her body. Her sartorial choice disrupted a common trope—that Afghan women who come to the United States will shed their veils as a public display of liberation. Despite extensive academic feminist literature that deconstructs and challenges this trope, it remains part of the mainstream media's representations of Afghan women specifically and Muslim women generally (Abu-Lughod 2013; Ayotte and Husain 2005). Some of the volunteers involved with WELO were either uncomfortable or disappointed with her headscarf choice. Several individuals asked Jennifer, "does she know she doesn't have to wear a veil here?" as if to suggest she needed to be told that she was allowed to shed her headscarf. Soraya knew she was not required to wear a veil, rather she *chose* to wear this garment as part of her personal identity and religious practices.

Soraya remained surprised and annoyed by the expectation that she would discard her headscarf while living in the United States. She spoke at length about this because she did not expect her decision to wear a headscarf to be an issue. Jane had told her that people in the United States valued individual choice and personal freedoms. Her personal choice, however, stood in stark contrast to the geopolitical and feminist imperialist ideologies about what constitutes personal corporeal freedom.

Conflicting Situated Knowledges and Gender Currencies

Soraya had convinced her parents to allow her to come to the United States with an expectation of sending remittances home.[4] Soraya had a well-paid local-Afghan position in Jane's NGO prior to leaving Afghanistan. Her salary provided a significant financial contribution to her family. Soraya's assurances to her parents that she would be able to work in the United States, combined with their understanding of the United States as a wealthy country, reinforced their expectation of financial remittances. Due to the stipulations of her U.S. visa, Soraya was not allowed to work; she could only be compensated for public presentations. The combined funds from her stipend for living expenses and the funds she received for speaking events did not meet her or her family's expectation of remittances. Although Nusha had forewarned her about financial constraints in the United States, Soraya had privileged Jane's representation and assurance that "everything would work out." She chose to believe the assertions of Jane, a U.S. citizen, over Nusha's own experiences in the United States. Soraya was invested in the U.S. development presence in Afghanistan through her work and relationship with Jane. She positioned Jane's representation of power and authority above local and contextualized forms of knowledge and experience as represented by Nusha.

Once Soraya was in the United States, she shared her desire to remain in the country in order to complete her bachelor's degree and go further with her education by obtaining a master's degree. Soraya's aspiration to stay in the United States was further complicated by her own competing emotions—loneliness and homesickness—and conflicting desires to please Jane, Jennifer, Rachel, her parents in Kabul, and WELO. She was reluctant to return home for multiple reasons, including not wanting to return home without a degree. Equally unbearable was the disappointment of providing a smaller financial return than she or her family had envisioned. Soraya's return to Afghanistan was fraught with anxieties about the amount of time she had spent away from home with little to show for it. The certificate of completion she received from WELO would not translate into a valuable form of currency for her in Afghanistan.

Soraya's gender and nationality translated into different forms of currency, which were contingent upon her spatial location. Soraya's facility with English and her ability to traverse space in Kabul without being accompanied by a mahram helped her to secure the position in Jane's NGO. Jane's attempt to help Soraya leave the country was part of her own desire to "save" Soraya from what she believed was an inevitable fate at the hands of local patriarchal structures and cultural mores. Soraya had seen the fellowship through Jane's eyes, believing that in the United States all of her desires would come to fruition. Soraya, by virtue of simply being an Afghan woman, represented a symbol of oppression to her American supporters. This symbol became the currency that helped to garner funds for the WELO fellowship. Soraya had indeed experienced suffering and hardship in her young life due to war-related conflicts and displacements. In many ways this suffering constituted part of her identity, but she was not comfortable with using the perception of her suffering as a method of currency. Soraya was unaware of the ways in which both Jane and WELO represented her as a "suffering subject" in need of saving.

Jane's methods for helping to achieve women's rights in Afghanistan included pushing against social and cultural mores. For example, Jane did not wear a headscarf; she was emphatic about her choice, describing this decision as her "brand." Not wearing a headscarf helped her to stand out among other privileged international workers as an advocate for Afghan women's rights. Another feature of her "brand" was that Jane drove her own car. The vast majority of women in Afghanistan (both local and international) do not drive; they hire taxis or cars with drivers. Jane defined her actions as modeling modern and progressive behavior for young Afghan women. Jane expressed her alternative lifestyle as resistance to local patriarchy. She called herself a *Kabuli*, which is a common distinction in Afghanistan to denote people with a long family history of living in Kabul. By calling herself *Kabuli*, she sought to connect herself with local-Kabul cosmopolitanism. However, her brand of cosmopolitanism resonated more with the international "scene" in Kabul, as discussed in chapter 2, than with local-Afghan *Kabulis*.

Nusha's criticisms of the program were not actively incorporated into the design, nor did the program retain enough flexibility to address the concerns of the fellowship recipient, Soraya (also see Sangtin Writers and Nagar 2006). Critical reflection is an important part of any organization or program, particularly those that seek to challenge existing social structures or provide international experiences. Part of the process of "empowering" women or altering oppression should include listening to marginalized people, even when they critique the very organizations that seek to assist them (Sharma 2008). As postcolonial scholar Gayatri Spivak (1988) argues, subaltern people can indeed speak for themselves; the problem lies in the inability or unwillingness of those in positions of political and economic power to recognize or acknowledge their voices as speech. Programs that are designed to assist are also constrained by policies, donors, and resources. Responsiveness to recipients is limited and rare; adjusting a program during implementation is even harder. Conditions of poverty, oppression, and marginalization are often defined by outsiders based on what communities lack (education, mechanization, resources, etc.). Outsiders are often blind to existing community resources and strengths (e.g., strong networks, family support systems, innovation). Lacking resources or access to political-economic power and influence does not render a community incapable or unwilling to shape the contours of their own lives or mechanisms of assistance.

Each person involved was operating from divergent standpoints or situated knowledges. The concept of situated knowledges, coined by Haraway (1988), includes disparate knowledge claims. This is a way of conceptualizing "knowledges that are explicitly about their positioning, sensitive to the structures of power that construct these multiple positions and committed to making visible the claims of the less powerful" (McDowell 1992, 413). This section examines the messiness of divergent situated knowledges when focused on a common purpose. For example, Jennifer's situated knowledges included being moved by Jane's concerns and Soraya's enthusiasm. Jennifer recognized that Nusha's ideas had been marginalized rather than respected. While researching intimate forms of geopolitics, and attempting to conduct research on services offered, Jennifer was faced with her own American-Afghan entanglement.

Nusha's situated knowledges were based on her own experiences within the United States and living and working in Kabul. As an Afghan woman with both international experience and acute local knowledge, her situated knowledges should have been privileged over those of others involved in formulating the fellowship. WELO's understanding of "how to help" was driven by the geopolitical discourses and ideologies they experienced through their previous work with Afghan women funded by the U.S. Department of State. Jane's interest in helping Soraya was based on her situated knowledges of feminist activism in the United States, negative views of Afghan patriarchy, and a desire to improve Afghan women's lives through a liberal-western feminist lens. The messiness and complications of this story highlight the difficulties associated with attempting to assist without a full understanding of *what is needed, who is in need,* and *how opportunity is defined and valued.* While this project intended to make "visible the claims of the less powerful" (McDowell 1992, 413), it did not succeed in respecting the situated knowledges of those in positions of less economic power or influence over this project, such as Nusha. However, Soraya's acceptance of the fellowship resulted in meeting Jane's, Jennifer's, WELO's, and her own goals.

Connecting the Intimate to the Geopolitical

Institutions and businesses in the United States regularly solicit feedback from customers or stakeholders. However, beneficiaries on the receiving end of assistance are rarely solicited for their input on program improvement. Similarly, requesting feedback or evaluating projects from the perspectives of individuals on the receiving end of internationally driven aid and development projects only occurs in rare or exceptional cases (see Collaborative Learning Projects 2010). Ultimately, WELO's reluctance to integrate Nusha's advice fell within the purview of conventional aid and development praxis—they saw neither Nusha nor Soraya as having an equal and shared relationship with WELO. Due to WELO's small size and their intimate connection to this project, they had, but did not seize, the opportunity to consider all stakeholders as equal participants, especially Nusha and Soraya.

WELO borrowed from the United States a geopolitically driven desire to save/ assist Afghan women. Jane's attempt to rescue Soraya can be seen within the broader context of U.S.-led intervention in Afghanistan. Numerous U.S.-led international interventions post-10/7/01 included "saving" Afghan women as a humanitarian justification for military actions in Afghanistan (Abu-Lughod 2002; Bricmont 2007; Hirschkind and Mahmood 2002; Hunt 2002). As discussed in chapter 1, First Lady Laura Bush, in an infamous radio address on November 17, 2001, claimed that U.S. military gains in Afghanistan were helping to liberate Afghan women. This pronouncement, in addition to similar political and popular discourses, inspired many individuals and groups to join in and be part of the United States' national attention toward Afghanistan. The geopolitical drive to liberate Afghan women translated into currency, as discussed in chapter 3, and enabled WELO to successfully raise funds for this fellowship.

Much of gender-focused programming in Afghanistan remains donor driven. Most large donors have not incorporated the input or needs of Afghan women. Few Afghan women have had direct operational control over programs or funds that propose to help or assist them. Most organizations employ privileged international workers in leadership positions, which may include foreign-passport-holding (and international salary–earning) Afghan expatriates and returnees. These jobs are also contingent on the robust existence of the international community in Afghanistan, rather than the sustained efforts of local organizations. The short-term gains for some women do not ensure longer-term gains for women more broadly. Several scholars have argued that Afghan women in positions of power or authority within organizations have been intensely protective of their positions because of the temporally limited resources and the modicum of power they have been afforded (Azarbaijani-Moghaddam 2006, 2009; Kandiyoti 2007b).

International programs that attempt to assist and "empower" women cannot successfully do so without the full participation of Afghan women across social, ethnic, locational, and class divides. Organizations' unwillingness to listen to and implement local-Afghan women's own articulation of their situation and ideas for change will remain a form of triage assistance that meets international rather than local women's needs and goals. The current modes of aid/development in Afghanistan in many respects attempt to replace the existing system of patriarchy with "new" hierarchical inequalities that in many instances have positioned Afghan women as an object of currency and exchange value. Afghanistan's patriarchal and development structures have made it difficult for women to effectively organize and collaborate. Many Afghan women continuously devise methods to alter, resist, and gain influence within their home lives and communities (Schneider 2005; Smith 2009; Smith and Manalan 2009; Wakefield 2004, 2005; Wakefield and Bauer 2005; Wordsworth 2007).

Privileged international aid and development workers often applaud Afghan women when they denounce or criticize local-Afghan patriarchal structures, while ignoring criticisms of international assistance. Recognizing and allowing Afghan women themselves, and on their own terms, to define the contours of their "empowerment" remains an essential yet overlooked aspect of international efforts. Many Afghan women have received and continue to seek assistance from foreign agencies.

Decision-making power and influence within informal family networks is based on a variety of intersectional factors such as gender, age, relational position within the family, knowledge, personality, and ability to navigate patriarchal structures. In many respects women retain more authority within this informal system than the more formalized structures being supported by international donors. Afghan women's existing positions of influence and authority, or feminist activism, remain highly dynamic while often unseen (or ignored) by international donors. Thus, power and influence is situational and spatially contingent. International development strategies seek to have Afghan women link liberation/freedom with western ideologies. This association encourages the view that neoliberal capitalism is a necessary structure for women's "empowerment."

In Soraya's case, certain aspects of her life can be seen as oppressed or victimized, while other features challenge this depiction. Her relative privilege, education, and skills countered the stereotype of the burqa-clad, suffering Afghan woman. She attempted to alter her own fate by effectively enrolling the assistance of her international employer. While Jane thought she was "saving" Soraya, Soraya was enlisting Jane to persevere on her behalf. In many respects, these different representations of Soraya exemplify situated forms of knowledge that offer different representations of "truth" (Haraway 1988). The belief that Soraya was "saved" because of international intervention rather than her own agency is an example of the more privileged and predominant "truth" that becomes neatly nested within the grand narratives discussed in chapter 1.

WELO was moved by a complicated mix of emotive aspirations to assist young Afghan women. The ways in which WELO organized its fellowship and interacted with Soraya were reminiscent of Kendall's (2002) research on privileged women and charitable organizations, which found that acts of assistance and charity for privileged women were either an expression of class, status, and exclusivity or a path toward upward socioeconomic mobility. Soraya often complained about being "shown-off" to WELO donors and supporters at public and privately held events and parties. Soraya lamented these encounters, stating that she was uncomfortable with these events because she felt like an object or showpiece. Being a showpiece required a particular "performance" that Soraya was both unwilling and unable to enact.

Performance, Performativity, and the Fourth Wall

Feminist philosopher Judith Butler (1990, 1993) employs the concept of gender *performativity* to critique the belief that gender is biologically determined rather than socially constituted. She defines *performativity* as the repetition of learned social behaviors over time, which due to repeated actions come to be learned and viewed as normative. She argues that gender is caused by *doing* rather than *being*. This doing requires extensive repetition of specific actions over time in order for individuals to be effectively performed by those actions. Butler argues that what has been assumed to be an internalized essence of gender is actually assembled through a continuous set of acts, which manifest through gender stylizations of the body. In our discussion of Soraya's behavior, her gender performativity reflected the spatial and situational contexts of her sociocultural experiences through repetition and *doing* rather than *being* female. As Nelson (1999) argues, performativity operates as a spatial process associated with the repetition of "doing gender" within a particular context.

This does not mean that Soraya was bound to her gender without agency or ability to alter her performativity. In many ways her gender performativity was produced through actions and changed through multiple influences, such as education and engagements with Islam. Soraya, as a devout Muslim, took comfort in her religion and found it to be particularly helpful during difficult periods in her life marked by war-related conflict and displacement. Thus, her clothing choices expressed the social and spatial contexts of her gender performativity along with a personal expression of faith. The theater concept of the "fourth wall" provides a helpful metaphor for explicating the differences between Soraya's gender performativity and the "performance" WELO expected. The fourth wall concept is used to highlight the ephemeral border between (1) Soraya's intersectional gender identity and performativity; and (2) WELO's expectation that Soraya would perform liberation through sartorial transgression.

The "fourth wall" is a term used by theater professionals to identify the invisible "wall" between the audience and stage performers. The audience members, by virtue of their placement in the theater, agree to suspend reality as part of their participation in the illusion created by the actors. Both the actors and the audience, when they enter into the theater space, agree to a temporally limited suspension of reality in order to enjoy the theatrical performance. When the actors perform poorly, the fourth wall begins to erode. In Soraya's case, WELO (as audience) expected a particular gender performance that they had scripted through their own mediated understandings of Afghanistan. Conversely, Soraya lived, believed, and delivered a much different script.

The fourth wall operated as an invisible border between Soraya's gender performativity and WELO's expected gender performance. The fourth wall had been crafted by a geopolitically infused expectation that Soraya would perform liberation on U.S. soil, similar to some of the public performances of unveiling discussed in chapter 1. WELO's expected gender performance from Soraya matched the geopolitical representations of Afghan women's liberation by way of U.S.-led interventions. The performance they anticipated from Soraya was also informed by the framing of Afghan women's living-suffering as a grievable object exchanged as currency, discussed in chapter 3. The currency of this grievable object was used by WELO to "sell" this fellowship (to donors) as a path to Afghan women's liberation. Since the grievable object of Afghan women's living-suffering *in* Afghanistan was the currency exchanged to garner funds for the fellowship, Soraya's oppression *had* to be altered by virtue of her locational transfer to the United States as expected by WELO and their donors in order to perform public displays of liberation.

As stated earlier, both Soraya and WELO entered into this arrangement with conflicting situated knowledges and specific goals, ideas, and hopes, which were challenged and altered as a result. As Soraya's gender performativity eroded the fourth wall, WELO attempted to maintain this invisible border. The spatial context of Soraya's gender performativity was not altered by way of her (temporally limited) relocation. Rather, she held onto her gender performativity as an expression of personal identity. Spatially, Soraya's performativity of her gender, while working for Jane in Afghanistan, met Jane's expectation of a woman in need of "saving." In the United States, Soraya's gender performativity did not meet WELO's expectations of a "newly liberated" woman. WELO expected a more dramatic transformation based largely on appearance. The performance they anticipated did not materialize.

Soraya's erasure of the fourth wall was viewed as her acting "off script"; she did not meet the geopolitical and mediated expectations of Afghan women shedding their veils as a sign of liberation. The individuals and groups that hold the purse strings of assistance projects build the fourth wall by writing the script and then directing, producing, and starring in the drama of development and aid. The recipient communities provide the set and support roles for the prescribed projects and expectations of the lead actors (i.e., development "experts"). Deviations or changes to these scripts, particularly from supporting actors, are subsequently identified as poor performances rather than flaws in the proverbial script.

Gender identities and conflict-driven displacements neither can nor should be reduced to mediated geographies, narrow representations of places and people, and dramatic representations of suffering or liberation. Everyday lived experiences are much more messy, complicated, and ordinary than suggested in mediated depictions.

Soraya found navigating through the various events, systems, and interactions associated with her fellowship stressful and difficult. Over time, Soraya continued to challenge WELO's expectations. Eventually she realized that the fourth wall was a border that reinforced her gender currency toward educational scholarships and other sources of funding. Nonetheless, she found it difficult to trade on the currency associated with perceptions of her suffering in Afghanistan and expected liberation in the United States. She further realized that stating, "I am going to become a leader for women's rights in Afghanistan" was part of the expected script. She discussed this at length with Rachel and Jennifer, identifying that some of her Afghan friends told her to say what Americans with money and influence to provide scholarships wanted to hear.

Each time she attempted to break through rather than reinforce the fourth wall, she found her gender currency, and subsequent ability to secure an educational scholarship in the United States, significantly diminished.

WELO

Let's look at the program from WELO's perspective. They raised and spent a considerable amount of money for this fellowship. They provided Soraya with new clothes, shoes, health care, housing, and transportation. Though highly valued by WELO, these funds did not have the same meaning and value to Soraya. Partly, this was due to her youth, inexperience living on her own, and lack of understanding about the program's funding mechanism. Although Soraya had earned an income in Afghanistan, she gave her earnings to her mother, who managed the household finances. Soraya did not have any prior experience managing financial resources. For example, she often overspent her generous monthly stipend. The cost of goods and services related to the fellowship translated into a particular form of economic value for WELO, which expected a performative return on their investment in Soraya.

Previous expressions of this story have met with reactions such as, "Well, Soraya knew what she was getting herself into, and she should be happy with what she was given considering her alternatives." This reaction, although common, reinforces existing unbalanced forms of assistance that do not involve beneficiaries as equal partners. Individuals living in conflict zones or areas marred by physical and structural violence *should* have just as much influence and control over the "well-meaning" individuals and organizations that propose to help, save, assist, or empower them. How can organizations propose to "empower" women without including them in decision making and implementation of programs?

An unequal relationship persists between Afghan women and the individuals and organizations poised to assist them. This inequality further perpetuates donor-driven approaches that propose to help, while directing and determining programs generally without any expectation of feedback or critique. The uneven relationship between donors and recipients grows deeper when these relationships demand uneven reciprocity (Silk 2004). Yeh's (2013) analysis of gift relationships identifies that once a gift is recognized as such by both giver and receiver, there is often an expected form of reciprocity determined by the giver. Thus, WELO's gift reciprocity was expected by way of Soraya's performance of liberation. As a gift provider, WELO did not view Nusha or Soraya as equal partners/stakeholders around the decision-making table. They were providing her with financial resources and expected to "show off" Soraya to their friends and donors by way of parties and public events. This required a particular type of gender performance to which Soraya was not accustomed; she found it insulting. Soraya was unable and unwilling to perform in the ways WELO and its supporters anticipated as reciprocity for their fellowship gift.

Arguably, Soraya had undergone varying degrees of gender-based marginalization, oppression, and suffering growing up in Afghanistan. The parameters of her experiences are hers to define; any changes to her gender performativity are hers to direct. Predesigned scripts intended to assist can lead to the aid and development trap of replacing one form of inequality with another. Such a pitfall suggests that recipients should view uneven and inadequate development or assistance as a preferred form of inequality. Soraya exemplifies the push-pull experienced by several Afghan women's groups and organizations that must navigate between competing interests. She experienced a multitude of pressures and expectations from her family in Afghanistan, WELO as her host organization, the schools where she studied, and her friends and acquaintances in Afghanistan and the United States.

Jane's assumptions about Soraya's "easier life" in the United States were based on her own experience and perspective. For Jane, life in the United States was exponentially easier than her own experiences living in Kabul. Conversely, for Soraya, life in the United States was exceedingly difficult. In the United States, most news and media reports focused on the war and the negative aspects of living in Afghanistan. Media reports about the positive aspects of Afghan life, the richness of the culture, the humor of the people, and the importance of family to both men and women remain rare or nonexistent. Soraya was used to being surrounded by her parents and seven siblings, along with uncles, aunts, and cousins. She had never slept in a room by herself before coming to the United States. She had never eaten alone, walked alone, or cooked by herself. Soraya's conflicting desires to both return to her family in Afghanistan and remain in the United States created a tremendous amount of stress and anxiety for her. Neither WELO nor Jane expected her to experience homesickness or unhappiness; they assumed that her life would seamlessly improve by virtue of locational transfer to the United States.

Soraya returned to Afghanistan at the end of the fellowship and continued her education. She worked with a diverse array of groups advocating for women's rights and responsibilities in her own country. Ultimately, traveling to the United States neither "saved" Soraya in the way Jane envisioned nor helped her to perform or articulate secular liberal feminism. However, she became a staunch and articulate advocate of Islamic feminism in Afghanistan. Upon her return home she focused her studies on Sharia (Islamic law) in order to articulate her rights within Islam. She identified this as the best strategy within her own sociopolitical context in Afghanistan. Soraya believed that respect for and belief in Islam within Afghanistan combined with the rights afforded to women within the Qur'an and other Islamic texts offered her (and other women) the best opportunity for increasing women's rights within her country.

Soraya was very much an agent of her own destiny rather than a passive victim of circumstance. Afghan women like Soraya and Nusha must be at the forefront of decision making, because they are the best people to define their "liberation" with respect to the parameters of their socioeconomic, political, and cultural contexts. For example, what appears to an outsider as docility and oppression may indeed be the very conditions from which a woman can secure influence, authority, or "empowerment" (Mahmood 2005).

As a leading scholar on gender and development, Naila Kabeer (1994, 2005), argued over twenty years ago, in order to assist women as part of the processes of development, those women must be included in drafting the proposals as well as implementing the projects that seek to move women out of economic poverty and sociopolitical marginalization. These women should have a prominent seat at the tables around which such projects are designed. Although this contention supports many of the arguments in this chapter, it is vital to recognize the reason many aid or development projects do not listen to recipients is not simply willful neglect or lack of interest. The actual "needs" of recipient communities do not push the bottom-line goals of geopolitically and geo-economically driven development metrics (Essex 2013). Geopolitics remains a primary rationale for fueling the engines of programs in order to *develop* a country's placement within the global economy that ultimately benefits donor countries and multinational donor organizations (Harvey 2006; Lawson 2014).

Conclusion

In spite of Nusha's misgivings, WELO proceeded with the fellowship program in an effort to more fully engage with Afghan women. Jennifer, feeling caught between Nusha's apprehensions, Jane's security concerns, and Soraya's desires, intervened by suggesting Soraya for the WELO fellowship. Jane, as a privileged international living in Kabul and as Soraya's employer, sought to engage in an act of feminist heroism by helping Soraya leave the country and to escape from local-Afghan patriarchal structures. Correspondingly, Soraya viewed relocation in the United States as a way to increase her currency and status in Afghanistan by way of foreign education. Soraya's relationship with Jane as her employer, mentor, and representative of the occupying power led her to privilege Jane's perspective over Nusha's expertise and experience.

Although the fellowship did not manifest in the ways Soraya anticipated, she gained additional skills, experienced living with people outside her family, and developed international friendships. The WELO fellowship can be considered a material manifestation of the geopolitical discourses discussed in chapters 1 and 2. WELO viewed Afghanistan generally, and by extension Islam, as the barrier to women's liberation and freedom (also see Abu-Lughod 2013). Conversely, Soraya found Islam as an important conduit for her salvation/liberation. Islamic feminism remains a cornerstone of Soraya's personal and professional work on women's rights in Afghanistan. Soraya's experiences exemplify that of many Afghan women who do not easily fit within existing metrics or two-dimensional portraits of oppression or suffering.

Afghan women such as Soraya have the support of their families to work and go to school; in return they help to support their families financially. Both popular and academic discussions about the Afghan family tend to highlight the negative aspects associated with patriarchy, domestic violence, and the practices of purdah (Jamal 2009). It is important to acknowledge that family structures *also* provide women (and men) with essential support networks to help foster their rights, education, employment, and political opportunities. For example, Afghan women who work in or lead organizations do so *with the support of their families* rather than in spite of their approval. The narrative presented in this chapter illustrates how international development projects operate as forms of imperial or neocolonial social engineering under the auspices of assistance or women's "empowerment."

The mediated images of Afghan women's suffering and oppression in Afghanistan, along with liberation by foreign invasion and intervention, set the backdrop for the WELO/Soraya performance. A theatrical fourth wall was constructed between Soraya's gender performativity and WELO's expectation of her liberation-performance. The geopolitically inspired assumptions of Soraya's liberation-performance ignored her own gender performativity and personal expressions of faith and identity. The story of "saving" Soraya illustrates several complications, complementary goals, and competing ideas on assistance. Soraya was both an agent of her own destiny and an object of need for those seeking to "save" her. This story further highlights the value of developing egalitarian relationships between those who give and receive assistance. Acknowledging Afghan women's agency requires the ability to listen and respond to the needs of others and develop equitable relationships, rather than privilege outsider knowledge as expertise.

Soraya performed neither her suffering nor her gender liberation in expected ways. Rather than speaking out about her suffering and subsequent acts of resistance against the Taliban or other forms of patriarchy, she took a much more subtle and introspective approach. She preferred writing to public speaking, and personal interaction to public demonstration. While her differentiated methods of expression ran counter to expectations in the United States, they aligned with comportment expectations in her home community. Outspoken women are regularly met with public scrutiny and gossip when they counter gendered behavioral expectations. Therefore, women who attempt to influence public discourse in Afghanistan must often contend with regular and significant social obstacles. The international donor community recognizes and often rewards these outspoken women as pioneers and trailblazers. Thus, publicly outspoken women often experience additional forms of backlash because of their perceived association with western liberal feminism. This attention often translates into actual international donor funds, suggesting yet another dimension to gender currency.

Other forms of women's rights or feminist activism that regularly go unnoticed by international workers and donors include subtler, discreet, private, and often tactical approaches that destabilize existing patterns of patriarchy. Both public and behind-the-scenes advocacy coexist in various intersecting, complementary, and at times conflicting ways. The complete picture of the numerous situational methods for gender-based activism in Afghanistan has not been included in the framing recognized by economically and geopolitically influential organizations.

Therefore, it is imperative to critically examine the ways in which certain representations of gender generate emotive responses and desires to give, assist, or save. The following chapter addresses this question by examining the public representations of grief for the victims of 9/11 and assistance programs devised by surviving family members. Chapter 7 discusses the ways in which the currency of surviving family members' grief allowed them to raise funds to assist Afghan women and children.

CHAPTER 7

"Our Hearts Break"
9/11 Deaths, Afghan Lives, and Intimate Intervention

This book has presented a critical examination of the ways in which the grievable-object of gendered Afghan living-suffering has been used and manipulated as geopolitical and geo-economic currency. In this chapter, we analyze two case studies to illustrate how the grievability of 9/11 deaths translated into currency, which was exchanged toward assistance projects in Afghanistan. The goal of this chapter is to explicate a more nuanced understanding of power geometries (Massey 1994) in an effort to illustrate the numerous categories of "morally deserving humanity" (Ong 2006, 24). The liberal and progressive ideologies of humanitarianism and feminism can and have been wielded as weapons to produce the violence and dispossession that rights-based claims seek to challenge (Slaughter 2007).

Constant critical reflection on economic and racial privilege, even during moments of grief, are necessary in order to dismantle the use of these privileged emotional geographies as a barrier to critical analysis. Emotional geographies attempt to understand affect through individual or collective experiences and conceptualizations of place (Davidson, Bondi, and Smith 2005). The emotional geographies associated with 9/11 were situated in place (i.e., locales such as New York, Pennsylvania, and Washington, D.C.) and ultimately mapped onto the U.S. nation as a whole. The intimate grief of individuals affected by the 9/11 attacks on the United States emotively resituated and rescaled personal losses to that of national tragedy. This chapter demonstrates the ways in which personal grief was scaled to national grief to elicit a particular political recognition of 9/11 victims. These deaths subsequently became geopolitical and geo-economic currency.

Grief is most often defined as an emotive response to tragedy and loss. This emotion can be a tactile feeling or animated to reflect a deep personal experience of loss or trauma. What happens when personal grief becomes public, collective, and even geopolitical? National tragedies such as the events of 9/11 (in the United States) have been expressed through public spectacles of grief. The articulation of public sorrow by way of presidential speeches, political discourses, and media narratives maneuvered and shaped national-collective suffering in order to legitimate political and military action (Burk 2003; Dahlman and Brunn 2003; Engle 2007; Fried 2006; Saal 2011; and Simko 2012). This examination of the geopolitics of grief demonstrates the intersections between intimate, national, and global appropriations of 9/11 grief and Afghan suffering.[1] Natural and human-caused disasters have a significant historical framing within the United States and have become part of the nation's collective identity (Rozario 2007). The tragedy of 9/11 exemplified a form of "mediated trauma" that incorporated nationalistic symbols and ideologies to situate this event within a framework of collective national identity and sorrow (Kaplan 2005).

For the individuals who lost loved ones on 9/11, their mourning is deeply personal, while simultaneously shared as a collective experience of suffering by citizens of an "injured nation." This grief was subsequently woven into various discourses that sought to validate the U.S. military response culminating in the October 7, 2001 invasion of Afghanistan (Engle 2007; Gunn 2004). Similar to Butler's (2006, 2009) theoretical discussion of grievability, Engle (2007) has argued that Afghan deaths were not framed as worthy of grief or as part of the political representations of 9/11 and its aftermath (i.e., the Global War on Terror). However, Afghan life portrayed through the frame of gendered suffering under the Taliban regime elicited a particular form of representational grief. This grief was not attached to Afghan civilian deaths but rather to the objectified oppression of Afghan life, predominantly symbolized by a burqa-clad woman.

On November 17, 2001, First Lady Laura Bush addressed the traumatized American nation as a self-appointed spokesperson for Afghan women. The following excerpt from her speech illustrates how she framed American sorrow and sympathy for Afghan women and children: "The plight of women and children in Afghanistan is a matter of deliberate human cruelty, carried out by those who seek to intimidate and control. Civilized people throughout the world are speaking out in horror—*not only because our hearts break for the women and children in Afghanistan*, but also because in Afghanistan we see the world the terrorists would like to impose on the rest of us" (emphasis ours).[2] This speech was intended to evoke an emotional response of sympathy and sorrow toward the "heart-breaking" plight of Afghan women and children. As discussed by several feminist scholars, this speech was a focal point for framing the "saving women" trope that helped to situate and further justify U.S. military actions in Afghanistan (Abu-Lughod 2002; Hirschkind and Mahmood 2002; Hunt 2002; Young 2003). This rallying cry also came at a time when the U.S.-led war in Afghanistan was marked by thousands of Afghan civilian deaths and the return of Afghanistan's civil war–era warlords. The invocation of these tropes helped to dehistoricize U.S. policies that abetted if not preempted the events of 9/11.[3] Simultaneously, "saving" Afghan women helped to reinforce the need for protracted U.S.-led intervention (Mamdani 2004; Rashid 2001, 2008). As

Mamdani (2004) reminds us, the United States was actively involved in perpetuating the conflict by helping to finance a pan-Islamic jihad against "godless communism" during the cold war. What international relations scholars often refer to as "blowback"—the growth of violent political Islam against the United States—grew from these foreign policy initiatives in the 1980s (Johnson 2000).

Grief as Currency—Setting the Stage for 9/11 and Beyond

Olds, Sidaway, and Sparke (2005) provide a sharp and poignant discussion about the way in which the representation of grief associated with 9/11 was racially contingent, focusing on a "white selfhood" that included " the geopolitical cover-up of the terror and death suffered by non-white people" (478). They argue that this racialized representation, in addition to the loss of life, includes "the loss of a critical lesson in how to respond to terror and mass death with justice and humanity" (ibid.). In light of these arguments, this chapter provides an overview of national grief and remembrances of 9/11 along with intimately personal responses to the loss of loved ones. By examining intimate responses to grief, we illustrate the ways in which 9/11 grief currency manifested into funds to help Afghan women and children. In these examples, Afghan women and children are geopolitically situated as grievable objects of living-suffering (as discussed in chapter 3). First, the following section reviews the ways in which 9/11 grief became nationalized and translated into currency.

Nationalized 9/11 Grief Currency

The visual portraits of 9/11 tragedies through the repetition of still and video photography served a central role in scaling personal loss as nationalized grief. Spatially visual language such as the "wounded skyline" was used to describe New York City on the afternoon of 9/11; the repetition of images of destruction were followed by both spontaneous and carefully constructed memorials. Street memorials provided a visual disruption to pedestrian traffic in an effort to demand reflection (Kaplan 2005). These memorials, combined with images of missing persons, were decidedly intimate—personal—and not immediately tied to communal expressions of national identity or patriotism (ibid.). Nationalistic themes were incorporated into the more institutionalized memorials and politically framed remembrances of the 9/11 dead. Political haranguing about how to permanently memorialize the dead included concerns that the World Trade Center site would be turned into a voyeuristic attraction and the surrounding area into a mall, much of which has materialized in recent years (Haskins and DeRose 2003).

Film, theater, and literature provided an avenue for shaping emotive summaries of 9/11 and how Americans were expected to reflect upon and remember these events (Greenberg 2003; Saal 2011). The *New York Times' Portraits of Grief* exemplified an individuation of sorrow in an effort to shape a sense of collective intimacy and shared pain.[4] These obituaries, and their accompanying photos, served to give meaning and to explain 9/11, which at that time was viewed as the unexplainable (Lule 2002). Lule (2002) further argues that these profiles affirmed dominant cultural values and beliefs in the United States at a time when people were questioning and challenging these beliefs in an effort to understand *why* the United States was attacked on 9/11. The emotive portraits in the *New York Times* distracted the populace from critically examining the "all-too-real consequences of the U.S. government's official policy of retaliation" (Engle 2007, 72). As one of the first institutionalized attempts to commemorate the deaths on 9/11, this collection of grief portraits offered a public expression of American values and featured an accounting of these deaths as grievable (Hume 2003; Butler 2006, 2009). This collective grief helped to situate 9/11 as an unfathomable drama and the United States as an innocent victim of terrorism rather than an imperial power that has continually exercised military force to secure its own political and economic interests. Public discussion and reflection on U.S. foreign policies and historical events that may have contributed to the violence of 9/11 were lacking at the time. However, public dissent eventually grew; a coalition of 9/11 surviving family members organized and demanded answers from the U.S. government. Their activism led to the formation of the 9/11 Commission in late 2002, and its completed report in 2004 (9/11 Commission 2004). Public reviews and popular criticisms of the aftermath of 9/11 continued through several mediated outlets. Challenges to the "grand narratives" emerged from public intellectuals such as Mahmood Mamdani's (2004) book *Good Muslim, Bad Muslim: America, the Cold War, and the Roots of Terror*, popular documentary filmmaker Michael Moore's Oscar-winning film *Fahrenheit 9/11*, and journalist and syndicated columnist Naomi Klein's (2008) best-selling book *The Shock Doctrine: The Rise of Disaster Capitalism*. These are just a few examples among others of vocal dissent to mainstream and government-mediated expectations of how to understand and remember 9/11.

The Smithsonian Institution, as a U.S. government museum, constructed an institutionalized framing and remembrance of 9/11.[5] The Smithsonian exhibit emphasized national unification around leaders and developed common symbols and icons to help discredit dissenting or alternative representations of 9/11. This exhibit was infused with nationalistic rhetoric and stood in stark contrast to spontaneous street and online memorials in New York and elsewhere (Haskins and DeRose 2003). Amy Fried (2006) argues that the Smithsonian's use of personal narratives in its 9/11 exhibit precluded meaningful critiques or multiple analyses of these events. In the early days after 9/11, although a disciplining and homogenizing of U.S. memorials and responses was actively being formed, "on the streets something fluid, personal and varied was taking place" (Kaplan 2005, 15). The street memorials generated by grieving loved ones and fellow citizens focused on the lives and deaths of individual people rather than the injured nation.

Memory and remembrance are important aspects of both personal and political grief. The political demands of the nation incorporated techniques of melodrama and storytelling to (1) define "America as a heroic redeemer," (2) depict Americans as a "unified and moral nation," and (3) authenticate American virtue "by the resolution to undertake retributive action in response to victimization" (Anker 2005, 35). Some U.S.-based imperialist-feminist responses, such as that of the Feminist Majority Foundation, supported the incorporation of Afghan women's rights as further justification for U.S. military actions (Russo 2006). Conversely, other U.S. and international feminist responses included multiple voices of caution, dissent, and concern about the U.S.-led invasion and occupation of Afghanistan (Hawthorne and Winter 2002). Lorraine Dowler (2002) critiques the removal or invisibility of women within the narrative of 9/11 heroes, which masculinized the space of ground zero through the visual embodiment of the former towers as a male police officer and male firefighter. The use of heroic-masculine terminology embraced "new" mythologies of supermen and heroes fighting to protect and save women (Kensinger 2009). This was further contextualized through various forms of popular geopolitics such as films, video games, and comic books, including the revival of the popular World War II hero, Captain America (Dittmer 2005, 2013). The masculinization of ground zero coupled with the protection of the now-feminized homeland was expanded by the imperative to "save" Afghan women. The rescue fetish has become its own objectified currency, producing the transition of Afghan women's living-suffering cum liberation into a consumer good (see chapter 4).

Some scholars have highlighted responses to 9/11 that were neither political nor motivated by personal economic gain. Dahlman and Brunn (2003, 277) argue that "The contribution of money, time, material aid and even blood mark significant forms of redistribution in society that do not conform to state or market institutions." While remembrances are not without contestation and challenge, the predominant messages and grand narratives shaped by nationally institutionalized remembrances of 9/11 positioned the United States as the wounded hero with the legitimate and even moral obligation to seek retributive justice (Däwes 2007).

9/11 Grief Currency

As discussed in chapter 3, the combination of grievable 9/11 deaths with the grievability of gendered Afghan aliveness (living-suffering) has translated into different forms of geopolitical gender currency. The geopolitics of grief currency produces a consumer culture through memorials and storytelling that are often reduced to the consumption of trinkets as objects of remembrance and loss (Fried 2006). Remembrances were marketed through the sale of souvenirs and commemorative gear. Walmart sold 4.96 million American flags within the first seven months after 9/11 compared with 1.18 million the previous year; the United States issued a 9/11 commemorative postage stamp that yielded $30 million in revenue; and both Qur'an and Bible sales increased by 800 percent and 30 percent, respectively (Brunn 2004). Organizations responding to 9/11 also garnered a certain level of social capital by attending to the social and emotional recovery of both New Yorkers and the nation as a whole (Fullilove et al. 2004).

This 9/11 grief currency can be calculated in terms of actual funds, consumptive practices, and the valuation of 9/11 deaths through compensation programs for surviving families. The families of those who died on 9/11 received much larger compensation packages than those who were injured or became ill as a result of rescue and recovery efforts (Gilbert and Ponder 2013). Therefore, the grievable deaths of victims had more currency—and, by extension, monetary value—than those who survived or assisted with recovery efforts.

Afghan civilian deaths may fall under the U.S. political rhetoric as expendable, collateral, and not grievable, although they retain geopolitical currency. For example, Afghan aliveness—portrayed through the gendered lens of Taliban- and Al-Qaeda-imposed living-suffering—expects a modicum of grievability within U.S. framings of Afghan women's oppression. This grief, when linked with development potentiality, has become its own form of currency, as discussed in chapter 3. The currency of 9/11 grief combined with Afghan need further situates assistance as by definition "good" and beyond critique. An undeniable good can and often does manifest into unequal power relations that manipulatively define assistance and development writ large as apolitical, benevolent, and altruistic. The following examination of American-Afghan entanglements illustrates differentiated forms of grief and gender currency.

9/11 Grief, Human Connection, and Currency

The organizations Beyond the 11th and the Peter M. Goodrich Memorial Foundation were each founded in response to the loss of loved ones on 9/11. Beyond the 11th was founded by Susan Retik and Patti Quigley, whose husbands were passengers on the planes that hit the World Trade Center towers. This organization raises funds for projects to assist widows in Afghanistan through Care International. Don and Sally Goodrich, the parents of Peter, who died on flight 175, founded the Peter M. Goodrich Memorial Foundation. This foundation has built schools in Afghanistan and provided young Afghans with the opportunity to study in the United States at secondary and collegiate levels. The following analysis of these organizations centers on the public representation of them through websites and documentary films made about these extraordinary people.

This analysis does not critique the personal actions and reactions of these individuals who attempted to formulate a nonviolent and humane response to their personal grief. Rather, this examination focuses on the public and nationalized framing of their private grief and healing. By evaluating the public framing of these organizations, we elucidate the ways in which the extraordinary actions of individuals became integrated into the geopolitical and geo-economic structures of gendered aid and development efforts in Afghanistan.

The documentary film about the Peter M. Goodrich Memorial Foundation is titled *Axis of Good: A Story from 9/11*, and the documentary about Retik and Quigley, the 9/11 widows who founded Beyond the 11th, is titled *Beyond Belief*.[6] The titles of both of these films offer poignant and emotive linguistic techniques to illustrate responses to grief as unique and exceptional acts of kindness in a time of crisis. The *Axis of Good* title suggests a counterframing to former President Bush's use of the term "Axis of Evil" to represent enemies of the U.S. state. It also situates the acts and actions contained in this film within the larger economic and geopolitical framing of humanitarian aid. *Beyond Belief* similarly focuses on the exceptionality of two 9/11 widows' responses to grief as one that does not seek revenge through violence but rather extends assistance through differentiated experiences of grief. In both cases these organizations operate from positions of relative economic privilege vis-à-vis the Afghans they engage with, and a modicum of power and authority associated with their status as Americans. Aid and development as a system is not critiqued in these films but rather represented as unquestionably benevolent.

The women featured in these respective documentaries are represented with a particular framing of intimacy through motherhood and home. Domestic spaces operate as a visual tool for drawing the viewer into their private lives, thus intimately connecting the viewer to the everydayness of these individuals and their grief. *Beyond Belief* provides several scenes of Retik and Quigley engaging in daily activities associated with motherhood, such as waking up their children, taking them to school, and preparing and eating meals. Similarly, the domestic sphere is a central technique for framing and drawing in the audience's intimacy with the Goodrich family in the *Axis of Good* documentary. The interviews and discussions with the respective families are also often portrayed in domestic spaces, and several shots in both films show connections between family members in kitchens, dining rooms, and bedrooms. The personal lens frames viewers' perception of these wounded families.

Sally Goodrich, as a mother who lost a son, is further represented as sacrificing time and attention toward her surviving children and grandchildren in order to become the benefactor of a school in Afghanistan. The representational use of gender resonates through the existing shibboleth of motherhood as virtuous, altruistic, and moral through various scenes and illustrations of care and kindness. A moral representation of motherhood and humanitarianism provides a form of authority for situating these actions as benevolent. The women and organizations depicted in the film show how each woman's personal sense of loss and relative privilege is the basis for making connections with individuals in Afghanistan. Retik and Quigley accomplish this by supporting widows in Afghanistan; Goodrich's focus is on education programs.

These documentary stories fit within a larger framework that depoliticizes and dehistoricizes U.S. geopolitical interventions in the region. The focus on the benevolent work of these individuals in Afghanistan removes a political tone and precludes any critique of U.S. foreign policy (Anker 2005; Maney, Woehrle, and Coy 2005; Wright 2012).[7] The American women's compassionate work with Afghans associates their American identities with morality similar to the institutionalized memorials and remembrances of 9/11. In addition to the shared response to 9/11 grief for both charitable organizations, three common themes are presented in each documentary: (1) an emphasis on nonviolence, love, and kindness; (2) the importance of making a personal connection through travel to Afghanistan to see the actual projects sponsored by their respective charities; and (3) "meaning making" as a method for processing and healing from profound loss.

The emphasis on nonviolence, love, and kindness is illustrated through the way in which Quigley and Retik are discussed by Paul Barker, director of CARE International in Kabul, Afghanistan, when he states: "Given the choice between violence and love they choose love."[8] Similarly, Don Goodrich states, "For every act of violence there needs to be an act of kindness or we devolve into violence." These films further underscore the importance placed by the Americans on making a personal connection with Afghans. Sally Goodrich connects her personal healing with a sense of shared grief and developing a common connection across difference. She states: "It wasn't until I encountered people who had suffered a great deal more, that I realized suffering is a bridge between people unlikely to communicate." Similarly Retik, in preparation for her first trip to Afghanistan, identifies her ultimate goal as making "a true connection with at least one of the women" that she will meet.

Both Susan Retik and Sally Goodrich identify their charitable work as an essential part of their own personal healing. For example, Retik, in response to the descriptions of her as "so generous," states, "well it really, really, really is as much for me as it's for the people we are trying to help. I need this to keep busy and focused and feeling productive." Similarly, Sally Goodrich connects the work she and her husband are doing for Afghans as part of "always trying to figure out how to reconstruct our lives." She also sees the work she is doing in Afghanistan as "living out the best part of my kid." Quigley, in describing the post-traumatic stress associated with profound grief, states that her healing process is a form of post-traumatic growth: "You also have post-traumatic growth and that's when you are able to positively make it through a tragedy. There's some kind of good or growth forward." Quigley and others contextualize their grief as a process of healing by attending to Afghan living-suffering. In the film Afghans are regularly identified as "having nothing." Nothing is represented in economic and resource terms. Therefore, the extensive networks among Afghans — along with their agency, resilience, and capabilities — are not discussed or highlighted in either film. However, the extensive suffering and need of Afghans is emphasized.

The focus on Afghan suffering incorporated into both films attempts to elicit viewer empathy. The 9/11 grief is continually represented through an intimate lens. Both films explicitly illustrate emotional expressions of the grievable deaths of the 9/11 victims. Afghan women are interviewed and included, particularly in *Beyond Belief*, with emotional scenes between the 9/11 widows and their Afghan counterparts. Individual interviews with Afghan women focus on their grievable living-suffering as widows and mothers and in situations of economic desperation and insecurity. In one scene there is mention of U.S.-sponsored violence, which is transferred to the Taliban and mitigated through a discussion of shared grief in the entangled conversations between the American and Afghan widows.

The scene begins with a number of widows in a room speaking (through a translator) to Retik and Quigley.

Modira Sahidi
> I have a 25-year-old daughter. When an American bomb hit our house her father died and she got injured. She was blinded. Her head and skull were fractured. The treatment she received didn't work, but I couldn't afford any more. My house is close, I wish you could come and visit her.

Retik
> Now that we've met you *(pause)*. Before we met you we wanted to help you. Now that we met you we *really* want to help you. We will tell your stories when we go home and we will let people know, and we will continue to help support you. We will continue to work hard.

The next scene is at Modira Sahidi's house.

Modira Sahidi
> She [Modira's daughter] was sitting with her father when the rocket came through the window. The ceiling fell and we all screamed, 'What happened?' We were afraid to move because another rocket might come. No one came, no neighbors, no one.

Retik
What do you think about the United States because your husband was killed as a result of bombing? Do you ... *(explaining to the translator)* before she answers tell her I won't be offended, whatever she says. To be honest ....

Zainab Wahidi, local representative of CARE Afghanistan, translates:
Your husband died in an American bombing. What do you think about America?

Modira Sahidi
It was from God, God's will.

Zainab Wahidi, translates:
What do you think about America? Tell us how you imagine it. Even if you think something bad don't be afraid to say it.

Modira Sahidi
Why should we say something bad about them? The Taliban are the bad people. Because of them, this is what happened.

Retik
It is the same living in the United States. Some people think blame Afghanistan for, or some of the people of Afghanistan, for the attacks on the United States, and this is why we're trying to reach out because it's a terrible situation that one hurts another, that gets the repercussion, I don't know if you can translate all of that but ....

Modira Sahidi
I think we have the same experience. In America's war—there and here—we became widows, and they became like us.

The scene ends.

Interestingly, the U.S. role in the death of Afghan civilians is identified, while Modira Sahidi blames the Taliban as "the bad people." The scene ends with a sense of shared experience, while identifying the conflict in both the United States and Afghanistan as "America's war." Retik signals a sense of common experience as operating outside the boundaries and cyclical aspects of political conflict, further depoliticizing international assistance. Sahidi's overall framing of her husband's death provides an "authentic" lens through which to reinforce U.S. violence as ultimately good for Afghanistan. This scene, along with the entire documentary, provides no historical or political context for U.S.-led military actions or development interventions.

In many respects, these examples illustrate profound and notable attempts to create intimately emotive linkages based on a belief in shared grief. The framing of Afghan and American civilians as common victims of the same terrorists responsible for 9/11 helps to shape a similar yet differentiated sense of victimhood. This victimhood operates to subtly erase the role of U.S. foreign policy and historical maneuvers in the region. The attempts by each organization to orchestrate projects beyond the bordered expectations of sovereign power can be viewed as operating above politics. Conversely, when compared with other institutionalized remembrances of 9/11 grief, these "heroic" efforts fit within a dehistoricized and depoliticized framing of the United States. These personal reactions suggest a "geography of care" as a counter to military efforts and militarized aid/development interventions (Lawson 2007). However, the representations of these stories dangerously situate them as apolitical. Paradoxically, these apolitical representations reinforce the United States as engaging in just, moral, and benevolent interventions in Afghanistan. These public representations, through documentary films and websites, are by definition geopolitical. The efforts of these individuals to situate themselves and their acts as above or outside of politics presents a complex, complicated, and at times confused entanglement (Donini 2007; Drury, Olson and Belle 2005; Duffield, Macrae, and Curtis 2001).

The use of documentary film attempts to articulate an alternative response to 9/11 while simultaneously reinforcing the grievability of 9/11 deaths and gendered Afghan living-suffering. The grievability of the men lost on 9/11 translates into grief currency for the respective families. The *Axis of Good* film begins at a church service where the reverend explains the Goodrich family's interest in building a school in Afghanistan in memory of Peter Goodrich, asking parishioners to donate money toward this cause. Sally Goodrich clearly states that, while they do not actively fundraise, people give them money in response to their story. "It is not that I don't need money, we do. It's that we don't actively fundraise, I believe that if we are doing something good, and people like it, they gravitate toward it—they will support it." Susan Retik more specifically links her grief and the sympathy of others with the ability of Beyond the 11th to successfully fundraise. For example, in one scene of the film, Patricia Quigley states that she wants to "get away from being the 9/11 widow" and Retik responds, "I hate to say it, but that's where the sympathy and that's where the money—[comes from]. People are like 'oh look at what they're doing'—and it's what we have to use." Retik articulates the currency of grief for their husbands (9/11 victims), as a necessity for successful fundraising efforts.

Conclusion

Americans and Afghans have been framed through a gender-specific and geopolitically inspired lens as suggested by the grievability-potentiality-currency matrix discussed in chapter 3. This framing positions Afghans as victims, embodied as women and children, and apolitical innocents in need of saving. Afghan women and children through objectified images of human suffering offer a poignant example that resonates symbolically and fits neatly within larger geopolitical saving narratives. The gendered framing of the family members of 9/11 victims does not challenge the hypermasculinized representation of the U.S. state and military. Rather it offers the expected feminine complement to masculine military aggression and revenge (Goldstein 2003).

The objectified grievability of Afghan women and children's living-suffering under the Taliban has been discursively reduced to a fetishized ontology of bare life in need of international rescue. The 9/11 grief currency is put to work to raise funds for the seemingly apolitical, innocent, and docile suffering of Afghan women and children. This resonates as geopolitical currency framed through the geopolitical tropes of saving and liberating Afghan women. Gendered currency operates in tandem with 9/11 grief currency. These emotive lenses shroud rather than illuminate the everyday lives of Afghan women and children. The *Axis of Good* and *Beyond Belief* documentaries have become subsumed within existing grand narratives rather than being used to effectively challenge them.

Small-scale attempts by Retik, Quigley, and Goodrich illustrate a more pluralistic connection between "morally deserving" humans (Ong 2006, 24). The public representations and frames through which these stories are told remain squeezed within existing tropes and grand narratives in order for them to be accessible to the general public. These tropes effectively elicit emotive responses that meet national imaginaries. The violence brought forth by U.S.-led military interventions, both historical and contemporary, suffers a veiled erasure through these intimately nationalized framings.

The careful crafting of how Americans were expected to cathartically respond to 9/11 through various political discourses (as discussed in this chapter) set the scene of masculine military revenge and feminine domestic comfort. The currency of grief, gendered victimhood, and suffering must be considered as part of intimate geopolitical analyses. It is imperative to be critically vigilant regarding the value and valuation of life and death by uneven development paradigms. Such paradigms, fueled by gendered-nationalist rhetoric, foster life, death, and grief currencies.

It is easy to admire human-to-human interactions across differentiated geographies and situational experiences of conflict-based grief. Despite this praiseworthiness, the entanglements discussed in this chapter should be open to comment and critique from the individuals on the receiving end of assistance, similar to arguments made about the organizations discussed in chapter 5 (Rubia) and chapter 6 (WELO). Despite the existing structures of the international aid and development industry, Retik, Quigley, and the Goodrich family attempted to make connections with Afghans based on mutual respect and human equality. Similar discourses are often used to represent international assistance and development, while the material practices of development significantly stray from these idyllic discourses.

One scene in the documentary *Beyond Belief* captures a strategy meeting in Boston, Massachusetts, with Retik, Quigley, and representatives from CARE International. Quigley questions her ability to decide what Afghan widows need by stating, "Here I am trying to help these women and make decisions that will impact their life, but I have never lived their life." In this way Quigley identifies the crux of the problem with much of aid and development.

Part of the ineffectiveness of assistance and development programs includes the design of programs in spaces outside the locations of the intended projects. Institutions in situations of economic and political privilege often "decide" on how to address both basic and larger economic needs without a thorough understanding of the places within which they will work or the people living in those places. Additionally, meetings to decide "how best" to assist do not generally include input from those communities.

The individual representatives of these organizations do indeed offer an alternative response to grief and loss that intends to provide charity, economic assistance, and service to make human-to-human connections across distant geographies. The intentions of these respective organizations are commendable, but not free from geopolitical and mediated representation. These commendable acts have been ripe fruit for manipulative geopolitical plucking. For example, Sally Goodrich was named ABC's person of the week (April 26, 2005), and Susan Retik received the Citizens Medal from President Obama in 2010.[9] The cathartic power of these stories provides an irresistible lens through which to view American geopolitical action as benevolent rather than violent.

CHAPTER 8

Gender Currency and the Development of Wealth

After the U.S.-led invasion of Afghanistan on October 7, 2001 and subsequent occupation, there was an extensive influx of international funds and workers tasked with development, construction, and mitigation of new forms of governance. The discursive political strategies that represented the U.S. role in Afghanistan included "saving" and "liberating" Afghan women from the Taliban. Afghan women's liberation was symbolized through women shedding the burqa, which had become geopolitically positioned as emblematic of their oppression. The extensive mediated political attention toward Afghanistan manifested into a series of grand narratives that attempted to define ensuing entanglements between the United States and Afghanistan. These grand narratives portrayed the United States as the victim of terrorism with a "moral" obligation to seek retributive justice (Anker 2005; Däwes 2007). The United States presented itself as a benevolent, just leader able to rescue and liberate Afghan women, and subsequently branded Afghanistan and Afghan culture as flawed and regressive.

Individuals and groups capitalized on the culmination of these grand narratives and the massive, U.S.-led international aid and development intervention in Afghanistan. Some Americans traveled to Afghanistan in an effort to participate in the national response, which identified Afghans—particularly women and children—as similar victims of terrorism. Additionally, highly paid international workers provided the monetary conditions for development of an auxiliary economy in Kabul that catered to their wants, needs, and desires. Some individuals seized on financial opportunities within the auxiliary aid and development economy, while others sought to capitalize on the currency of Afghan women's "liberation" by selling Afghan women's stories or the products of their labor. Other entanglements between Americans and Afghans included globally intimate attempts to make connections across bordered differences.

This book has explored how the grand narratives associated with the geopolitical "saving" of Afghanistan translated into different forms of gender and grief currency. The multiple ways in which these currencies were exchanged by individuals and organizations often occurred in the pursuit of personal profit or professional gain. Other exchanges included representing Afghan women and children as victims of insurgent violence. For example, when Afghan women and children were victims of suicide bombings or other forms of insurgent violence, their deaths were discursively used to discredit the use of violence by the enemy. Afghan women and children were thus represented as apolitical innocents in need of foreign "saving" so that this form of political currency could be effectively exchanged for public and political support of the war effort. This narrative also helped to mediate the information war in the United States that concurrently accompanied military violence. The information war refers to the ways in which the United States mediated information about political conflict to ensure continued nationalism and public support from its citizenry. This form of intervention also reinforces common tropes that fuel the grand narratives about Afghanistan and the United States.

As discussed in detail in chapters 3 and 4, gender currency was developed from the objectified, grievable living-suffering of Afghan women in need of rescue and the subsequent tales of their liberation. International organizations exchanged this currency in various ways. Programs involving Afghan women have proliferated in order to become more attractive to larger donors. Gender currency also manifested in new forms of employment in Afghanistan for internationals as "gender specialists." This title was given to development workers tasked with improving women's rights and gender relations in Afghanistan. Interestingly, most of these gender specialists had little or no background knowledge or understanding of Afghanistan's multivarious societies, cultures, gender norms, and relations.[1] This begs the question of how one can be a "gender specialist" without understanding the social and cultural contexts that signify the contours of "doing gender." As Judith Butler's (1990) seminal work on gender performativity shows, it is the *doing of gender* that is the mechanism of its construction and reproduction through repetition. Gender occurs by *doing*, and this *doing* is mediated by spatial, social, cultural, and political contexts of daily life repeated over time (Nelson 1999). Thus, many international workers have reduced the contextual and spatially significant aspects of gender performativity in Afghanistan to narrow representations of culture that are ascribed to gendered geopolitics and imperial neoliberal feminist approaches to women's rights. As demonstrated throughout this book, gender categories are as dynamic for men and women in Afghanistan's diverse societies as they are in the United States and elsewhere.

Other forms of gender currency include the exchange of Afghan women's labor for liberation. In this way, women's low-wage labor was communicated as "liberty," and this labor-as-liberty was portrayed as necessary for alleviating women's oppression in Afghanistan. While women's labor was being translated as liberation, many projects fell within existing neoliberal economic structures rather than providing new or novel approaches to gender equality, whether locally or globally. Many of these projects reinforced, rather than challenged, existing capitalist systems of low-wage labor production for the sale of products in higher-wage-earning countries. Linking women's labor with liberation became a currency exchanged through advertising in the United States. In this way the concept of women's labor as liberation was capitalized upon by advertising "labor-liberation" as a commodity for sale. Other individuals, such as Debbie Rodriguez, capitalized on Afghan women's currency by writing a pseudomemoir about her work at the Beauty School of Kabul. She traded on Afghan women's currency to secure her own personal wealth. Similar to women's labor, the public face and beauty of Afghan women became symbols of liberation. These symbolic representations helped to further entrench existing and false binaries between the covered and uncovered body.

As this book has shown, the development of gender currency situates women's liberation into a narrow frame that has been designed and depicted by internationals rather than Afghans. The expectation of suffering in order to receive assistance, combined with the geopolitics of this suffering, created the grand narratives and related currencies. Afghan life persists in a cyclical state of triaged assistance and development that serves some acute humanitarian needs, while at the same time rendering the economy anemic and dependent upon temporally limited funds from donor countries.

Debord's (2009) conceptualization of social spectacle provides an interesting critical examination of the way the visual display of Afghan women's localized oppression and foreign saving were capitalized upon. Due to the consistent and continued decline of use value, Debord argues that workers are incorporated as laborers who must submit to the parameters set by capitalist structures or die. For consumers, Debord states:

> The real consumer has become a consumer of illusions.... The spectacle thus becomes a generalized expression of this illusion. (Debord 2009, 32)

The use value of the product is further obscured by the exchange value of Afghan women's liberation currency—represented through geopolitical spectacles. The "consumer's illusion" became the imagined ability of U.S. (and other international) consumers to participate in Afghan women's liberation by purchasing goods made by Afghan women. This illusionary form of consumption manifests when Afghan women's labor is discursively represented as liberation. This depiction of liberation meets the goals of the geopolitical grand narratives, and subsequently becomes a marketing tool for the sale of Afghan-women-made goods. In this way, the commodity being sold as a materialized illusion of liberation is discursively embedded into the advertisement for the product.

Afghan women's use value thus manifests through the advertised illusion of their labor-as-liberation. This use value has been materialized as currency, which is exchanged for capital and in some cases wealth. Afghan women's geopolitical "usefulness" transpires predominantly in terms of its exchange value. The currency of Afghan women's liberation has been exchanged for political/public support for the United States to spend its state resources (i.e., taxes) on militarized violence and development. Afghan women's "value" to internationals operates as another form of exchange by way of their discursive labor and revealed face in an effort to strengthen the grand narratives.

The currency associated with the grievable-object of Afghan women's and children's living-suffering and foreign rescue was exchanged by WELO (see chapter 6) to raise funds for the fellowship program that brought Soraya to the United States. WELO's commitment to helping Afghan women was mired in a limited understanding and unwillingness to incorporate Afghan women as equal partners in the design and implementation of its program. WELO members privileged their own visions and beliefs in assistance over those of their Afghan adviser (Nusha) and the recipient of their fellowship (Soraya).

As discussed in chapter 6, WELO, Jane, and Jennifer sought to save/assist Soraya. WELO did not redesign the program, despite being urged to do so by their primary Afghan interlocutor, Nusha. As reciprocity for its fellowship-gift, WELO expected Soraya to embody and perform corporeal and sartorial liberation in the United States. Jane, as Soraya's mentor in Afghanistan, sought to "save" her based on Jane's feminist beliefs and negative perceptions of the Afghan patriarchy. Jane emphasized Soraya's urgent need to leave Afghanistan as a method of rescue. She convinced Jennifer that Soraya had to "get out" of Afghanistan to ensure her security. Jennifer, moved by Jane's representation of Soraya's predicament, privileged Jane's assessment over Nusha's objections.

Soraya enlisted Jane's assistance to improve her education by leaving Afghanistan. She expected to increase her currency toward future job prospects and the opportunity to send remittances home. This narrative illustrated several interconnected and conflicting situated knowledges about oppression, rescue, and assistance. The inherent pitfalls of assistance projects often occur because all stakeholders are not equally consulted and involved in the design, development, and enactment of projects. Those on the receiving end of assistance are rarely if ever considered equal stakeholders in the provisioning of aid and development.

Soraya's expected performance of gender was analyzed by incorporating the fourth wall as a discursive border. The terminology of "the fourth wall" is used to highlight the invisible border between *gender performativity* (the doing of gender) and *performing gender-liberation* as reciprocity for WELO's fellowship-gift. The fourth wall is both spectacle and border. It positions simplified epistemologies about Afghan women above a more complex and complicated understanding of Afghans' diverse expressions of gender performativity. The fourth wall, as discussed in chapter 6, was an ephemeral border between Soraya's gender performativity and the gendered performance expected of her by WELO. The fourth wall operated as an expression of the grand narratives (Afghan women's local oppression and foreign saving), which subsequently informed WELO's "understanding" or ways of knowing Afghanistan and the lives and experiences of Afghan women.

The U.S. aid worker, Jane, claimed she was modeling modern feminist behavior for Afghan women. However, her gender performativity was often read locally as performing the male gender, because she acted in ways that were associated with Afghan-male gender performativity. Afghans did not mistake Jane as a man, but rather her way of *doing* gender signaled masculinity rather than femininity. Despite Jane's mode of dress, which was gendered feminine, her comportment was more closely associated with Afghan-male rather than Afghan-female ontologies. Similarly, Sarah Chayes, a former NPR correspondent, wore Afghan-male clothing in an effort to appear as a man in public spaces and ensure her own mobility and security (Chayes 2006). Although both her dress and comportment were socially and behaviorally read as male, Afghans with whom she worked knew she was biologically female. Afghan girls (and some women) have also been dressed or have chosen to dress as men to access spaces and economic opportunities that are available to boys/men but that exclude girls/women (Billaud 2015). This practice is known as *bacha posh* ("dressed like boy"). These examples highlight that the corporeality of dress is gender-coded in addition to certain behavioral traits, both of which are paramount to the doing of gender and how others interpret these gender codes. The fourth wall illustrates the bordered divisions between gender performativity (the doing of gender) and gender performances scripted by geopolitical discourse.

Jane further distinguished herself in Kabul by identify her office as western. She described "being western" based on her expectations of the Afghan women she hired. She stated that she would only hire Afghan women who came to interview for a job without being accompanied by a mahram. The presence of a male relative signaled to Jane that a prospective female assistant would have restricted mobility, and she needed her assistants to travel unaccompanied throughout the city as part of the stipulations of employment. In comparison, the organization Rubia (chapter 5) expected and preferred to hire women who were accompanied by a mahram. These examples illustrate differences associated with Afghan and internationally directed programs. Jane's NGO operated within internationally dominated spaces in Kabul, while Rubia worked largely with rural populations with limited access to the Kabul-based donor community. These examples demonstrate western approaches in comparison with an Afghan-community-driven project.

In some respects, the development paradigms being perpetuated for women in Afghanistan requested them to exchange existing patriarchal bargains with capitalist gambles. Gambling on neoliberal capitalist frameworks for gender liberation has been embedded into the various ways individuals and groups in Afghanistan engage with economic development programs. These gambles have manifested into different forms of opportunity as well as new forms of debt and continued poverty. For example, the expectations of development organizations such as USAID's Afghan Small and Medium Enterprise Development (ASMED) program exemplify the geopolitical desire for quick and identifiable success, rather than taking the time needed to build up struggling businesses with long-term strategies. Rubia (the organization discussed in chapter 5) participated in a handicraft-sector meeting held by ASMED in which the participants were told if they were not making a profit within the first year they were considered a failing business and would no longer receive support from ASMED. Many attendees, including Rubia, found this confusing because, although they had never earned a profit, they earned enough to keep their businesses operational and were able to pay their respective employees. Rubia's business model did not fit ASMED's definition of profit-based success. The materials Rubia used to create its goods were often produced on a small scale, such as fine natural materials, hand-spun silk threads, and hand-loomed cotton and yarns that were batch-dyed with plants and other natural color sources. Women worked in their homes, at their own pace. The business was designed to fit their lifestyle, not the other way around. Gambling on the probability of entrepreneurial success situated small-scale businesses like Rubia with the odds stacked against them. This was partly due to the better odds offered to organizations operating with donor subsidies in order to maintain and grow their businesses.

The material implications of geopolitical grand narratives also operate as disciplinary frameworks toward incorporating Afghanistan into international development paradigms. For example, donors and advisers regularly attempted to discipline Rubia to fit within the grand narratives and to trade on gender currency associated with these narratives. Rubia and T&B illustrate several intersecting and divergent methods of assistance, which explicate the opportunities, challenges, and drawbacks of engaging with market capitalism. Both organizations engaged in small-scale businesses toward securing employment and income for women. T&B, in an effort to effectively market its materials, incorporated the "saving women" trope by discursively representing labor as liberation. This liberation trope was embedded into the advertising of these products. In several magazine articles, T&B is discursively represented as privileging the market over its workers. Conversely, Rubia found it difficult to trade on this currency, which in some cases limited its sales opportunities and decreased its value to potential donors. T&B and Rubia focused on design and aesthetics as paramount for the sale and marketing of products. Both found niche marketing and sales events to be the most effective methods to compete in a crowded marketplace, which was reliant on low-wage human labor and mechanized production.

Some have argued that "selling" the idea of labor-as-liberation would effectively attend to the immediate economic needs of laborers. However, positing labor-liberation as a marketing tool reduces labor and economic need to a trend or style, in an effort to "charm" the consumer (see Thrift 2008). Positioning labor-liberation as a style trend communicates a dangerous temporal fluidity. Clearly, fashion has been imbued with political meaning (Gökariksel and Secor 2009). However, this type of geopolitical marketing is subject to the temporal limitations of passing fashion trends, which further privilege consumer desire over laborers' experiences or incomes. The idea that consumption can liberate laborers subtly erases the stark veracities of low-wage, long-hour, unregulated, and insecure labor practices.

The critiques of international intervention and social engineering, discussed in this book, have challenged hierarchal and uneven power relations within and beyond patriarchy. Internationals should not be the primary designers or determiners for achieving women's rights in Afghanistan. Afghan women and men must necessarily lead any efforts to change gender relations or improve women's roles and rights in society. International individuals and organizations can and should help to fund and support these efforts, but not drive them. The constant and continual leadership of Afghan women and men is necessary for the development and sustenance of women's roles and rights in society. As Afghanistan's own history illustrates, former attempts by international occupiers (e.g., the former Soviet Union, foreign resistance soldiers) to socially engineer gender roles led to extensive local backlash directed most acutely at women (Edwards 2002). Thus, any "gains" for women that are associated with outside intervention have been the primary targets of criticism and retrogressive actions.

Individualism, Autonomy, and Neoliberalism

Debord's (2009) concept of the spectacle when applied to these case studies further underscores the way in which certain individualized dramas perpetuate grand narratives and contribute to gender currency. These stories fit within neoliberal economic structures that privilege autonomy and individualism over that of collectivities. Collectivities come with their own sets of complications, hierarchies, and inequalities (Joseph 2002). Simply replacing relational social value with individually based structures dependent on market-driven capitalism can be problematic. This also does not necessarily improve women's or men's lives or society as a whole. Individualism requires and relies on mechanized and mediated technologies for social reproduction, rather than solely depending on the support of family, community, or other interrelational structures. Mechanized independence perpetuates consumption and necessitates the reproductive aspects of neoliberal capitalism.

Most international workers in Afghanistan have relied on the importation of goods and various technologies, such as generator-produced electricity. This has helped to perpetuate an insulated and more individualized experience of Afghanistan. Privileged international workers have also helped to form a temporally limited and spatially distinct conflict-subsidized cosmopolitanism in Kabul. The privileged international worker enjoys various forms of wartime cosmopolitanism. This cosmopolitanism includes the migration of international workers from neighboring countries to work within various aspects of the auxiliary war economy largely catering to the needs, wants, and desires of predominantly privileged and professionalized international workers.

Being a privileged international worker has become its own form of currency in Afghanistan. This currency allows such individuals access to international organizations and donor funds; for some it is a means to secure employment within international organizations with inflated salaries. The auxiliary geo-economy relies on the disposable incomes of well-paid international workers as well as the excesses of imported goods. For example, the "Bush market," named for former U.S. president George W. Bush, is a space in Kabul that sells secondhand materials. These goods have been discarded or pilfered from military bases, embassies, and other international civilian compounds. The dwindling of this market and other manifestations of the auxiliary geo-economy in Kabul as a result of the drawdown of troops, international funds, and workers further highlights the temporality of these wartime economies.

In summary, various forms of personal wealth generated by privileged international workers in Afghanistan, as discussed in chapter 2, include:

- International salaries composed of danger pay and post-differential additions to base salaries.
- Inflated rental prices that are perpetuated by the ability of well-funded international organizations and embassies to secure space in central Kabul.
- Private logistics, security, and military corporations capitalizing on the need for their services.
- An extensive amount of subcontracting that produces substandard outcomes.[2]

It is crucial to consider the ways in which funds and resources have been used and misused by internationals rather than ascribing these irregularities to common tropes such as "Afghan lack of capacity." Economic deprivation is rarely viewed in comparison to the privileged side of global economic hierarchies. Aid, assistance, and development are positioned and measured against need and suffering rather than conditions associated with the so-called good life (Tuan 1986). The "good life" is admittedly a contested term with multiple definitions from various perspectives (Berlant 2011).

Privileged international workers earning inflated salaries live a much more physically comfortable and mechanized lifestyle than their Afghan contemporaries. Their way of living is rarely if ever compared to Afghans, while Afghan desperation and poverty are the very conditions necessary for aid/development workers' employment. Consider if international workers' standard of living in Afghanistan were more similar to the Afghans they are there to assist. Therefore, imagine the provisioning of resources such as potable water, sanitation, electricity, and housing through horizontal rather than hierarchical forms of aid distribution and development projects and programming.

Chapter 3 discussed the currency of 9/11 grief by drawing upon Butler's (2006, 2009) theoretical explanation of precarious life. Butler identifies the expectation of grief over life when it is extinguished as necessary for viewing that former life as recognizable and subsequently valuable. The loss of Afghan life when caused by U.S.-led military violence is indeed grievable among Afghan families and friends. This grief does not however translate as such in the United States. The loss of U.S. lives remains grievable in the United States, while Afghan deaths are predominantly represented as anonymous. Chapter 7 analyzed how the grievability of 9/11 deaths translated into currency, which was exchanged to raise funds in an effort to assist and alleviate Afghan women's and children's suffering. Although Afghan deaths are not represented as grievable in the United States, the living-suffering of Afghan women and children has been manipulated to elicit a modicum of U.S. grief. Grievable representations of Afghan living-suffering, combined with geopolitical rescue and development potentiality, become the currency that fuels opportunistic practices under the guise of aid and development.

The geopolitics of bare life provides a geopolitical tool that reduces full life to the biological basics without political access or participation. This positions bare life as grievable and in a constant state of potentiality toward rescue by international aid and development. In this representation, bare life precludes any space for understanding the complexities and complications of Afghans' everyday lives. Thus, bare-life ontologies operate most effectively as a political tool. This political tool manipulates the intimacy of individual suffering by situating it within a macroscale frame, which geopolitically situates suffering/oppression locally and assistance/liberation internationally. Afghan ontologies become bare life through the discursive representation of Afghan women and children's living-suffering and the invisibility of Afghan men as grievable subjects, living or dead.

The "hyper-visibility" of Afghan women's and children's living-suffering (Russo 2006), along with the geopolitical currency of their deaths, renders Afghan male deaths invisible, without currency, and their living-suffering as ungrievable. Afghan women's and children's living-suffering was examined in chapters 5, 6, and 7. Members of the Afghan community discussed in chapter 5, who were in a situation of economic need, neither saw themselves as bare life nor viewed their lives as grievable. Therefore, the women working for Rubia, like Soraya (chapter 6), could not and would not perform or represent their lives in this way, despite the potential currency they could have exchanged from these performances.

The grievable living-suffering of Afghan women and children requires a performance to an audience that has come to expect a specific form of misery. Both parties pay a price—dignity lost, funds proffered. In many of these entanglements both suffering/need and its alleviation/assistance have been imagined by the donor rather than explicated by those in situations of economic need. For example, donors regularly told Rachel that the Afghans associated with Rubia did not look desperate enough for assistance. The dignity of people in situations of economic deprivation often manifests as fundamental concerns over personal, family, and community appearance, the importance of which remains unrecognizable to donors (Edin and Kefalas 2011).

Donors have also dictated the appearance of poverty (Kennedy 2009; Wilson 2011). These representations of bare-life ontologies have become part of the spectacle of conflict development and its associated geographies. In the United States, the repetition of images of burqa-clad suffering women with children in Afghanistan came to embody the political ontology of bare life as a spectacle (Debord 2009; Butler 2009). The reduction of full to bare life is not simply a process of killing with impunity, but also the ability to rescue bare life through development potentiality. Grievable-aliveness is gendered female and associated with children as an apolitical category. The apolitical gendering of bare life is situated within a state of potentiality toward geopolitical (and military) and geo-economic (development) rescue. This indirectly attempts to dichotomize violence by positioning the U.S. military as humane and benevolent, and insurgent violence as savage and malevolent.

As argued throughout this book, the subject of gendered living-suffering becomes an object of geopolitical saving and subsequent liberation. Geopolitical gendered suffering has been translated into a currency to be exchanged through the material practices of market-driven capitalist development. The apolitical rendering of bare life discursively assumes a lack of female agency. Gendered suffering reinforces the trope that local-Afghan men are unable or unwilling to participate in caring for women and children. This trope both marginalizes women's agency and places men as adversaries, thus rendering invisible their participation in home-family reproduction and security. In so doing, this trope simultaneously discredits female agency and male victimhood (Carpenter 2006, 2013).

Although Afghan deaths are not necessarily grievable within Butler's (2006, 2009) framework, they do retain currency as part of the discursive strategy of counterinsurgency. Afghan civilian deaths, particularly those of women and children, retain a modicum of grievability that has been exchanged as currency in an effort to delegitimize insurgent violence. Focusing on Afghan women and children both highlights their status as apolitical innocents and reinforces the "saving" trope. All sides of the conflict have made civilian deaths geopolitical in an attempt to discredit each other's legitimate use of violence.

"ConflictSpace" is a term used to quantify the dynamic areas over and upon which a multitude of military "logics" are played (Flint et al. 2009). Qualitatively, civilian and conflict spaces have become intermeshed in many locations within Afghanistan; bodies and battlegrounds have been intersected as part of everyday life. Civilian lives are geopolitical sites of potentiality through development; they are fodder for geopolitical meaning when extinguished by the enemy, and lacking grievability when killed by the United States.

Grieving family members of 9/11 victims turned toward Afghanistan in an effort to seek a connection based on their belief in a shared grief. Assistance projects in Afghanistan became part of the healing process for surviving family members. Although these individuals and the Afghans they worked with had both experienced the loss of loved ones, their grief and its related currencies were (un)common. We purposely bracket "(un)" to highlight the shared and distinct forms of grief and related currencies. The 9/11 deaths retain much more grievability and associated currency in the United States because personal grief was both recognizable and scaled to represent the nation's grief (chapter 7). Conversely, Afghan loss of life remains largely anonymous, unrecognized, and subsequently not grievable (in the United States). The tabular matrix (figure 3.1, chapter 3) illustrates the linkages between grievability, development potentiality, and currency in the U.S. geopolitical gendered framing of grief.

Intimate Entanglements

This book has included several examples of intimate entanglements between Americans and Afghans. Many of the Americans discussed throughout this text sought to forge a connection, while others opportunistically seized upon gendered currencies associated with the geopolitically driven grand narratives and billions of U.S. dollars directed toward this ongoing conflict and its aftermaths (Bashir and Crews 2012). Small-scale and intimately global projects have had the advantage of being able to operate autonomously from large-scale structures of international aid and development. In many respects, the attempts by small groups to forge connections in Afghanistan exemplify the individuation of "do it yourself" (DIY) approaches. Many individuals and some groups charted an alternative path and sought to conduct projects outside of existing matrices of aid and development. Many of the individuals and groups discussed throughout this book were not themselves development professionals or seasoned aid workers. Their interests in Afghanistan were in most cases driven by personal responses and reactions to 9/11/01 and 10/7/01. The desire to make a connection across geographic boundaries, cultures, and belief structures further exemplifies an alternative attempt at assistance. However, all of the entanglements discussed in this book underscore the power of grand narratives to seduce individuals into becoming part of (or co-opted into) the existing matrices of U.S.-led international development in Afghanistan. Despite different approaches, the overwhelming majority of Americans in our respective research and experiences view current structures of aid and development as the best or only path for connection through assistance. As discussed in chapter 5, Rubia's purposeful attempts to operate outside a development paradigm were continually challenged, including efforts to discipline the organization into a framework that was more recognizable to donors.

Macroscale assistance intends to build political and economic relationships and reciprocity such as allegiance building, geopolitical influence, and resource extraction (Klare 2001, 2012). Structural inequalities, violence, and unevenness accompany macroscale development ideologies, discourses, and structures. At the microscale, these unjust structures can be resisted and challenged in divergent ways. The intimate entanglements between Americans and Afghans, discussed here, illustrate many efforts that pushed against or disrupted the structures of development. Conversely, the power and influence of grand narratives and other imagined geographies about Afghanistan have been a continual and constant barrier for organizations that attempt to operate outside of development structures. The architecture of macroscale and donor-country-led development perpetuates deep-seated forms of structural violence that grease the machine of neoliberal global capitalism.

The structural conditions that allow projects to fail require the need for continual funding. The cyclical nature of development depends on continuous reallocation of funds, despite their sustained lack of effectiveness (Lawson 2014). The critiques of aid and development in Afghanistan by international aid workers themselves demonstrate that while most saw a vast amount of funds and resources wasted, they remained actively involved as cogs in the proverbial wheel of development. Some continued to operate as part of the structure of the aid and development machine because of well-paid salaries, résumé building, and other professional development pursuits. International development persists as predominantly hierarchical and linked to multinational organizations and banks and geopolitically and geo-economically powerful donor countries.

It is essential to look at aid and development from the ground up. The poverty and conflict on the ground, combined with geopolitical attention and funds, helped to create conditions for corruption, greed, and the generation of personal wealth. The conditions of desperation and need provide enormous salaries for internationals. Horizontal rather than hierarchal development assistance would require working oneself out of a job, while the professionalization of aid and development remains continual and cyclical (Roberts 2014). Popular mediated representations of aid and development identify international workers as altruistic beings, sacrificing their easy lives to help others in situations of desperation (Richey and Ponte 2011). These discursive representations marginalize the actualization of development, which produces wealth for the privileged few on the backs of the impoverished many. Assistance in places like Afghanistan exemplifies the global capitalist economy's trope of creating prosperity and opportunity. Economic need therefore becomes the structure upon which the seductive promises of global capitalism are constructed.

Afghans who do not privilege the market (or global capitalist economy) over the circadian procedures of their daily lives, families, and communities are often viewed by development workers as lacking capacity or as being in a "childlike" state of potentiality. The unrecognized capacity of these communities rests with their ability to live outside the global capitalist economy. They may and often do borrow from it when needed, while they resist full participation (Gibson-Graham 2006). Full participation would require becoming disciplined subjects at the bottom rungs of global production as low-wage or disposable laborers (Wright 2006). In many respects, refusal expresses an unwillingness to participate in the way U.S.-led development projects have been structured in Afghanistan. Participation would ultimately provide minimal and temporally limited currency, for example, exchanging economic need for the extraction and exploitation of land and labor, respectively.

The U.S.-led development ideologies, which are beholden to capitalist frameworks, have sought to include women in Afghanistan (and elsewhere) into the paid workforce. This attempt further separates the spaces of home and work, while demarcating clear distinctions between unpaid domestic labor and paid labor outside the home. Therefore, home-based work for women that relies on a fluidity of time between paid and unpaid labor does not fit into the time-labor divisions of contemporary global capitalism. The often-repeated joke among Afghans, "Americans have watches and Afghans have time," summarizes the disparate ways of thinking about technology, time-to-labor burdens, and the differentiated meanings and value placed on time. This also highlights the ways in which development and military technologies (i.e., watches) operate as disciplinary techniques over land and people. When Afghans stated that they have "time," this signaled the lack of importance placed on attending to the rigors of capitalist development.

Similarly, Soraya (chapter 6) found the extensive amount of receipting and numbering she experienced in the United States as oppressive. The banal practice of receiving a receipt after a purchase, along with numbers being attributed to nearly everything, including people (i.e., Social Security numbers), seemed to Soraya as overwhelmingly structured and repressive. Soraya's visceral reactions and rejections of this system illuminated the structural oppression of quantification and disciplined order that has (in an acutely Foucauldian manner) become normalized in the United States. Her reactions to these practices highlighted the violence of modern docility that has been rendered obscure by its ordinariness. While her headscarf symbolized an oppression she did not feel, the invisibility of regulation, control, and power was starkly evident to her through her daily attempts to make sense of the United States as a so-called country of liberty.

This analysis does not suggest that Afghanistan is incapable of participating in the capitalist economy. Rather, this book highlights the ways in which Afghanistan, due to its precarious political position, endemic corruption, and the extensive occupation by foreign troops, has remained beholden to and dependent upon external funds in order to participate in global capitalism. Afghanistan continues to be a "country of interest" for various political players both regionally and beyond, due in part to its extensive mineral wealth and strategic geopolitical location. As the United States withdraws its political and economic attention away from Afghanistan, other regional powers (e.g., Pakistan, India, Iran, China, and Russia) are poised to expand their existing economic and political interests in an effort to influence their own futures through spatial, situational, and resource advantage in Afghanistan (Klare 2012).

Examining the connections between the global and the intimate has become a salient aspect of critical scholarship and feminist research. Our analyses throughout this book draw on this instrumental and insightful scholarship in order to examine geopolitics and geo-economics at the intersection of various spatial and situational scales. While intimate analyses are paramount to our research methods and practice, we argue for continual and constant vigilance. Various forms of manipulation and exploitation of the global-intimate have increasingly become embedded into the geopolitics and representations of aid and development.

Large-scale and multinational assistance organizations, both governmental and nongovernmental, continually seek to develop a connection, albeit a virtual one, between middle- and upper-middle-class individuals (largely from donor countries) and those on the receiving end of assistance. These attempts at manufacturing intimate connections simultaneously reinforce existing orientalized and essentialist stereotypes of gender, race, and poverty (Wilson 2011). Objectified images of suffering and its alleviation through aid have become coded through disparate representations of black and brown (mostly women's or children's) bodies. Headscarves and the burqa have been another method for racializing female bodies as the *other* in a state of oppression in need of foreign saving (Abu-Lughod 2013; Spivak 1988). Attempts to initiate personal, individual, and virtually intimate connections between donors/consumers and women in need fits within neoliberal frameworks by commodifying concepts of need and liberation.

Currently, trends in conflict development position desperation and need as the basis upon which all forms of assistance are measured. Focusing on need and poverty can help to sideline or erase the historical and contemporary geopolitical maneuvers that led to political violence and subsequent conditions of resource deprivation and poverty. Focus on privation yields discursive tropes that define work and low wages as charity (Roy 2010). As such, work is seen as something given or provided, for which one should be grateful rather than critical. By contrast, when the money a woman earns is viewed separately from discursive descriptions of liberation, it is more difficult to view her work as charity (Roy 2010). Therefore, rights-based claims associated with economic assistance and development do not include labor rights or human rights violations perpetuated by international workers (Hiatt and Greenfield 2004).

Contemporary conceptualizations and presentations of need in Afghanistan and other conflict zones have commercialized and commoditized poverty and desperation. These forms of commodification have paved an entryway for enterprising individuals (operating from positions of relative economic and political privilege) to develop various forms of *personal wealth*. The associated gender currencies that have been exchanged further exemplify entrenched forms of capitalism that do not operate equitably. The American-Afghan entanglements discussed throughout this book underscore the symbiotic relationship between geopolitical discourse, material practices of aid and development, and the exchange of gender currencies as part of market-driven capitalist "logics." When a person or organization trades on manufactured tropes by way of these currencies, their actions further fuel the engines of geopolitics and global capitalism. Those who purposefully move away from these structures lose currency, such as Soraya in chapter 6 and Rubia in chapter 5. For many the cost of losing this currency translates as a preservation of dignity and honor. Their poverty and deprivation are not for sale. Within a capitalist framework, poverty remains a necessary conduit to the production of wealth. As capitalist development illustrates, particularly in situations of conflict, poverty becomes the condition for building new forms of wealth that are representationally and discursively identified as assistance.

Throughout this book we have employed intimate encounters at a microscale to complicate and dispute the ways in which Afghan people and Afghanistan have been imagined, described, fetishized, politicized, vilified, and rescued. The geopolitical discourses that emerged have been used to narrowly categorize Afghan men and women as perpetrators and victims, respectively. This book has interrogated these discourses by examining the intricacy and evolving messiness of multiple American-Afghan entanglements. In Afghanistan, where oral culture is deeply appreciated, the exploits of the wise fool, Mullah Nasruddin, illustrate succinctly a mosaic of circumstances. It is therefore fitting that we conclude this book with a famous Mullah Nasruddin story told repeatedly to depict the entangled intersection between the intimate and the geopolitical. We heard this story from men commenting on the sartorial demands of performing whiteness to gain access to privileged international spaces. This story was also told to us by women to express how the chadri/burqa or headscarf had been used as a misguided measure of Afghan women's liberation. "Mullah Nasruddin was invited to attend a wedding banquet. Having come from the fields he was dirty and poorly dressed and was not admitted to the gathering. He went home, bathed, dressed in his best clothing and returned. He was invited inside the banquet and was offered the seat of honor, next to the host. When the soup was served, Mullah Nasruddin reached over and dipped his sleeve into his bowl declaring, 'Eat sleeve, it was you who was invited to this wedding, not me!'" The wise fool clearly recognized that his appearance rather than his person was the one actually invited to the banquet. This parable characterizes how appearance *feeds* the shallowness of geopolitical discourse and aid and development practice. As discussed throughout this book, appearance has framed many representations of gendered suffering, liberation, and grief through various spectacles and performances. The currency of Mullah Nasruddin's clothes further exemplifies the misappropriation of bodies, exchanged through geopolitical and geo-economic currencies of gender and grief. Currency exchanges made for personal profit or professional gain, on the backs of those in situations of economic or political privation, epitomizes the intimately global practices of Kabul's carpetbaggers.

NOTES

Preface

1. Additional presentations both individually and collectively included the Choices Program Summer Teaching Institutes, the Scholars online project, the Vermont Geography Alliance, and speaking at universities and in other public and private settings.

2. These surveys were conducted with the assistance of Haley Bolin, who was at that time an undergraduate student at Dartmouth College.

3. McKittrick's (2006) analysis of the currency of female bodies during the North Atlantic slave trade argues that the meaning of race was reinforced both geographically and ideologically through various processes of economic exchange.

Chapter 1. Introduction

1. This led to the formation of the Durand Line and Wakhan Corridor, which the British used to split the Pashtun majority areas of Afghanistan and to ensure that British India and the Russian Empire had no common border.

2. This is particularly pronounced in colonial accounts and more recently in military analyses and memoirs.

3. While *mujahedin* is the term used to describe individuals who fought against the communist government in Afghanistan, as well as the invasion and occupation by the Soviet Union, it is often translated as "holy war warrior"; however, when the United States was supporting the mujahedin, the word was often interpreted as "freedom fighter." During the Soviet occupation, the United States supported the mujahedin with arms and funding, providing the bulk of support to Hezb-e-Islami, led by Gulbuddin Hekmatyar, who was known for throwing acid on unveiled female students at Kabul University. Hekmatyar later became the prime minister of Afghanistan (1993–94) with support from the United States. The United States now considers him a terrorist, and he lives in self-imposed exile in Iran.

4. Rashid tells two stories; in one of the stories girls are being raped, and in another a boy is about to be sodomized. Rashid credits the story of the girls as the most credible.

5. For example several books written about RAWA were released shortly after 9/11. Most were in the making prior to 9/11, but international interest in this organization

helped to increase the sale and distribution of these books (Benard 2002; Brodsky 2003; Chavis 2004). RAWA had been operating orphanages, schools, literacy programs, and small-scale development projects as part of their platform toward social and political change in Afghanistan. One could argue that RAWA's portrayal of issues and events was also skewed by their own sociopolitical position and goals as a political women's rights organization. They have been under threat in Afghanistan since their founding, and several members have been imprisoned and killed including Meena, RAWA's founding leader, who was assassinated in 1987 (Mehta 2002; RAWA 2002).

6. Mavis Leno's appeal to Unocal (Russo 2006).

7. Several RAWA members identified that when Oprah mentioned their organization it had a huge impact on the number of hits they received on their website, emails, and financial support from individuals in the United States (Fluri 2006, Fluri 2008a, Fluri 2009b).

8. For additional critical examinations of the co-optation of women's rights by the Bush administration see Abu-Lughod (2002), Hirschkind and Mahmood (2002), and Hunt (2002).

9. The Taliban also required men to meet corporeal expectations. For example, they had to grow their beards to meet a particular length, and wear specific styles of clothing.

10. To view this image see http://www.buzznet.com/2010/12/lil-kims-mugshot-1996/lil-kim-in-a-burqa-on-the-cover-of-one-world-magazine-jan-2003/, accessed December 8, 2015.

11. For example, Holly Collins is the first U.S. citizen who sought and was granted asylum by the Dutch government for herself and her children on the grounds of domestic abuse. L. Michael, December 5, 2011, "New Documentary by BU Professor Tackles Flawed Family Court System," *The Quad: BU's independent online magazine*, http://buquad.com/2011/12/05/no-way-out-but-one-bu-professor-presents-a-documentary-highlighting-americas-flawed-family-court-system/, accessed October 31, 2012.

12. Zarmeena's execution on RAWA's website: http://www.rawa.org/murder-w.htm. For additional academic analyses see Tickner (2002); Moghadam (2002b).

13. See Fluri (2009b) for an analysis of RAWA's documentation and international interventions in Afghanistan.

Chapter 2. The Carpetbaggers of Kabul

1. According to the office of the Special Inspector General for Afghanistan Reconstruction (SIGAR), created by Congress to provide independent oversight of Afghanistan reconstruction activities and funds, "as of June 30, 2013, the United States had appropriated approximately $96.57 billion for relief and reconstruction in Afghanistan since fiscal year 2002" (http://www.sigar.mil/about/, accessed January 15, 2014).

2. "The Afghanistan health survey, 2006, reveals that 24.9% of households have no toilet facilities while the remaining households have access to some kind of sanitation facilities, e.g., a traditional latrine within their compounds and households. Sanitary means of excreta disposal are scarce. Sanitations systems in major cities are lacking, resulting in a high number of waterborne diseases, especially during the summer months (e.g., outbreaks of cholera)." Country Cooperation Strategy for WHO and Afghanistan 2009–2013, 27 (http://www.who.int/countryfocus/cooperation_strategy/ccs_afg_en.pdf, accessed August 25, 2013).

3. Traffic lights were only introduced in Kabul in 2009, a city population estimated at three to four million.

4. Skimming begins before the contract is awarded. It is a widely circulated "secret" that vendors pay a "fee" equal to a percentage of the contract in order to be considered for a contract (Nawa 2006).

5. A comparison study conducted by the author Fluri in 2006, on the use of local resources (water, food, and electricity), identified that on average one privileged international worker used the same amount of resources as nine local residents.

6. The term "cosmopolitan" refers to those with the social, political, and economic ability to travel globally and easily between different countries.

7. We realize that while these are ordinary brands within a U.S. context, they are sold at relatively high prices to provide comfort and convenience foods for some international workers.

8. For further information, please refer to the U.S. Department of State Standardized Regulations 652 (f) at: http://aoprals.state.gov/content.asp?content_id=271&menu_id=78 (accessed January 15, 2014). The U.S. Department of State Danger Pay Allowance and Post (Hardship) Differential percentages are available at: http://aoprals.state.gov/Web920/danger_pay_all.asp; http://aoprals.state.gov/Web920/hardship.asp.

9. "In country" is a popular expression used by aid/development workers to distinguish between workers in the field versus those in home offices.

10. This quote was based on rates in 2006. Rates have since increased while local-Afghans' salaries remain fractional by comparison to international worker rates. Quoted in Fluri (2009a, 989). Also see Wilder (2007).

11. In general, these workers are not ethnically Tajik or Uzbek but rather ethnically Russian living in these former Soviet Republics.

12. Afghan Scene Facebook Page, https://www.facebook.com/Afghan.Scene (accessed July 22, 2014).

13. Many refugees in Pakistan also participated in aid/development projects orchestrated or funded by USAID and related agencies in the 1980s and early 1990s. This led to the development of networks and connections that helped some to secure positions in Afghanistan after the fall of the Taliban.

14. Additionally, Afghan national language proficiency among Afghan Americans raised in the United States ranges from minimal to fluent. Many can speak their mother tongues but cannot read or write in them.

15. Security protocols are specifically outlined and vary by organization.

16. Residents may be targeted by insurgents for working with internationals or by criminals who assume they have money because of the presence of internationals.

17. When the brief drive between the U.S. embassy and the airport is considered too dangerous to navigate by vehicle, U.S. government employees and contractors are transported by helicopter.

18. The term "attractive passports" refers to individuals from countries (such as the United States) that experience international mobility to many destinations without visa requirements, or with relatively easy visa expectations (also see Sparke 2006).

19. Until recently, the U.S. embassy only issued visas on a limited basis and to individuals on programs sponsored by the U.S. State Department. Afghans were required to travel to the U.S. embassy in Islamabad, Pakistan to seek a travel visa. In 2009, the Af-

ghan Allies Act allocated 7,500 U.S. visas for Afghan citizens who have worked with the U.S. government in specific capacities (such as translators) (http://travel.state.gov/visa/immigrants/info/info_4495.html, accessed March 6, 2013).

20. These transportation services are much more expensive, but having been vetted, they are considered more trustworthy. These examples illustrate the mobility currencies of this cosmopolitan war zone.

21. In 2015 a young female Afghan artist wore a sculpture she made of body armor in the shape of exaggerated female breasts and buttocks on the streets of Kabul in an effort to protest street harassment. A month later a woman fully covered in a black niqab was brutally beaten to death by a mob after being accused of burning the Qur'an. These events signal changing ideas about women's corporeal protections in public space in the Afghan capital; see Fluri and Lehr (forthcoming).

22. The fortified compound known as Green Village—offering numerous amenities, office space, and residence to 1,500 individuals—boasts they have been repeatedly attacked but never breached.

23. This is based on informal interviews with Afghan men. Also these men stated that they dress in *shalwar kamiz* at home. *Shalwar kamiz* consists of loose-fitting pants and a long tunic and is worn by most Afghans, both men and women, although style and color differences vary by gender, age, and region.

24. The field-visit bingo game has appeared on the following websites/blogs: WanderLust: Notes from a Global Nomad, http://morealtitude.wordpress.com/2012/05/26/field-visit-bingo/ (accessed March 15, 2013); Afghan Scene: http://www.afghanscene.com/july-issue-july-issue/10180-field-visit-bingo (accessed March 15, 2013); and Stuff Expat Aid workers Like: http://stuffexpataidworkerslike.com/tag/field-visit-bingo/ (accessed December 8, 2015).

Chapter 3. Gender and Grief Currency

1. Petraeus was later appointed as CIA director and resigned when his longtime affair with his biographer became public. He was eventually charged with mishandling classified documents. In 2015 he pled guilty to these charges and received a fine and two years probation.

2. A content analysis of the Afghan News Center revealed the continual use of civilian deaths to challenge the violence enacted by the perpetrator, both international forces and insurgents.

Chapter 4. "Conscientiously Chic"

1. This information is based on a study conducted by Jennifer Fluri during 2006–8.
2. Tarsian & Blinkley's website, www.tarsian.com.
3. Employees earned about $5/day, which T&B identifies as "above average wages." Relative to the wages of other women in similar positions in Afghanistan, this could be classified as "above average," while we critique both these comparisons and the representation of low-wage labor as liberation.
4. See Barlas (2002) for a critique of these assumptions through her identification and discussion of the covered/veiled body as a private space.
5. For example, T&B has been lauded or advertised in the *New York Times* Fashion section, *In Style Magazine*, *The Guardian*, *Time Out*, *People* magazine, *Organic Style*, *Accessories* magazine, *Lucky*, *Breathe*, *O* magazine, and *Marie Claire*.

6. Complaints about Rodriguez's involvement in the Beauty School were discussed on National Public Radio; see Nelson (2007).

Chapter 5. "We Should Be Eating the Grant, but the Grant Eats Us"

1. The hierarchies of class between elites and nonelites exist in both urban and rural settings.

2. Most of the original participants in Rubia belonged to an extended kinship network who were living in close proximity as refugees.

3. "It is now widely accepted by UNHCR itself that current official refugee figures for Afghanistan are well short of the actual number. Official figures have been based on those registered with the UNHCR in Pakistan and Iran, but there have been large influxes of refugees that remain undocumented either because of their unwillingness to be identified for fear of being repatriated, or the incapacity or unwillingness of UNHCR and host governments to offer assistance to new waves of refugees. According to the U.S. Committee for Refugees, at the end of 2000 there were some 3.6 million Afghan refugees worldwide and perhaps 375,000 IDPs; more have fled since October 2001. Official UNHCR figures put the number of refugees at 3.6 million, and just more than 980,000 IDPs. The UNHCR, however, conceded unofficially in 1999–2000 that there are up to two million refugees in Pakistan without documentation. This would take the total number of refugees and internally displaced to more than 6 million. Whatever the actual figures, Afghan refugees constituted the largest refugee population in the world in 2000–2001, as they have done for much of the past two decades" (Jazeyery 2002, 240).

4. In the highly stratified class system that defines their society, crafts production, such as weaving, carpentry, pottery, etc., are set at the lowest rung. The community members with whom Rachel was working were landowners and farmers in Afghanistan. Despite their difficult straits as Taliban-era refugees in Pakistan, the adoption of these crafts, even as a means of income, would not have been appropriate.

5. *Purdah* refers to the practice of women remaining predominantly in the home. In this community, women's mobility outside the home included wearing a chadri/burqa and being accompanied by a mahram (close male relative acting as an accompanying escort).

6. Rubia Organization for Development Afghanistan RODA was the registered name of the local NGO in Afghanistan, a separate entity from Rubia, Inc., the nonprofit organization registered in the United States. Rachel was the executive director for Rubia, Inc., the volunteer international support network for RODA, from 2000 to 2011. We refer to both organizations in this chapter as "Rubia" for simplicity.

7. All aspects of family reproduction involve children as a valuable resource. The participation of children in family enterprise is akin to chores, not the same as exploitive child labor.

8. Rubia and other embroiderers were hired to do their piecework in studio settings. This failed due to the physical demands of embroidering continuously for many hours a day and also because of the separation of women from the home.

9. The Rubia embroidery community in Pakistan was not abandoned; as long as there were trained women still residing in Lahore they were provided with work and income.

10. Ultimately, over a process of five years, they were able to register as an NGO through the intervention and $500 "fee" paid to a fixer.

11. Access to international donor organizations is channeled through local-Afghan employees, those with the language and skills currency to obtain those jobs, as discussed

in chapter 2. These individuals serve as gatekeepers, reserving access and funding for their own networks.

12. An office in Kabul was necessary for product distribution, to network with the international community to seek funding, and to participate with other handicrafts projects in sales events and services.

13. Sakhi's honorable behavior in building a business that benefited his community, while respecting social norms, increased his prestige, status, and trust. Such deportment can be seen to reinforce rather than challenge the preexisting trust networks of kinship and community.

14. The idea of a school did have value; it just was not their most pressing need. Six months into the program the women requested a school for their children, whose education had been neglected through the course of war and displacement. Many Afghans did not allow their children to attend local Pakistani schools because, as illegal immigrants, they were afraid of being noticed, investigated, and deported. Rubia's intimate scale and flexibility made it possible to garner funds and materials to organize a small primary school for the Afghan children in the neighborhood.

15. A *malik* is a local leader and acts as a representative of a given group (or clan) to the provincial and federal/central government.

16. In general, people enjoy taking and having their pictures taken, but images of women and men are carefully protected. They are meant to be shared among close friends and family members, and not to be sold or traded for public consumption. This is in accordance with the purdah practices of this community.

17. For example, see Women for Women International's Sponsor a Sister Program, https://give.womenforwomen.org/sponsorship/ (accessed April 11, 2015).

18. Women were able to identify each other's handwork by the quality, size, and shape of the individual stitches. Once, when a woman tried to subcontract her stitching out to another embroiderer, the managers challenged her because "her" stitched signature did not match her style of embroidery.

Chapter 6. "Saving" Soraya

1. Involvement in this project was associated with the author's interest in conducting service research as discussed in Trauger and Fluri (2014).

2. At that time, the U.S. embassy in Kabul was only issuing U.S. visas for State Department–sponsored travel. All other visa requests and interviews were conducted at the U.S. embassy in Islamabad, Pakistan.

3. The ninth month of the lunar calendar, during which fasting is required (Oxford Dictionary of Islam 2003).

4. The term "situated knowledges" is drawn from the work of Donna Haraway (1988).

Chapter 7. "Our Hearts Break"

1. Throughout this chapter we use grief, sorrow, anguish, and pain interchangeably to mean an experience of intense sorrow caused by the loss of a loved one or similar trauma.

2. The full content of this speech is archived through the American Presidency Project: http://www.presidency.ucsb.edu/ws/?pid=24992 (accessed April 13, 2014).

3. The U.S. role in Afghanistan is marked by support of several fundamentalist groups (1980–92) in their fight against Soviet occupation (Maley 2009; Mamdani 2004).

4. The 9/11 obituaries ran in the *New York Times* from September 15 thru December 31, 2001, and were later published in a book containing a total of 1, 910 "Portraits of Grief" (Miller 2003).

5. The Smithsonian continues to archive and display objects from 9/11, through online and physical exhibitions titled *September 11: Bearing Witness to History* (http://amhistory.si.edu/september11/, accessed June 21, 2014).

6. The film about the Peter M. Goodrich Memorial Foundation is still in production, but can be viewed in its current form at http://www.axisofgoodmovie.com/. Information about the Peter M. Goodrich Memorial Foundation can be found on their website, http://www.goodrichfoundation.org/. The *Beyond Belief* film is available on Netflix and through the Beyond the 11th website, http://www.beyondthe11th.org/.

7. For example, the efforts of 9/11 families—particularly those who fought for investigations of the Bush administration culminating in the 9/11 Commission—remain absent.

8. Authors' transcript of the film *Axis of Good: A Story of 9/11*; all subsequent quotes in this section are from authors' transcript of film dialogue in *Axis of Good: A Story of 9/11* or *Beyond Belief*, unless otherwise noted.

9. Sally Goodrich named ABC Person of the Week, http://abcnews.go.com/WNT/PersonOfWeek/story?id=1071393 (accessed February 7, 2014). President Obama Honors Winners of the 2010 Citizens Medal, http://www.whitehouse.gov/the-press-office/president-obama-honors-winners-2010-citizens-medal (accessed February 7, 2014).

Chapter 8. Gender Currency and the Development of Wealth

1. This information is based on a study conducted by Jennifer Fluri during 2006–8.

2. The combination of subcontracting, corruption, security, and logistics attached to a given project has drained the allocated resources, which were then siphoned from materials and labor costs leading to low-wage labor and substandard supplies for construction.

GLOSSARY

This book contains words used in Dari (Afghan Persian) and Pashto. Many of these words are used in both languages; some are of Arabic origin. This glossary employs a general system of transliteration based on Afghan Persian pronunciation and does not distinguish between Pashto and Dari origins.

Afghan living-suffering: Mainstream media images of Afghan suffering as embodied by living women and children.
aleatory sovereignty: As quoted in Dunn and Cons (2014, 3): "rule by contingency—a concept that replaces Agamben's monolithic sovereign power with a systemic accounting of how the iterative process of enacting sovereignty makes it fragile, unpredictable and haphazard."
bare life: Life that exists in the "zone of indistinction" between political life and death. Often used to identify lives that are completely dependent upon institutions of government for survival or elimination, such as a concentration camp.
bios: Used by Agamben (who draws on Aristotle) to identify political life and its separation from natural life (*zoë*).
chadri (also called "burqa"): An outer garment or veil worn in public spaces by some women in Afghanistan. This garment has a caplike headpiece to which pleated fabric is attached, draping the entire body. A small mesh screen over the eyes allows women to see without being seen. The front of this garment generally ends just below the hips to allow for easier movement of the arms. During the Taliban era, all women were required to wear this garment.
COIN: U.S. military acronym for counterinsurgency.
conflict development: Development projects occurring in an active conflict zone.
corporeal currency: Identifies when bodies are used as a form of economic or political exchange.
corporeal modernity: The association of unveiled bodies with concepts such as freedom and liberty.
cosmopolitanism: The social, political, and economic conditions associated with groups of people who travel globally and easily between different countries.

Eid: A Muslim celebration to mark the end of Ramadan, known as Eid-al-Fitr (feast of the breaking of the fast). Eid-al-Adha (feast of the sacrifice) is another celebration to commemorate the willingness of Ibrahim (Abraham) to sacrifice his son to God.

emotional geographies: The study of spatial aspects of emotion and affect. Emotional geographies include examining spaces that are intended to elicit catharsis, such as memorials or cemeteries, and an individual or group's emotional connection to specific places.

expatriate Afghans: Afghans who have emigrated to locations outside the country and have returned to Afghanistan to work within the international aid and development mission.

gender currency: The way in which ideas about gender have been used as a unit of exchange between groups, organizations, or individuals.

gender mainstreaming: The development strategy for promoting gender equality and bringing gender issues into the mainstream of society.

geo-economy: The economic processes associated with the spatial configuration of international development.

good life: The subjective identification of a full, enjoyable, and comfortable life.

grand narrative: A dominant public narrative, usually produced by way of political influence on media representations of a particular idea or event.

grief currency: The use of grief as a unit of exchange between groups, organizations, or individuals.

grievability: Coined by Judith Butler to identify the sociopolitical extent to which different individuals' lives are grieved over after they have been killed.

grievable life: As quoted in Butler (2009, 14): "Precisely because a living being may die, it is necessary to care for that being so that it may live. Only under conditions in which the loss would matter does the value of the life appear. Thus, grievability is a presupposition for the life that matters."

implementing partner: Contracting organizations that implement programs and projects for USAID in Afghanistan.

information war: The way in which information is mediated, influenced, or controlled by governments to portray particular information about their role in a particular war or conflict.

intimately global: The connection between global processes such as globalization and intimate or personal activities and experiences.

izzat: Honor.

Kabuli: A person who lives in Kabul and identifies him/herself with modern urban lifestyles associated with this city.

legal exception: The suspension of law, often due to a state of emergency.

local-Afghans: Afghans who live in Afghanistan and have remained in Afghanistan (or who lived briefly in neighboring countries) during various phases of conflict.

mahram: A term commonly used in Afghanistan to refer to a close male relative of a woman who can accompany her as a protector while traversing public spaces.

malik: Community or village man of influence. Often elected as liaison between the tribe/community and the government.

mujahedin: Fighters in a holy war, jihad (s., mujahed; pl., mujahedin). In Afghanistan this designation was used to refer to resistance fighters against the Soviet occupation of Afghanistan.

necropolitics: The relationship between sovereign power and control over life and death.

neoliberal economics: The liberalization of the market economy including deregulation. This form of capitalism began with the economic policies of Ronald Reagan in the United States and Margaret Thatcher in the United Kingdom (known as the Washington Consensus).

ontology: A branch of metaphysical philosophy concerned with the nature of being.

Pashtunwali: Traditional moral and legal code of conduct among Pashtuns.

performativity: The repetition of behaviors and social processes associated with "doing" gender, or becoming a male or female.

potentiality: (1) Referring to a child, whose potentiality requires him/her to "suffer an alteration (to become other) through learning" in order to gain knowledge; and (2) referring to an adult who possesses knowledge while remaining in a state of potentiality until he/she brings his/her knowledge into actuality (Agamben 1999, 179).

power geometries: Term coined by Doreen Massey (1994) to identify the ways in which time-space compression of globalization affects people differently.

privileged international workers: International workers in Kabul, Afghanistan working for Tier 1 or Tier 2 organizations.

purdah: Meaning "curtain," this term is often used to identify the seclusion of women from public space.

Ramadan: Ninth month in the Islamic calendar during which Muslims fast from sunrise to sunset. Fasting during Ramadan is one of the five pillars of Islam.

regional-international workers: International workers in Kabul from neighboring countries predominantly working in the service economy or for Tier 3 organizations.

rentier state: A state that receives a significant amount of its operational funding from other countries.

secular liberal feminism: A type of feminism associated with second-wave liberal feminism in the United States. Liberal feminism focuses on gender equality within capitalist economic structures through pay equity.

situated knowledges: Identified by Donna Haraway (1988) to incorporate forms of producing knowledge based on personal experiences, which challenges the concept of objective disembodied knowledge.

sovereign exception: When a sovereign government suspends existing laws or rights, usually during a state of emergency.

spectacle: Visually striking performance or public display.

structural violence: A term coined by Johan Galtung (1969), referring to institutional structures that cause harm or prevent people from accessing basic resources.

translocal: Interactive economic and political processes within several different locales that are in general spatial proximity to one another.

use value: The usefulness of a commodity. Marx separated use value from exchange value in order to identify exchange value as an abstraction from the usefulness of a commodity.

whiteness: The structural social, economic, and political advantage based on colonial histories and cultural practices that positioned white people into a noncategory and represented their bodies as the ideal norm.

Glossary

zoë: Used by Agamben (1998) (who draws on Aristotle) to identify natural life and its separation from political life, *bios*.

zone of indistinction: Agamben (1998) uses this term to identify the political zone between political (*bios*) life and natural (*zoë*) life. This zone is indistinct because of the ways in which modern politics seeks to orchestrate and control the interrelationship between natural/physical life and political life.

WORKS CITED AND CONSULTED

Abirafeh, L. 2005. "Lessons from Gender-Focused International Aid and Post-Conflict Afghanistan . . . Learned?" Friedrich-Ebert-Stiftung, Division of International Cooperation Department for Development Policy (1–28).
———. 2009. *Gender and International Aid in Afghanistan: The Politics and Effects of Intervention*. London: MacFarland.
Abu-Lughod, L. 1990. "The Romance of Resistance: Tracing Transformations of Power through Bedouin Women." *American Ethnologist* 17 (1): 41–55.
———. 2002. "Do Muslim Women Really Need Saving? Anthropological Reflections on Cultural Relativism and Its Others." *American Anthropologist* 104 (3): 783–90.
———. 2013. *Do Muslim Women Need Saving?* Cambridge, Mass.: Harvard University Press.
Adamec, L. 2012. *Historical Dictionary of Afghanistan*. 4th ed. Lanham, Md.: Scarecrow Press.
Agamben, G. 1998. *Homo Sacer: Sovereign Power and Bare Life*. Translated by Daniel Heller-Roazen. Stanford: Stanford University Press.
———. 1999. *Potentialities: Collected Essays in Philosophy*. Stanford: Stanford University Press.
———. 2005. *State of Exception*. Translated by K. Attell. Chicago: University of Chicago Press.
Ahmed, A. S. 1978. "An Aspect of the Colonial Encounter in the North-West Frontier Province." *Asian Affairs* 9 (3): 319–27.
Ahmed-Ghosh, H. 2013. "A History of Women in Afghanistan: Lessons Learnt for the Future or Yesterdays and Tomorrow: Women in Afghanistan." *Journal of International Women's Studies* 4 (3): 1–14.
Alcoff, L. 1991. "The Problem of Speaking for Others." *Cultural Critique* 20: 5–32.
Anker, E. 2005. "Villains, Victims, and Heroes: Melodrama, Media, and September 11." *Journal of Communication* 55 (1): 22–37.
Armitage, L. 2003. "Miss Afghanistan 2003." Afghanland.com, http://afghanland.com/entertainment/missafgh2003.html (accessed December 8, 2005).
Ayotte, K. J., and M. E. Husain. 2005. "Securing Afghan Women: Neocolonialism, Epistemic Violence, and the Rhetoric of the Veil." *NWSA Journal* 17 (3): 112–33.

Azarbaijani-Moghaddam, S. 2004. "Afghan Women on the Margins of the Twenty-First Century." In *Nation-Building Unraveled? Aid Peace and Justice in Afghanistan*, edited by A. Donini, N. Niland, and K. Wermester, 95–116. Sterling, Va.: Kumarian Press.

———. 2006. *Women's Groups in Afghan Civil Society: Women and Men Working towards Equitable Participation in Civil Society Organizations*. Kabul: Research Conducted for Counterpart International.

———. 2007. "On Living with Negative Peace and a Half-Built State: Gender and Human Rights." *International Peacekeeping* 14 (1): 127–42.

———. 2009. "The Arrested Development of Afghan Women." In *The Future of Afghanistan*, edited by J. Alexander Their, 63–72. Washington, D.C.: United States Institute for Peace.

Barfield, T. 2004. "Radical Political Islam in an Afghan Context." *Asia Program Special Report* (15–27). Woodrow Wilson International Center for Scholars.

———. 2010. *Afghanistan: A Cultural and Political History*. Princeton, N.J.: Princeton University Press.

Barlas, A. 2002. *Believing Women: Un-reading Patriarchal Interpretations of the Quran*. Austin: University of Texas Press.

Bashir, S., and R. D. Crews, eds. 2012. *Under the Drones: Modern Lives in the Afghanistan-Pakistan Borderlands*. Cambridge, Mass.: Harvard University Press.

Benard, C. 2002. *Veiled Courage: Inside the Afghan Women's Resistance*. New York: Broadway Books.

Berkeley Community Profiles. N.d. "Sarah Takesh." http://mba.haas.berkeley.edu/community/alumni/profiles/takesh_sarah.html (accessed February 10, 2013).

Berlant, L. G. 2011. *Cruel Optimism*. Durham, N.C.: Duke University Press.

Billaud, J. 2015. *Kabul Carnival: Gender Politics in Postwar Afghanistan*. Philadelphia: University of Pennsylvania Press.

Bligh, M. C., J. C. Kohles, and J. R. Meindl. 2004a. "Charisma under Crisis: Presidential Leadership, Rhetoric, and Media Responses before and after the September 11th Terrorist Attacks." *Leadership Quarterly* 15 (2): 211–39.

———. 2004b. "Charting the Language of Leadership: A Methodological Investigation of President Bush and the Crisis of 9/11." *Journal of Applied Psychology* 89 (3): 562.

Bordo, S. 2004. *Unbearable Weight: Feminism, Western Culture, and the Body*. 2nd ed. Berkeley: University of California Press.

Bricmont, J. 2007. *Humanitarian Imperialism: Using Human Rights to Sell War*. New York: Monthly Review Press.

Brodsky, A. E. 2003. *With All Our Strength: The Revolutionary Association of the Women of Afghanistan*. New York: Routledge.

Brooks, E. C. 2007. *Unraveling the Garment Industry: Transnational Organizing and Women's Work*. Minneapolis: University of Minnesota Press.

Brooks, K. 2006. "The Tailor of Kabul." *People Magazine*, February 28.

Brunn, S. D. 2004. *11 September and Its Aftermath: The Geopolitics of Terror*. New York: Routledge.

Burk, A. L. 2003. "Private Griefs, Public Places." *Political Geography* 22 (3): 317–33.

Bush, G. W. 2001a. "Radio Address by Mrs. Bush," November 17. Online at *The American Presidency Project*, by Gerhard Peters and John T. Wooley. http://www.presidency.ucsb.edu/ws/?pid=24992 (accessed March 4, 2014).

———. 2001b. "The President's News Conference," October 11. Online at *The American Presidency Project*, by Gerhard Peters and John T. Woolley. http://www.presidency.ucsb.edu/ws/?pi (accessed May 29, 2014).

———. 2001c. *The Global War on Terrorism: The First 100 Days*. Washington, D.C.: Coalition Information Centers. http://www.dtic.mil/dtic/tr/fulltext/u2/a408814.pdf (accessed March 4, 2014).

Butchy, L. 2006. "Sewing Clothes Mending Lives: Interview with Sarah Takesh." Columbia College Today, www.college.columbia.edu/cct.archive/nov05/cover.php (accessed February 2, 2016).

Butler, J. 1990. *Gender Trouble: Feminism and the Subversion of Identity*. New York: Routledge.

———. 1993. *Bodies That Matter: On the Discursive Limits of "Sex."* New York: Routledge.

———. 2006. *Precarious Life: The Powers of Mourning and Violence*. London: Verso.

———. 2009. *Frames of War: When Is Life Grievable?* London: Verso.

Campbell, Duncan. 2004. "Kabul Tunes into Capital Pursuits" *Guardian*, June 17.

Carpenter, R. C. 2006. "Recognizing Gender-Based Violence against Men and Boys in Conflict Situation." *Security Dialogue* 37: 83–103.

———. 2013. *"Innocent Women and Children": Gender, Norms and the Protection of Civilians*. Farnham, U.K.: Ashgate.

Centlivres-Demont, M. 1994. "Afghan Women in Peace, War, and Exile." In *The Politics of Social Transformation in Afghanistan, Iran, and Pakistan*, edited by M. Weiner and A. Banuazizi. Syracuse, N.Y.: Syracuse University Press.

Chavis, M. E. 2004. *Meena, Heroine of Afghanistan: The Martyr Who Founded RAWA, the Revolutionary Association of the Women of Afghanistan*. New York: Saint Martin's Press.

Chayes, S. 2006. *The Punishment of Virtue: Inside Afghanistan after the Taliban*. New York: Penguin Books.

Cohen, C. B., R. Wilk, and B. Stoeltje, eds. 1996. *Beauty Queens on the Global Stage: Gender, Contests, and Power*. New York: Routledge.

Collaborative Learning Projects. 2010. *Listening Project: Field Visit Afghanistan, May–April 2009, Revised August 2010*. www.cdainc.com (accessed October 15, 2011).

Collins, J. M. 2002. "And the Walls Came Tumbling Down: Sharing Grand Jury Information with the Intelligence Community under the USA PATRIOT Act." *American Criminal Law Review* 39: 1261.

Crews, R. D., and A. Tarzi, eds. 2009. *The Taliban and the Crisis of Afghanistan*. Cambridge, Mass.: Harvard University Press.

Dahlman, C., and S. Brunn. 2003. "Reading Geopolitics beyond the State: Organisational Discourse in Response to 11 September." *Geopolitics* 8 (3): 253–80.

Damjanov, M. ed. N.d. "Green without Hippie: Help the Environment—and Don't Sacrifice an Ounce of Style." *Lucky Life*, July.

Daulatzai, A. 2006. "Acknowledging Afghanistan Notes and Queries on an Occupation." *Cultural Dynamics* 18 (3): 293–311.

Davidson, J., L. Bondi, and M. M. Smith, eds. 2005. *Emotional Geographies*. Farnham, U.K.: Ashgate.

Däwes, B. 2007. "On Contested Ground (Zero): Literature and the Transnational Challenge of Remembering 9/11." *Amerikastudien/American Studies* 52: 517–43.

Debord, G. 2009. *The Society of the Spectacle*. Translated by Ken Knabb. Sussex: Soul Bay Press.

De Certeau, M. 1984. *The Practice of Everyday Life*. Berkeley: University of California Press.

De Waal. A. 1997. *Famine Crimes: Politics and the Disaster Relief Industry in Africa*. Bloomington: Indiana University Press.

Dittman, A. 2007. "Recent Development in Kabul's Shar-e-Naw and Central Bazaar Districts." *ASIEN* 104: 34–43.

Dittmer, J. 2005. "Captain America's Empire: Reflections on Identity, Popular Culture, and Post-9/11 Geopolitics." *Annals of the Association of American Geographers* 95 (3): 626–43.

———. 2013. *Captain America and the Nationalist Superhero: Metaphors, Narratives, and Geopolitics*. Philadelphia: Temple University Press.

Donini, A. 2007. "Local Perceptions of Assistance to Afghanistan." *International Peacekeeping* 14 (1): 158–72.

Dowler, L. 2002. "Women on the Frontlines: Rethinking War Narratives Post 9/11." *Geojournal* 58 (2–3): 159–65.

Drury, A. C., R. S. Olson, and D. A. V. Belle. 2005. "The Politics of Humanitarian Aid: U.S. Foreign Disaster Assistance, 1964–1995." *Journal of Politics* 67 (2): 454–73.

Duffield, M. 2001. *Global Governance and the New Wars: The Merging of Development and Security*. Vol. 87. London: Zed Books.

———. 2007. *Development, Security and Unending War: Governing the World of Peoples*. Cambridge, Mass.: Polity.

Duffield, M., J. Macrae, and D. Curtis. 2001. "Editorial: Politics and Humanitarian Aid." *Disasters* 25 (4): 269–74.

Dunn, E. C., and J. Cons. 2014. "Aleatory Sovereignty and the Rule of Sensitive Spaces." *Antipode* 46 (1): 92–109.

Edin, K., and M. Kefalas. 2011. *Promises I Can Keep: Why Poor Women Put Motherhood before Marriage*. Berkeley: University of California Press.

Edwards, D. 1996. *Heroes of the Age: Moral Fault Lines of the Afghan Frontier*. Berkeley: University of California Press.

———. 2002. *Before Taliban: Genealogies of the Afghan Jihad*. Berkeley: University of California Press.

El Guindi, F. 1999. *Veil: Modesty, Privacy and Resistance*. New York: Berg Publishers.

Elden, S. 2013. "Secure the Volume: Vertical Geopolitics and the Depth of Power." *Political Geography* 34: 35–51.

Ellin, A. 2007. "Shades of Truth and Account of the Beauty School of Kabul Is Challenged." *New York Times*, April 29. http://www.nytimes.com/2007/04/29/fashion/29kabul.html?pagewanted=all&_r=0 (accessed February 10, 2013).

Engle, K. J. 2007. "Putting Mourning to Work Making Sense of 9/11." *Theory, Culture & Society* 24 (1): 61–88.

Enloe, C. H. 2000a. *Bananas, Beaches and Bases: Making Feminist Sense of International Politics*. Berkeley: University of California Press.

———. 2000b. *Maneuvers: The International Politics of Militarizing Women's Lives*. Berkeley: University of California Press.

———. 2004. *The Curious Feminist*. Berkeley: University of California Press.

Escobar, A. 2011. *Encountering Development: The Making and Unmaking of the Third World*. 2nd ed. Princeton, N.J.: Princeton University Press.
Essex, J. 2013. *Development, Security, and Aid: Geopolitics and Geoeconomics at the U.S. Agency for International Development*. Athens: University of Georgia Press.
Evans, J. C. 2001. Hijacking Civil Liberties: The USA PATRIOT Act of 2001. *Loyola University Chicago Law Journal* 33: 933.
Expat Women Entrepreneur Blog. http://www.expatwomen.com/expat-women-entrepreneur-business-ideas/tarsian-and-blinkley-sarah-takesh.php (accessed January 28, 2013).
Fahmy, S. 2004. "Picturing Afghan Women: A Content Analysis of AP Wire Photographs during the Taliban Regime and after the Fall of the Taliban Regime." *Gazette* 66 (2): 91–112.
Faria, C., and S. Mollett. 2014. "Critical Feminist Reflexivity and the Politics of Whiteness in the 'Field.'" *Gender, Place and Culture* 23 (1): 79–93.
Fishstein, P., and A. Wilder. 2012. "Winning Hearts and Minds? Examining the Relationship between Aid and Security in Afghanistan." Feinstein International Center, Tufts University, Medford, Mass.
Flint, C., P. Diehl, J. Scheffran, J. Vasquez, and S. H. Chi. 2009. "Conceptualizing Conflictspace: Toward a Geography of Relational Power and Embeddedness in the Analysis of Interstate Conflict. *Annals of the Association of American Geographers* 99 (5): 827–35.
Fluri, J. L. 2006. "Our Website Was Revolutionary: Virtual Spaces of Representation and Resistance." *ACME: An International E-Journal for Critical Geographies* 5 (1): 89–111.
———. 2008a. Feminist-Nation Building in Afghanistan: An Examination of the Revolutionary Association of the Women of Afghanistan (RAWA). *Feminist Review* 89: 34–54.
———. 2008b. "'Rallying Public Opinion' and Other Misuses of Feminism." In *Feminism and War: Confronting U.S. Imperialism*, edited by R. Riley, C. T. Mohanty, and M. B. Pratt, 143–60. London: Zed Books.
———. 2009a. "'Foreign Passports Only': Geographies of (Post)Conflict Work in Kabul, Afghanistan." *Annals of the Association of American Geographers* 99 (5): 989.
———. 2009b. "Geopolitics of Gender and Violence 'from Below.'" *Political Geography* 28: 259–65.
———. 2009c. "The Beautiful 'Other': A Critical Examination of 'Western' Representations of Afghan Feminine Corporeal Modernity." *Gender, Place, and Culture: A Journal of Feminist Geography* 16 (3): 241–57.
———. 2011a. "Armored Peacocks and Proxy Bodies: Gender and Geopolitics in Aid/Development Spaces." *Gender, Place, and Culture: A Journal of Feminist Geography* 18 (4): 519–36.
———. 2011b. "Bodies, Bombs, and Barricades: Gendered Geographies of (In)Security." *Transactions of the Institute of British Geographers* 36 (3): 280–96.
———. 2012. "Capitalizing on Bare Life: Sovereignty, Exception, and Gender Politics." *Antipode* 44 (1): 43.
———. 2013. "Women." In *The Ashgate Research Companion to Critical Geopolitics*, edited by K. Dodds, M. Kuus, and J. P. Sharp, 509–26. Farnham, U.K.: Ashgate.

———. 2014. "States of (In)security: Corporeal Geographies and the Elsewhere War." *Environment and Planning D: Society and Space* 32: 795–814.
Follain, J., and R. Cristofari. 2003. *Zoya's Story: An Afghan Woman's Struggle for Freedom*. New York: Harper Collins.
Forsythe, D. P. 2005. *The Humanitarians: The International Committee of the Red Cross*. Cambridge: Cambridge University Press.
Foucault, M. 1977. *Discipline and Punish: The Birth of the Prison*. Translated by A. Sheridan. New York: Pantheon Books.
Fremont-Barnes, G. 2009. *The Anglo-Afghan Wars 1839–1919*. New York: Osprey.
Fridell, G. 2007. *Fair Trade Coffee: The Prospects and Pitfalls of Market-Driven Social Justice*. Vol. 28. Toronto: University of Toronto Press.
Fried, A. 2006. "The Personalization of Collective Memory: The Smithsonian's September 11 Exhibit." *Political Communication* 23 (4): 387–405.
Fullilove, M. T., L. Hernandez-Cordero, J. S. Madoff, and R. E. Fullilove. 2004. "Promoting Collective Recovery through Organizational Mobilization: The Post-9/11 Disaster Relief Work of NYC RECOVERS." *Journal of Biosocial Science* 36 (4): 479–90.
Gall, C. 2004. "Silk and Human Kindness." *New York Times Magazine*, Style section, February 22, 2004. http://www.nytimes.com/2004/02/22/magazine/silk-and-human-kindness.html (accessed December 15, 2005).
———. 2014. *The Wrong Enemy: America in Afghanistan, 2001–2014*. New York: Houghton Mifflin Harcourt.
Gallagher B. 2012. "Coming Home." In *The New Violent Cartography: Geo-Analysis after the Aesthetic Turn*, edited by S. O. Opondo and M. J. Shapiro. London: Routledge.
Galtung, J. 1969. "Violence, Peace, and Peace Research." *Journal of Peace Research* 6 (3): 167–91.
Geiser, U. 2013. "Producing Civil Society, Ignoring *Rivaj*." In *Beyond Swat: History, Society, and Economy along the Afghanistan-Pakistan Frontier*, edited by M. Marsden and B. Hopkins. New York: Columbia University Press.
Gibson-Graham, J. K. 2006. *"The" End of Capitalism (as We Knew It): A Feminist Critique of Political Economy; with a New Introduction*. Minneapolis: University of Minnesota Press.
Gilbert, E., and C. Ponder. 2013. "Between Tragedy and Farce: 9/11 Compensation and the Value of Life and Death." *Antipode* 46 (2): 404–25.
Gökariksel, B., and A. Secor. 2009. "New Transnational Geographies of Islamism, Capitalism and Subjectivity: The Veiling-Fashion Industry in Turkey." *Area* 41 (1): 6–18.
Goldstein, J. S. 2003. *War and Gender: How Gender Shapes the War System and Vice Versa*. Cambridge: Cambridge University Press.
Goodhand, J. 2002. "Aiding Violence or Building Peace? The Role of International Aid in Afghanistan." *Third World Quarterly* 23 (5): 837–59.
———. 2006. *Aiding Peace?: The Role of NGOs in Armed Conflict*. Boulder, Colo.: Lynne Rienner Publishers.
Graham, S. 2004. "Vertical Geopolitics: Baghdad and After." *Antipode* 36 (1): 12–23.
Greenberg, J. 2003. *Trauma at Home: After 9/11*. Omaha: University of Nebraska Press.

Gregory, D. 2004. *The Colonial Present: Afghanistan, Palestine, Iraq*. Malden, Mass.: Blackwell.
Grewal, I. 2003. "Transnational America: Race, Gender, and Citizenship after 9/11." *Social Identities* 9 (4): 535–61.
Grima, B. 1992. *The Performance of Emotion among Paxtun Women: "The Misfortunes Which Have Befallen Me."* Vol. 17. Austin: University of Texas Press.
Guindi, F. 1999. *Veil: Modesty, Privacy, and Resistance*. Oxford: Berg.
Gunn, J. 2004. "The Rhetoric of Exorcism: George W. Bush and the Return of Political Demonology." *Western Journal of Communication (Includes Communication Reports)* 68 (1): 1–23.
Gupta, A. 2012. *Red Tape: Bureaucracy, Structural Violence, and Poverty in India*. Durham, N.C.: Duke University Press.
Hancock, G. 1989. *Lords of Poverty: The Power, Prestige, and Corruption of the International Aid Business*. New York: Atlantic Monthly Press.
Hannah, M. 2006. "Torture and the Ticking Bomb: The War on Terrorism as a Geographical Imagination of Power/Knowledge." *Annals of the Association of American Geographers* 96 (3): 622–40.
Haraway, D. 1988. "Situated Knowledges: The Science Question in Feminism and the Privilege of Partial Perspective." *Feminist Studies* 14: 575–99.
Haroon, S. 2013. "Public Visibility of Women." In *Beyond Swat: History, Society, and Economy along the Afghanistan—Pakistan Frontier*, edited by M. Marsden and B. Hopkins. New York: Columbia University Press.
Hartnett, S. J., and L. A. Stengrim. 2006. "War Rhetorics: The National Security Strategy of the United States and President Bush's Globalization-through-Benevolent-Empire." *South Atlantic Quarterly* 105 (1): 175–205.
Harvey, D. 2006. *Spaces of Global Capitalism: Towards a Theory of Uneven Geographical Development*. New York: Verso.
Haskins, E. V., and J. P. DeRose. 2003. "Memory, Visibility, and Public Space Reflections on Commemoration(s) of 9/11." *Space and Culture* 6 (4): 377–93.
Hawthorne, S., and B. Winter, eds. 2002. *September 11, 2001: Feminist Perspectives*. Melbourne, Australia: Spinifex Press.
Herod, A. 2010. *Scale*. New York: Routledge.
Herod, A., and M. W. Wright, eds. 2002. *Geographies of Power: Placing Scale*. Oxford: Blackwell.
Hiatt, J. P., and D. Greenfield. 2004. "Importance of Core Labor Rights in World Development." *Michigan Journal of International Law* 26: 39.
Hirschkind, C., and S. Mahmood. 2002. "Feminism, the Taliban, and Politics of Counter-Insurgency." *Anthropological Quarterly* 75 (2): 339–54.
Hopkins, B. 2008. *The Making of Modern Afghanistan*. New York: Palgrave Macmillan.
House Session. 2001. Carolyn Maloney presentation before Congress wearing a burka. October 16. http://www.c-spanvideo.org/program/166698-3 (accessed October 5, 2012, time segment 04:09:24).
Hume, J. 2003. "'Portraits of Grief,' Reflectors of Values: The *New York Times* Remembers Victims of September 11." *Journalism & Mass Communication Quarterly* 80 (1): 166–82.

Hunt, K. 2002. "The Strategic Co-optation of Women's Rights." *International Feminist Journal of Politics* 4 (1): 116–21.
Hunt, L. 2007. *Inventing Human Rights: A History*. New York: W. W. Norton & Co.
Hyndman, J. 2007. "Feminist Geopolitics Revisited: Body Counts in Iraq." *Professional Geographer* 59 (1): 35–46.
Hyndman, J., and M. De Alwis. 2004. "Bodies, Shrines, and Roads: Violence, (Im)mobility and Displacement in Sri Lanka." *Gender, Place & Culture* 11 (4): 535–57.
Innocent, M. 2011. "Should America Liberate Afghanistan's Women?" *Survival* 53 (5): 31–52.
Issa, C., and M. K. Sardar. 2007. "Kabul's Urban Identity: An Overview of the Sociopolitical Aspects of Development." *ASIEN* 104: 51–64.
Jain, D. 2005. *Women, Development, and the UN: A Sixty-Year Quest for Equality and Justice*. Bloomington: Indiana University Press.
Jamal, A. 2009. "Gendered Islam and Modernity in the Nation-Space: Women's Modernism in the Jamaat-e-Islami of Pakistan." *Feminist Review* 91 (1): 9–28.
Jay, M. 1993. *Downcast Eyes: The Denigration of Vision in Twentieth-Century French Thought*. Berkeley: University of California Press.
Jazayery, L. 2002. "The Migration-Development Nexus: Afghanistan Case Study." *International Migration* 40 (5): 231–54.
Jetter, A., A. Orleck, and D. Taylor, eds. 1997. *The Politics of Motherhood: Activist Voices from Left to Right*. Lebanon, N.H.: University Press of New England.
JICA. 2006. *The Study on the Kabul Metropolitan Area Urban Development in the Islamic Republic of Afghanistan*. Japan International Cooperation Agency Final Report, RECS International Inc.
Johnson, C. 2000. *Blowback: The Costs and Consequences of American Empire*. New York: Henry Holt.
Johnson, C., and J. Leslie. 2002. "Afghans Have Their Memories: A Reflection on the Recent Experience of Assistance in Afghanistan." *Third World Quarterly* 23 (5): 861–74.
———. 2004. *Afghanistan, the Mirage of Peace*. London: Zed Books.
Jones, S. G. 2010. *In the Graveyard of Empires: America's War in Afghanistan*. New York: W. W. Norton.
Joseph, M. 2002. *Against the Romance of Community*. Minneapolis: University of Minnesota Press.
Kabeer, N. 1994. *Reversed Realities: Gender Hierarchies in Development Thought*. London: Verso.
———. 2005. "Gender Equality and Women's Empowerment: A Critical Analysis of the Third Millennium Development Goal 1." *Gender & Development* 13 (1): 13–24.
Kakar, P. 2004. "Tribal Law of Pashtunwali and Women's Legislative Authority." *Afghan Legal History Project*. Harvard Law School. http://www.law.harvard.edu/programs/ilsp/research/kakar.pdf (accessed September 19, 2007).
Kamp, M. R. 2008. *The New Woman in Uzbekistan: Islam, Modernity, and Unveiling under Communism*. Seattle: University of Washington Press.
Kandiyoti, D. 1988. "Bargaining with Patriarchy." *Gender and Society* 1 (3): 274–90.
———, ed. 1991. *Women, Islam, and the State*. Philadelphia: Temple University Press.

———. 2005. "Rethinking Bargaining with Patriarchy." In *Feminist Visions of Development: Gender Analysis and Policy*, edited by C. Jackson and R. Pearson, 135–150. London and New York: Routledge.

———. 2007a. "Old Dilemmas or New Challenges? The Politics of Gender and Reconstruction in Afghanistan." *Development and Change* 38: 169–99.

———. 2007b. "Between the Hammer and the Anvil: Post-Conflict Reconstruction, Islam and Women's Rights." *Third World Quarterly* 28: 503–17.

Kaplan, E. A. 2005. *Trauma Culture: The Politics of Terror and Loss in Media and Literature*. New Brunswick, N.J.: Rutgers University Press.

Kattak, S. G. 2002. "Violence and Home: Afghan Women's Experience of Displacement." In *Understanding September 11*, edited by C. Calhoun, P. Price, and A. Timmer. New York: New Press.

Katz, C. 2001. "Vagabond Capitalism and the Necessity of Social Reproduction." *Antipode* 33 (4): 709–28.

———. 2004. *Growing Up Global: Economic Restructuring and Children's Everyday Lives*. Minneapolis: University of Minnesota Press.

Katzman, K. 2009. *Afghanistan: Politics, Elections and Government Performance*. Washington, D.C.: Library of Congress, Congressional Research Service.

Kendall, D. 2002. *The Power of Good Deeds: Privileged Women and the Social Reproduction of the Upper Class*. Lanham, Md.: Rowman & Littlefield.

Kennedy, D. 2009. "Selling the Distant Other: Humanitarianism and Imagery—Ethical Dilemmas of Humanitarian Action." *Journal of Humanitarian Assistance*. http://jha.ac/2009/02/28/selling-the-distant-other-humanitarianism-and-imagery—ethical-dilemmas-of-humanitarian-action.

Kennedy, M. 2007. "Selling Afghanistan." *Marketplace*, March 16. http://www.marketplace.org/topics/life/selling-afghanistan (accessed February 10, 2013).

Kensinger, L. 2009. "Radical Lessons: Thoughts on Emma Goldman, Chaos, Grief, and Political Violence Post 9/11/01." *Feminist Teacher* 20 (1): 50–70.

Kent, V. 2007. "Protecting Civilians from UN Peacekeepers and Humanitarian Workers: Sexual Exploitation and Abuse." In *Unintended Consequences of Peacekeeping Operation*, edited by C. Aoi, C. de Coning, and R. Thakur, 44–66. Tokyo and New York: United Nations University Press.

Kessler-Harris, A. 2004. "Reframing the History of Women's Wage Labor: Challenges of a Global Perspective." *Journal of Women's History* 15 (4): 186–206.

Khalid, A. 2006. "Backwardness and the Quest for Civilization: Early Soviet Central Asia in Comparative Perspective." *Slavic Review* 65 (2): 231–51.

Klare, M. 2001. *Resource Wars: The New Landscape of Global Conflict*. New York: Metropolitan Books.

———. 2012. *The Race for What's Left: The Global Scramble for the World's Last Resources*. New York: Macmillan.

Klein, N. 2008. *The Shock Doctrine: The Rise of Disaster Capitalism*. New York: Picador.

Kothari, U. 2005. "Authority and Expertise: The Professionalisation of International Development and the Ordering of Dissent." *Antipode* 37 (3): 425–46.

Kristof, N. 2009. "Where Sweat-Shops Are a Dream." *New York Times*, January 14, http://www.nytimes.com/2009/01/15/opinion/15kristof.html?_r=0 (accessed February 5, 2013).

Kristof, N., and S. WuDunn. 2009. *Half the Sky: Turning Oppression into Opportunity for Women Worldwide*. New York: Alfred A. Knopf.

Lawson, V. 2007. "Geographies of Care and Responsibility." *Annals of the Association of American Geographers* 97 (1): 1–11.

———. 2014. *Making Development Geography*. 2nd ed. New York: Routledge.

Lim, J., and A. Fanghanel. 2013. "'Hijabs, Hoodies and Hotpants': Negotiating the 'Slut' in SlutWalk." *Geoforum* 48: 207–15.

Lister, S., and Z. Karaev. 2004. *Understanding Markets in Afghanistan: A Case Study of the Market in Construction Materials*. Kabul: Afghanistan Research and Evaluation Unit.

Lucky Life Advertisement. 2005. "Green without Hippie." *Lucky Magazine*, July.

Lule, J. 2002. "Myth and Terror on the Editorial Page: The *New York Times* Responds to September 11, 2001." *Journalism & Mass Communication Quarterly* 79 (2): 275–93.

Mabro, J. 1991. *Veiled Half-Truths: Western Travellers' Perceptions of Middle Eastern Women*. New York: I. B. Tauris.

Mahmood, S. 2005. *Politics of Piety: The Islamic Revival and the Feminist Subject*. Princeton, N.J.: Princeton University Press.

Maley, W. 2006. *Rescuing Afghanistan*. Kensington, Australia: University of New South Wales Press.

———. 2009. *The Afghanistan Wars*. New York: Palgrave Macmillan.

Mamdani, M. 2004. *Good Muslim, Bad Muslim: America, the Cold War, and the Roots of Terror*. New York: Pantheon Books.

Mandel, R. 2008. *Cosmopolitan Anxieties: Turkish Challenges to Citizenship and Belonging in Germany*. Durham: Duke University Press.

Mandel, R., and C. Humphrey, eds. 2002. *Markets and Moralities: Ethnographies of Postsocialism*. New York: Berg/NYC Press.

Maney, G. M., L. M. Woehrle, and P. G. Coy. 2005. "Harnessing and Challenging Hegemony: The U.S. Peace Movement after 9/11." *Sociological Perspectives* 48 (3): 357–81.

Marsden, M. 2009. "Talking the Talk: Debating Debate in Northern Afghanistan." *Anthropology Today* 45 (2): 20–24.

———. 2013. "Trade and Traders in Afghanistan." In *Beyond Swat: History, Society, and Economy along the Afghanistan-Pakistan Frontier*, edited by M. Marsden and B. Hopkins. New York: Columbia University Press.

Marsden, M., and B. D. Hopkins. 2011. *Fragments of the Afghan Frontier*. New York: Columbia University Press.

Massey, D. 1994. *Space, Place, and Gender*. Minneapolis: University of Minnesota Press.

Mbembé, J. A. 2003. "Necropolitics." *Public Culture* 15 (1): 11–40.

McDowell, L. 1992. "Doing Gender: Feminism, Feminists, and Research Methods in Human Geography." *Transactions of the Institute of British Geographers* 17 (4): 399–416.

McKittrick, K. 2006. *Demonic Grounds: Black Women and the Cartographies of Struggle*. Minneapolis: University of Minnesota Press.

Mehta, S., ed. 2002. *Women for Afghan Women: Shattering Myths and Claiming the Future*. New York: Palgrave Macmillan.

Menon, N. 2005. "Between the Burqa and the Beauty Parlor." In *Postcolonial Studies and Beyond*, edited by A. Loomba, S. Kaul, M. Bunzl, A. Burton, and J. Esty, 134–43. Durham: Duke University Press.
Mermin, L. 2004. *The Beauty Academy of Kabul*. New York: Magic Lantern Media.
Miller, N. 2003. "'Portraits of Grief': Telling Details and the Testimony of Trauma." *Differences: A Journal of Feminist Cultural Studies* 14 (3): 112–35.
Mills, M. 2012. "Victimhood as Agency: Afghan Women's Memoirs." In *Orientalism and War*, edited by T. Barkawi and K. Stanski, 197–222. New York: Columbia University Press.
Minca, C. 2007. "Agamben's Geographies of Modernity." *Political Geography* 26 (1): 78–97.
Mirzoeff, N., ed. 2002. *The Visual Culture Reader*. London: Routledge.
Mitchell, T. 2002. *Rule of Experts: Egypt, Techno-Politics, Modernity*. Berkeley: University of California Press.
Moghadam, V. M. 2002a. "Islamic Feminism and Its Discontents: Toward a Resolution of the Debate." *Signs: Journal of Women in Culture and Society* 27 (4): 1135–71.
———. 2002b. "Patriarchy, the Taleban, and Politics of Public Space in Afghanistan." *Women's Studies International Forum* 25 (1): 19–31.
Mohanty, C. T. 2004. *Feminism without Borders*. New Delhi, India: Zubaan Books, Kali for Women.
Momsen, J. 2004. *Gender and Development*. London: Routledge.
Monsutti, A. 2006. "Afghan Transnational Networks: Looking beyond Repatriation." Kabul: Afghanistan Research and Evaluation Unit. http://www.areu.org.af/EditionDetails.aspx?EditionId=144&ContentId=7&ParentId=7 (accessed October 25, 2013).
———. 2013. "Anthropologizing Afghanistan: Colonial and Postcolonial Encounters." *Annual Review of Anthropology* 42: 269–85.
Mosse, D. 2005. "Global Governance and the Ethnography of International Aid." In *The Aid Effect: Giving and Governing in International Development*, edited by D. Mosse and D. Lewis, 1–36. London: Pluto Press.
———, ed. 2013. *Adventures in Aidland: The Anthropology of Professionals in International Development*. Vol. 6. New York: Berghahn Books.
Munshi, S. 2001. "Marvelous Me: And the Construction of the 'Modern' Indian Woman." In *Images of the "Modern Woman" in Asia: Global Media, Local Meanings*, edited by S. Munshi, 78–93. Richmond, Va.: Curzon.
Munster, R. V. 2004. "The War on Terrorism: When the Exception Becomes the Rule." *International Journal for the Semiotics of Law* 17 (2): 141–53.
Naghibi, N. 2007. *Rethinking Global Sisterhood: Western Feminism and Iran*. Minneapolis: University of Minnesota Press.
Narayan, U. 1997. *Dislocating Cultures: Identities, Tradition, and Third World Feminism*. New York: Routledge.
Nawa, F. 2006. *Afghanistan, Inc: A CorpWatch Investigative Report*. Oakland, Calif.: CorpWatch.
Nayak, A. 2006. "After Race: Ethnography, Race, and Post-Race Theory." *Ethnic and Racial Studies* 29 (3): 411–30.

Nelson, L. 1999. "Bodies (and Spaces) Do Matter: The Limits of Performativity." *Gender, Place and Culture* 6 (4): 331–53.

Nelson, S. S. 2007. "Subjects of 'Kabul Beauty School' Face New Risks." *All Things Considered*, June 1. National Public Radio. http://www.npr.org/templates/story/story.php?storyId=10634299 (accessed August 9, 2013).

9/11 Commission. 2004. *The 9/11 Commission Report*, http://avalon.law.yale.edu/sept11/911Report.pdf (accessed December 9, 2015); http://www.9-11commission.gov/report/ (accessed December 9, 2015).

Norland, R. 2013. "Despite a Whiff of Unpleasant Exaggeration, a City's Pollution Is Real." *New York Times*, January 21, http://www.nytimes.com/2013/01/22/world/asia/kabuls-pollution-is-real-despite-unpleasant-exaggeration.html?_r=0 (accessed February 4, 2016).

Olds, K., J. D. Sidaway, and M. Sparke. 2005. "White Death." *Environment and Planning D: Society and Space* 23: 475–79.

Ong, A. 2006. *Neoliberalism as Exception: Mutations in Citizenship and Sovereignty*. Durham, N.C.: Duke University Press.

Oyěwùmí, O. 1997. *The Invention of Women: Making an African Sense of Western Gender Discourses*. Minneapolis: University of Minnesota Press.

Papanek, H. 1973. "Purdah: Separate Worlds and Symbolic Shelter." *Comparative Studies in Society and History* 15 (3): 289–325.

Peet, R., and E. Hartwick. 2015. *Theories of Development: Contentions, Arguments, Alternatives*. 3rd ed. New York: Guilford Press.

Petchesky, R. P., and M. Laurie. 2007. "Gender, Health, and Human Rights in Spaces of Political Exclusion." Background paper prepared for the Women and Gender Equity Knowledge Network of the WHO Commission on Social Determinants of Health.

Petraeus, D. H., and J. F. Amos. 2006. "Counterinsurgency." Headquarters Department of the Army. Field Manual 3-24, Marine Corps Warfighting Publication 3-33.5.

Potts, Tracey J. 2012. "'Dark Tourism' and the 'Kitschification' of 9/11." *Tourist Studies* 12 (3): 232–49.

Pratt, G., and V. Rosner, eds. 2012. *The Global and the Intimate: Feminism in Our Time*. New York: Columbia University Press.

Qazi, N. 2012. "The Afghan Commute." *Financial Times*, April 21, http://www.ft.com/intl/cms/s/2/fcc6ee56-849e-11e1-b6f5-00144feab49a.html#axzz2JHUfqP8S (accessed April 16, 2016).

Qazi, S. H. 2010. "The 'Neo-Taliban' and Counterinsurgency in Afghanistan." *Third World Quarterly* 31 (3): 485–99.

Rashid, A. 2001. *Taliban: Militant Islam, Oil, and Fundamentalism in Central Asia*. New Haven: Yale University Press.

———. 2008. *Descent into Chaos: The U.S. and the Disaster in Pakistan, Afghanistan, and Central Asia*. New York: Penguin.

RAWA. 2002. "Statement on the U.S. Strikes on Afghanistan." In *September 11, 2001: Feminist Perspectives*, edited by S. Hawthorne and B. Winter, 95–96. North Melbourne, Australia: Spinifex Press.

Rennie, R., S. Sharma, and P. K. Sen. 2008. *Afghanistan in 2008: A Survey of the Afghan People*. Kabul: Asia Foundation, Afghanistan Office.

Richey, L. A., and S. Ponte. 2011. *Brand Aid: Shopping Well to Save the World*. Minneapolis: University of Minnesota Press.

Roberts, S. M. 2014. "Development Capital: USAID and the Rise of Development Contractors." *Annals of the Association of American Geographers* 104 (5): 1030–51.

Rodriguez, D. 2007. *Kabul Beauty School: An American Woman Goes Behind the Veil*. Paperback reprint ed. New York: Random House.

Routledge, P. 2010. "Sensuous Solidarities: Emotion, Politics and Performance in the Clandestine Insurgent Rebel Clown Army." *Antipode* 44 (2): 428–52.

Roy, A. 2002. *The Algebra of Infinite Justice*. New York: Penguin.

———. 2010. *Poverty Capital: Microfinance and the Making of Development*. New York: Routledge.

Roy, O. 1990. *Islam and Resistance in Afghanistan*. Vol. 8. Cambridge: Cambridge University Press.

Rozario, K. 2007. *The Culture of Calamity: Disaster and the Making of Modern America*. Chicago: University of Chicago Press.

Rubin, B. R. 2002. *The Fragmentation of Afghanistan: State Formation and Collapse in the International System*. New Haven: Yale University Press.

———. 2015. *Afghanistan from the Cold War through the War on Terror*. Oxford: Oxford University Press.

Russo, A. 2006. "The Feminist Majority Foundation's Campaign to Stop Gender Apartheid: The Intersections of Feminism and Imperialism in the United States." *International Feminist Journal of Politics* 8 (4): 557–80.

Saal, I. 2011. "'It's about Us!' Violence and Narrative Memory in Post 9/11 American Theatre." *Arcadia-International Journal for Literary Studies* 45 (2): 353–73.

Said, E. 1979. *Orientalism*. New York: Vintage Books.

Saldahna, A. 2007. *Psychedelic White: Goa Trance and the Viscosity of Race*. Minneapolis: University of Minnesota Press.

Sangtin Writers and R. Nagar. 2006. *Playing with Fire: Feminist Thought and Activism through Seven Lives in India*. Minneapolis: University of Minnesota Press.

Schneider, I. 2005. "The Position of Woman in the Islamic and Afghan Judiciary." In *The Shari'ia in the Constitutions of Afghanistan, Iran, and Egypt: Implications for Private Law*, edited by N. Yassari. Tubingen: Mohr Siebeck.

Schütte, S. 2013. "Living with Patriarchy and Poverty: Women's Agency and the Spatialities of Gender Relations in Afghanistan." *Gender, Place & Culture* 21: 1–17.

Schwartz-DuPre, R. L. 2010. "Portraying the Political: *National Geographic*'s 1985 Afghan Girl and a U.S. Alibi for Aid." *Critical Studies in Media Communication* 27: 336–56.

Scott, J. W. 2009. *The Politics of the Veil*. Princeton, N.J.: Princeton University Press.

Sediqi, A. 2012. "A Preliminary Assessment of Air Quality in Kabul." Afghanistan Ministry of Mines. http://moph.gov.af/Content/Media/Documents/Kabul-Air-2003-03-18-20102912201015593917.pdf. (last accessed June 25, 2016)

Seuter, E., and C. Rubin. 2005. "The Tailor of Kabul." *People Magazine*, February 28, 127–28. http://www.tarsian.com/catalog/img/peoplemagazine_feb2005.jpg (accessed February 10, 2013).

Shabir, G., S. Ali, and Z. Iqbal. 2011. "U.S. Mass Media and Image of Afghanistan: Portrayal of Afghanistan by *Newsweek* and *Time*." *South Asian Studies* 26 (1): 83.

Shaheed, A. L. F. 2009. "Dress Codes and Modes: How Islamic Is the Veil?" In *The Veil: Women Writers on Its History, Lore and Politics*, edited by J. Health, 290–306. Berkeley: University of California Press.

Sharma, A. 2008. *Logics of Empowerment: Development, Gender, and Governance in Neoliberal India*. Minneapolis: University of Minnesota Press.

Shepherd, L. J. 2008. *Gender, Violence, and Security: Discourse as Practice*. New York: Zed Books.

Sheppard, E., P. W. Porter, D. R. Faust, and R. Nagar. 2009. *A World of Difference: Encountering and Contesting Development*. New York: Guilford Press.

Sibley, D. 1995. *Geographies of Exclusion: Society and Difference in the West*. London: Routledge.

Silk, J. 2004. "Caring at a Distance: Gift Theory, Aid Chains and Social Movements." *Social & Cultural Geography* 5 (2): 229–51.

Silverstein, P. 2004. "Headscarves and the French Tricolor." *Middle East Report Online* 29, http://www.merip.org/mero/mero013004?ip_login_no_cache=f7b6a8cf371e9cf9da95b74d68ce6b06 (accessed April 19, 2016).

Simko, C. 2012. "Rhetorics of Suffering: September 11 Commemorations as Theodicy." *American Sociological Review* 77 (6): 880–902.

Slaughter, J. 2007. *Human Rights, Inc.: The World Novel, Narrative Form, and International Law*. New York: Fordham University Press.

Smith, D. 2009. *Decisions, Desires, and Diversity: Marriage Practices in Afghanistan*. Kabul: Afghanistan Research and Evaluation Unit.

Smith, D., and S. Manalan. 2009. *Community-Based Dispute Resolution Processes in Bamiyan Province*. Kabul: Afghanistan Research and Evaluation Unit.

Sopko, J. M. 2013. "Testimony before the Committee on Oversight and Government Reform: U.S. House of Representatives, Challenges Affecting U.S. Foreign Assistance to Afghanistan," April 10, 2013. Special Inspector General for Afghanistan Reconstruction. http://oversight.house.gov/wp-content/uploads/2013/04/Sopko-Testimony-Final.pdf (accessed August 25, 2013).

———. 2014. "SIGAR 15–24 Audit Report: Afghan Women: Comprehensive Assessments Needed to Determine and Measure DOD, State, and USAID Progress." Office of the Special Inspector General for Afghanistan Reconstruction (SIGAR), 1–44.

Sparke, M. 2006. "A Neoliberal Nexus: Economy, Security, and the Biopolitics of Citizenship at the Border." *Political Geography* 25 (2): 151–80.

Spivak, G. C. 1988. "Can the Subaltern Speak?" In *Marxism and the Interpretation of Culture*, edited by C. Nelson and L. Grossberg. Chicago: University of Chicago Press.

Stabile, C. A., and D. Kumar. 2005. "Unveiling Imperialism: Media, Gender, and the War on Afghanistan." *Media, Culture & Society* 27 (5): 765–82.

Stewart, R. 2006. *The Places in Between*. New York: Mariner Books.

Stigter, E., and A. Monsutti. 2005. *Transnational Networks: Recognizing a Regional Reality*. Kabul: Afghanistan Research and Evaluation Unit.

Strüver, A. 2007. "The Production of Geopolitical and Gendered Images through Global Aid Organisations." *Geopolitics* 12: 680–703.

Sturken, M., and L. Cartwright, L. 2009. *Practices of Looking: An Introduction to Visual Culture*. 2nd ed. Oxford: Oxford University Press.

Suhrke, A. 2007. "Reconstruction as Modernisation: The 'Post-Conflict' Project in Afghanistan." *Third World Quarterly* 28 (7): 1291–1308.

Sultana, F. 2007. "Reflexivity, Positionality, and Participatory Ethics: Negotiating Fieldwork Dilemmas in International Research." *ACME: An International E-Journal for Critical Geographies* 6 (3): 374–85.

Takesh, S. 2004. *Afghan Scene Magazine*, Issue 1: 17–18.

———. 2005. "Sarah Takesh, Clothing Entrepreneur, Kabul, Afghanistan. Collaborating with Afghan Women to Produce Gorgeous Designs, Wages, and a Taste of Liberty." *OrganicStyle.com*, May.

Thrift, N. 2008. "The Material Practices of Glamour." *Journal of Cultural Economy* 1: 9–23.

Tickner, J. A. 2002. "Feminist Perspectives on 9/11." *International Studies Perspectives* 3 (4): 333–50.

Time Out New York Holiday Gift Guide. 2004. November 18–24.

Trauger, A., and J. L. Fluri. 2012. "Getting Beyond the 'God Trick': Toward Service Research." *Professional Geographer* 66 (1): 32–40.

Tuan, Y. F. 1986. *The Good Life*. Madison: University of Wisconsin Press.

Tyner, J. 2011. *Space, Place, and Violence: Violence and the Embodied Geographies of Race, Sex, and Gender*. New York: Routledge.

UNEP. 2008. *Afghanistan Environment*. United Nations Environment Programme Special Report. http://reliefweb.int/sites/reliefweb.int/files/resources/37FB695F399DC788C1257582004CA11E-Full_Report.pdf (accessed August 25, 2013).

U.S. Congress. 2001. "Afghan People vs. the Taliban: The Struggle for Freedom Intensifies." Committee on International Relations.

U.S. Senate Foreign Relations Committee. 2000. "The Taliban: Engagement of Confrontation?" Hearing of the Near Eastern and South Asian Affairs Subcommittee of the Senate Foreign Relations Committee, July 20.

Van Munster, R. 2004. "The War on Terrorism: When the Exception Becomes the Rule." *International Journal for the Semiotics of Law* 17 (2): 141–53.

Vandenberg, M. 2005. "Peacekeeping, Alphabet Soup, and Violence against Women in the Balkans." In *Gender, Conflict, and Peacekeeping*, edited by D. Mazurana, A. Raven-Roberts, and J. Parpart, 150–67. Lanham, Md.: Rowman & Littlefield.

Velásquez, S. 2001/2002. "Ms. News." *Ms. Magazine*, December 2001/January 2002, 11.

Wakefield, S. 2004a. *Gender and Local Decision Making: Findings from a Case Study in Panjao*. Kabul: Afghanistan Research and Evaluation Unit.

———. 2004b. *Gender and Local Decision Making: Findings from a Case Study in Samangan*. Kabul: Afghanistan Research and Evaluation Unit.

———. 2005. *Field Notes and Observations on Gender and Decision-making in Herat*. Kabul: Afghanistan Research and Evaluation Unit.

Wakefield, S., and B. Bauer. 2005. *A Place at the Table: Afghan Women, Men, and Decision-Making Authority*. Kabul: Afghanistan Research and Evaluation Unit.

Walker, R. 2004. *Body Outlaws: Breaking the Rules of Beauty and Body Image*. 2nd ed. New York: Seal Press.

Whitlock, G. 2005. "The Skin of the Burqa: Recent Life Narratives from Afghanistan." *Biography* 29 (1): 54–76.

———. 2007. *Soft Weapons: Autobiography in Transit*. Chicago: University of Chicago Press.

Wilder, A. 2007. *Cops or Robbers? The Struggle to Reform the Afghan National Police*. AREU Issues Paper Series 75. Kabul: Afghanistan Research and Evaluation Unit.

Wilder, A., and S. Gordon. 2009. "Money Can't Buy America Love." *Foreign Policy* 1, http://foreignpolicy.com/2009/12/01/money-cant-buy-america-love/ (accessed April 19, 2016).

Wiles, J. L., M. W. Rosenberg, and R. A. Kearns. 2005. "Narrative Analysis as a Strategy for Understanding Interview Talk in Geographic Research." *Area* 37 (1): 89–99.

Wilson, K. 2011. "'Race,' Gender, and Neoliberalism: Changing Visual Representations in Development." *Third World Quarterly* 32 (2): 315–31.

Wilson, K. J., B. Everdene, and F. Klijn. 2012. "The Markets for Afghan Artisans Approach to Women's Economic Empowerment." *Gender and Development* 20 (1): 81–94.

Wolf, N. 2002. *The Beauty Myth: How Images of Beauty Are Used against Women*. Reprint ed. New York: Harper Perennial.

Wordsworth, A. 2007. *A Matter of Interests: Gender and the Politics of Presence in Afghanistan's Wolesi Jirga*. Kabul: Afghanistan Research and Evaluation Unit.

World Bank. 2005. *Kabul: Urban Land in Crisis: A Policy Note*. South Asian Energy and Infrastructure Unit of the World Bank. http://siteresources.worldbank.org/SOUTHASIAEXT/Resources/223546-1150905429722/PolicyNote4.pdf (accessed May 30, 2014).

Wright, M. W., ed. 2006. *Disposable Women and Other Myths of Global Capitalism*. New York: Routledge.

———. 2009. "Gender and Geography: Knowledge and Activism across the Intimately Global." *Progress in Human Geography* 33 (3): 379–86.

———. 2012. "Witnessing, Feminicide, and a Politics of the Familiar." In *The Global and the Intimate: Feminism in Our Time*, edited by G. Pratt and V. Rosner. New York: Columbia University Press.

Yeh, E. T. 2013. *Taming Tibet: Landscape Transformation and the Gift of Chinese Development*. Ithaca: Cornell University Press.

Young, I. M. 2003. "The Logic of Masculinist Protection: Reflections on the Current Security State." *Signs: Journal of Women in Culture and Society* 29: 1–25.

Zeiger, D. 2008. "That (Afghan) Girl! Ideology Unveiled in *National Geographic*." In *The Veil: Women Writers on Its History, Lore, and Politics*, edited by J. Heath. Berkeley: University of California Press.

Zulfacar, M. 2006. "The Pendulum of Gender Politics in Afghanistan." *Central Asian Survey* 25 (1–2): 27–59.

INDEX

Abu-Lughod, Lila, 6, 16, 54, 57
Afghan languages, 28, 135n14
Afghan men: dress code for, 7, 34–35, 136n23; female agency and, 126; grievability of, 49; performativity of, 121; Taliban treatment of, 14–15, 134n9
Afghan Scene, 26–28
Afghan women: currency of, 61–62; as distinct category, 2–3; educational opportunities for, 86–90; efforts to nationalize, 2–4; international donors and, 79–80; living-suffering of, 20, 47–48, 62, 97–98, 125–26; media representations of, x–xi, 12–14; saving/liberating, 9–11, 15, 38, 51, 53–55, 105, 117–18. *See also* veiling/unveiling practices; women's liberation
Agamben, Giorgio: potentiality analysis, 48; sovereignty and bare life theories, 43–45
agency: abandonment of, 16; Afghan women's, 91, 96, 102, 126; community, 84; victimhood as, 17
aid/development: to alleviate suffering, 47–48; documentary films on, 110–14; gender-specific funding, 53–54; patriarchal systems and, 95; precarity/precariousness and, 49–50; shallowness of, 132; structural conditions for, 127–28; temporal limitations to, 78; U.S. government funding, 22; U.S. military, 9–11, 15, 50. *See also* development programs
alcohol consumption, 35, 36
Al-Qaeda, 49–50, 109
autonomy, 18, 70, 123
Axis of Good (2009 film), 110, 114, 115

bare life: of Afghan lives, 46–47, 49, 52, 125–26; Agamben's concept, 44–45; gendering of, 126; rescuing, 62, 126; zone of indistinction and, 45–46
Barfield, Thomas J., 1
Barker, Paul, 111
beauty: pageants, 12–13; schools and parlors, 60–62, 63, 119
Beauty Academy of Kabul, 60–62, 119
Beyond Belief (2007 film), 14, 110–12, 115–16
Beyond the 11th, 109–10, 114
bios, 44
bodies: beauty and, 12–13, 60–62; control over, 6; currency of, 19, 133n3; misappropriation of, 132; production and consumption of, 6, 19; security for, 33–34, 136n21; of sex workers, 39; as war weapon, 3. *See also* dress codes
Brunn, Stanley, 108
building construction, 24
burqa: description of, 4; for protection, 33–34; sexualization of, 13; as symbol of oppression, 7–8, 9–10, 15, 81, 130; used in marketing, 81–82; women's liberation and, 132
Bush, Laura, 11–12, 94, 105
Bush administration, 9, 11, 139n7
Butler, Judith: on performativity, 96–97, 118; on precariousness and grief, 20, 43–44, 48, 125; on sustaining life, 49

capacity, lack of, xii, 48, 124, 129
capitalism: conflict-zone, 26; consumer, 6; global, 50, 128–31; market-driven, xii, 63,

162 Index

capitalism (*continued*)
  83, 84, 123, 126, 131; neoliberal, 56, 96, 121, 123; violence of, 56
CARE International, 109, 111, 116
carpetbagger, usage of term, xii, 21
celebrity advocacy, 7, 134n7
chadri. *See* burqa
Chayes, Sarah, 121
children, 34, 71, 137n7; education for, 138n14; living-suffering of, 47, 51–52, 105–6, 115, 120, 125–27; political currency of, 46, 49; victimization of, 10, 117–18
clothing companies, 55–56, 58–60
collectivities, 123
Collins, Holly, 134n11
colonizers, x, 2
commodification of time, 71, 76, 77
commodity, 131; gendered suffering as, 52; spectacle and, 51, 119
conflict development, 47, 56, 126, 131
"ConflictSpace," usage of term, 127
conflict zones, 45, 131; international workers in, 25–26, 29, 33, 36
Cons, Jason, 46
consumers: conscientious, 59–60, 63, 80; of illusion, 119; virtual connections of, 82–83
consumption: cosmopolitan, 25, 33; foreign, 85; illusionary form of, 119; labor-liberation and, 57–58, 123; of 9/11 commemorative gear, 109; of women's bodies, 6, 19
corporeal modernity, 12, 62
corruption, 41
cosmopolitanism, 25, 33, 93, 124, 135n6
counterinsurgency (COIN), 46, 47, 126

Dahlman, Carl, 108
Daulatzai, Anila, 55
deaths, Afghan civilian, 113, 136n2; caused by Taliban, 52; geopolitical currency of, 109, 126–27; grievability of, 45–49, 105, 125
Debord, Guy, 43, 51, 119, 123
development programs: approaches and implementation, xii, 39, 41, 127–28; critical reflection of, 93, 116; donor agendas and, 17–18; expectations of, 122; feedback and evaluation of, 94; ideologies, 128–29; potentiality and, 48; unequal relationships in, 99–100
discipline, 77–78
docility, 9, 16, 101, 130
domestic labor, 69–72, 74

donors: access to, 137–38n11; gender currency and, 122; incentives and expectations, 72, 76–77, 79–80, 86; Kabul's dependence on, 18, 25; local-Afghan women and, 54; needs of recipients and, 95, 99–100
Dowler, Lorraine, 108
dress codes: Afghan men, 7, 34–35, 136n23; Afghan women, 6, 35; *bacha posh* ("dressed like boy"), 121
Duffield, Mark, 49
Dunn, Elizabeth Cullen, 46

education: for children, 138n14; donor attempts at, 76–77; WELO exchange program, 86–90
Eid, 90
El Guindi, 5
elites and nonelites, 2, 19, 49, 54, 65, 137n1
embroidery work: branding and sales, 80–83; community-driven, 67–69, 78–79; education and, 76–77; home-based, 69–72; markets for, 79–80; stitch signatures on, 82–83, 138n18
emotional geographies, 104
Engle, Karen J., 48, 105
English language, 28, 72
executions, 14–15
expatriate Afghans, 22, 27, 28, 30

fair trade, 56, 80
family networks, 95, 102
femininity, 12, 121
feminist activism: of Afghan women, 54–55, 96, 100, 102–3; situated knowledges of, 94; Taliban regime and, 6; transnational, 9, 19, 89
Feminist Majority Foundation (FMF), 9–10, 108
fourth wall, concept, 97–99, 102, 120

Gall, Carlotta, 10
gender currency: appearance and, 132; of bodies, 19, 133n3; donor funding and, 98–99, 118, 122; grievable living-suffering as, 49, 51–52, 92, 108–9, 118; labor-liberation and, 53–55, 63–64, 118–20; saving Afghan women and, 117–18
gender equality, 53, 58, 119
gender mainstreaming, 53
gender performance/performativity, 96–98, 100, 102, 118, 120–21
gender politics, 2–6, 16
gender roles, 16, 17, 62, 123; labor and, 69–72; social changes and, 53, 72

gender specialists, 53, 118
geo-economy: Afghan women and, 51, 63; definition of, 22; in Kabul, 25–26, 41–42, 124; security and, 34; sex work and, 38
geography of Afghanistan, 1–2, 133n1
geopolitical currency: of Afghan civilian deaths, 46–47, 52, 109, 126–27; of saving/liberating Afghan women, 60–61, 94–95, 115, 117–18
geopolitics: in Afghanistan history, 1–2; of Afghan women, 5–6, 15, 16–17; of aid/development, 18, 50, 101; of bare life, 125; capitalism and, 131; of human rights, 50–51; intimate forms of, 93–94; popular, 108
gift reciprocity, 99–100, 120
Gökariksel, Banu, 6
Goodrich, Sally, 109, 110–11, 114, 116
gossip, 73, 75, 78, 102
Gregory, Derek, 45, 49
Grewal, Inderpal, 51
grief: as currency, 47, 48–49, 52, 104–6, 114, 115, 125; healing and, 111–12, 127; nationalized, 106; public responses to, 110–14; remembrances and memorials, 51, 106–8; value of life and, 43, 45
grievability: of Afghan civilian deaths, 45–49, 105, 125, 127; definition of, 43; of living-suffering, 20, 52, 97–98, 114, 126

handicraft production, 67, 122, 137n4, 138n12. *See also* embroidery work
Haraway, Donna, 19, 93
Haroon, Sana, 71
hero mythology, 108
honor, 71, 73, 75
housing, 23, 30, 73–75
human rights: concepts, 18; geopolitical manipulation of, 50–51; Taliban and, 7–8, 15

individualism, 18, 50, 123
information war, 118
Inside Man (2006 film), 21
international workers: behavior and political ideologies, 35–36; criticisms of, 128; living conditions of, 23–24; media representations of, 129; regional, 22; salaries, 25–26, 125, 135n10; sexual harassment and, 38–39; types of, 22; upward mobility of, 29–30. *See also* privileged international workers

intimate analyses, 127–28, 130. *See also* personal connections
Islam, 100, 101, 106
izzat, 71

Kabeer, Naila, 101
Kabul: cosmopolitanism in, 33, 124; economy, 18–19, 25, 41–42, 124; entertainment and restaurants, 36; home/office spaces in, 73–75; international workers in, 25–28; reconstruction and infrastructural changes, 23–24, 134n2, 135nn3–5; security in, 34; souvenirs of, 31, 33
Kabuli, usage of term, 93
Kendall, Diana, 96
knowledge. *See* situated knowledges
Kristof, Nicholas, 56–57

labor: customer and, connection, 82–83; home-based, 69–72, 129; liberation and, 54–58, 59–60, 63–64, 67–69, 118–20, 123; wages, 59, 136n3; of widows, 54–55. *See also* embroidery work
Lahore, 65–67
legal exception, 44, 47
liberation. *See* women's liberation
Lil' Kim, 13
literacy, 76–77
living-suffering: currency of, 51–52, 108; efforts to relieve/liberate, 50–51, 62, 82, 85; gendered, 126; grievable, 20, 47–49, 52, 97–98, 112, 114–15, 125–26
local-Afghans: employment opportunities, 28–29, 137–38n11; English-language skills, 28, 72, 137–38n11; housing, 23; patriarchal structures, 95, 101; salaries, 25–26, 135n10; security and mobility, 30; usage of term, 22
Lule, Jack, 107

MacMakin, Mary, 60–61
Mahmood, Saba, 16
mahram, 4, 6–7, 68, 121; security purposes of, 33–34, 92
maliks, 78, 138n15
Maloney, Carolyn, 10
Mamdani, Mahmood, 106, 107
markets: "Bush market," 124; for international workers, 25, 33; local and regional, 90; niche or fair trade, 55, 58–59, 77, 79–81, 85, 86
Marsden, Magnus, 84
masculinity, 108, 115, 121

Mbembé, Joseph-Achille, 47
McKinney, Cynthia A., 10–11
mehman khana, 75
mobility: career, 29; limitations, 75; security and, 30–31, 121, 136n20; of widows, 54
modernist movements, 5
Moghadam, Valentine M., 6
motherhood, 110–11
mujahedin: CIA cash payments to, 21, 23; usage of term, 133n3; U.S. support of, 12
Mullah Nasruddin story, 131–32
Muslim women, 11, 16, 91

Nangarhar Province, 65–66, 72–73
National Geographic "Afghan Girl" (1985), 12, 13
necropolitics, 10, 47
Nelson, Lise, 97
neoliberalism, 56, 96, 121, 123, 128
9/11: Afghan activists and, 14; Afghan women and, 9–12, 16; collection and compensation programs, 90–91, 109; consumptive practices of, 109; deaths, 48; documentary films on, 109–16; grief, 43–44, 52, 104–6, 108–9, 114, 125, 127; institutionalized memorials of, 51, 106–8; obituaries, 107, 139n4
nongovernmental organizations (NGOs), 22, 41, 74; local-Afghan, 28–29; registration, 72, 137n10

Ong, Aihwa, 45–46
ontology, 115
otherness, x, 45, 82

passports, 30, 35, 36, 135n18
patriarchy: international workers and, 88, 93, 95, 103, 120; U.S. representations of, 15, 81, 94; women's liberation and, 68, 84
personal connections, 82–83, 111, 115, 130
Peter M. Goodrich Memorial Foundation, 109–10
Petraeus, David, 46, 136n1
Places in Between, The (Stewart), 2
political life, 44–45
potentiality: Agamben's analysis, 48; learned, 52; rescue and development, 43, 47–49, 52, 109, 125–27
poverty, 50, 56, 85, 126, 131
precarity/precariousness: aid/development and, 49–50; bare life and, 44; Butler's concept, 19, 43, 125; of security, 88

privileged international workers: attitudes, 48, 95; career mobility, 29–30; currency of, 124; definition of, 22; housing for, 23; marketing and, 55, 59; security and mobility of, 30–31; wealth generated by, 58, 61–62, 119, 124, 139n2
property ownership, 23
public spaces, 136n21; mobility in, 54; women's access to, 2, 4, 6, 76, 121
purdah, 67, 71, 102, 137n5, 138n16

Quigley, Patricia, 109–14, 115–16

race, 35, 133n3
Ramadan, 90
rape, 3, 15, 37, 133n4
refugees, 65–66, 135n13, 137nn2–4
remittances, 91–92
Retik, Susan, 109–14, 115–16
Revolutionary Association of the Women of Afghanistan (RAWA): background, 133–34n5; documentation of Taliban punishments, 14–15; political/public support of, 8–9, 134n7; utilization of burqa, 8
Rodriguez, Debby, 61–63, 119
Rohrabacher, Dana, 7, 10–11
Roy, Ananya, 57
Rubia, Inc.: background, ix, 137n6, 138n14; donors and funding, 75–77, 79–80, 128; embroidery project plan, 66–69, 122; grassroots organizing, 78–79; hiring preferences, 121; home-based operations, 70–71, 137n8; Kabul office, 73–75, 138n12; Pakistan operations, 69, 72, 137n9; relocation to Afghanistan, 72–73; sales and marketing strategy, 80–85
Russo, Ann, 10

Said, Edward, x
Samadzai, Vida, 12
Secor, Anna, 6
security: community, 34, 136n22; companies, 33, 34, 38; gender-based, 33–34, 121; for international workers, 30–31
service workers, 26
sex trafficking, 37–39
sexual harassment, 38–39
situated knowledges, 19, 93–94, 98, 120
Slaughter, Joseph, 50
Smithsonian Institution, 107, 139n5

social responsibility, 58–59
Soraya, Queen, 5
sovereignty: Agamben's theories, 44–45; aleatory, 46; violence and, 43–44
Soviet Union, 3, 12, 133n3
Special Investigator General for Afghanistan Reconstruction (SIGAR), 39, 54, 134n1
spectacle: bare life as, 126; social/societal, 43, 51, 119, 123
Spivak, Gayatri, 93
state of emergency, 44
stereotypes, 5, 11, 57, 96, 130
Stewart, Rory, 2
sweatshops, 56

Takesh, Sarah, 59–60
Taliban: abuses and punishments, 14–15, 134n9; treatment of women, 3–4, 6, 10; U.S. operations against, 112–13
Tarsian and Blinkley (T&B), 58–60, 63, 122, 136n3
Thrift, Nigel, 63
time, importance of, 77–78, 129
Time magazine, 13

UNHCR, 137n3
United States: fight against Soviet occupation, 15, 138n3; foreign policy, 107, 111, 114; geopolitics, 9; intervention in women's liberation, 9–13, 94–95, 117; invasion/occupation of Afghanistan, 4, 9, 21–22, 105–6, 108, 112–13, 117
United States Agency for International Development (USAID), 49, 54, 135n13; Afghan Small and Medium Enterprise Development (ASMED), 122; Rubia project, 73, 78, 79; use of implementing partners, 41
USA PATRIOT Act, 44
U.S. Congress, 7–8, 10, 14
U.S. embassy: in Islamabad, 135–36n19, 138n2; in Kabul, 24, 31, 135n17, 138n2
use value, 119–20
U.S. military: aid/development assistance, 15, 50; COIN strategy, 46, 47, 50; liberation of Afghan women, 9–11, 95; operations against Taliban, 23, 112–13; response to 9/11, 105; violence, 112–14, 115, 118, 125

veiling/unveiling practices: geopolitics of, 5–6; personal choice and, 91, 92; post-9/11 context, 9–12; Taliban requirements, 3–4
victimhood, 10, 17, 112–13, 115, 117–18
violence: attempts to dichotomize, 126; civilian deaths and, 46–47; domestic, 13; insurgent, 118; military, 50, 112–14, 115, 125; of 9/11, 107; political, 131; production of, 104; sovereignty and, 43–45; structural, 128
volunteers: Rubia's U.S.-based, 79–83, 84, 86; WELO, 91

war profiteering, 21, 62
wealth: generated by international workers, 58, 61–62, 119, 124, 139n2; production of, 50, 52, 56, 131
"whiteness," 35, 36, 132
widows: 9/11, 109–10, 112–14, 116; as workers, 54–55
Winfrey, Oprah, 7, 134n7
womanhood, 6
Women's Educational Leadership Organization (WELO): candidate's experiences with, 89–92, 96, 129–30; critical reflection of, 93–94; exchange program background, 86–89; geopolitics and, 94–95; performance expectations, 97–100, 102, 120–21
women's liberation: beauty and, 12, 60–62, 63, 119; branding and marketing, 58; commercialization of, 51; labor and, 54–58, 59–60, 63–64, 67–69, 82, 118–20; performative aspects of, 97–98, 102; U.S. intervention in, 9–12, 94–95, 117
women's rights: celebrity advocates, 7, 134n7; efforts of international workers, 53, 88, 92–93, 123; global, 6–7; promoted by Afghan women, 100; RAWA's achievements, 8; U.S. military and, 108; U.S. politicians and, 10–11
WuDunn, Sheryl, 56–57

Yeh, Emily, 99

zoë, 44
zone of indistinction, 44–46

GEOGRAPHIES OF JUSTICE AND SOCIAL TRANSFORMATION

1. *Social Justice and the City*, rev. ed.
by David Harvey

2. *Begging as a Path to Progress: Indigenous Women and Children and the Struggle for Ecuador's Urban Spaces*
by Kate Swanson

3. *Making the San Fernando Valley: Rural Landscapes, Urban Development, and White Privilege*
by Laura R. Barraclough

4. *Company Towns in the Americas: Landscape, Power, and Working-Class Communities*
edited by Oliver J. Dinius and Angela Vergara

5. *Tremé: Race and Place in a New Orleans Neighborhood*
by Michael E. Crutcher Jr.

6. *Bloomberg's New York: Class and Governance in the Luxury City*
by Julian Brash

7. *Roppongi Crossing: The Demise of a Tokyo Nightclub District and the Reshaping of a Global City*
by Roman Adrian Cybriwsky

8. *Fitzgerald: Geography of a Revolution*
by William Bunge

9. *Accumulating Insecurity: Violence and Dispossession in the Making of Everyday Life*
edited by Shelley Feldman, Charles Geisler, and Gayatri A. Menon

10. *They Saved the Crops: Labor, Landscape, and the Struggle over Industrial Farming in Bracero-Era California*
by Don Mitchell

11. *Faith Based: Religious Neoliberalism and the Politics of Welfare in the United States*
by Jason Hackworth

12. *Fields and Streams: Stream Restoration, Neoliberalism, and the Future of Environmental Science*
by Rebecca Lave

13. *Black, White, and Green: Farmers Markets, Race, and the Green Economy*
by Alison Hope Alkon

14. *Beyond Walls and Cages: Prisons, Borders, and Global Crisis*
edited by Jenna M. Loyd, Matt Mitchelson, and Andrew Burridge

15. *Silent Violence: Food, Famine, and Peasantry in Northern Nigeria*
by Michael J. Watts

16. *Development, Security, and Aid: Geopolitics and Geoeconomics at the U.S. Agency for International Development*
by Jamey Essex

17. *Properties of Violence: Law and Land-Grant Struggle in Northern New Mexico*
by David Correia

18. *Geographical Diversions: Tibetan Trade, Global Transactions*
by Tina Harris

19. *The Politics of the Encounter: Urban Theory and Protest under Planetary Urbanization*
by Andy Merrifield

20. *Rethinking the South African Crisis: Nationalism, Populism, Hegemony*
by Gillian Hart

21. *The Empires' Edge: Militarization, Resistance, and Transcending Hegemony in the Pacific*
by Sasha Davis

22. *Pain, Pride, and Politics: Social Movement Activism and the Sri Lankan Tamil Diaspora in Canada*
by Amarnath Amarasingam

23. *Selling the Serengeti: The Cultural Politics of Safari Tourism*
by Benjamin Gardner

24. *Territories of Poverty: Rethinking North and South*
edited by Ananya Roy and Emma Shaw Crane

25. *Precarious Worlds: Contested Geographies of Social Reproduction*
edited by Katie Meehan and Kendra Strauss

26. *Spaces of Danger: Culture and Power in the Everyday*
edited by Heather Merrill and Lisa M. Hoffman

27. *Shadows of a Sunbelt City: The Environment, Racism, and the Knowledge Economy in Austin*
by Eliot M. Tretter

28. *Beyond the Kale: Urban Agriculture and Social Justice Activism in New York City*
by Kristin Reynolds and Nevin Cohen

29. *Calculating Property Relations: Chicago's Wartime Industrial Mobilization, 1940–1950*
by Robert Lewis

30. *In the Public's Interest: Evictions, Citizenship, and Inequality in Contemporary Delhi*
by Gautam Bhan

31. *The Carpetbaggers of Kabul and Other American-Afghan Entanglements: Intimate Development, Geopolitics, and the Currency of Gender and Grief*
by Jennifer L. Fluri and Rachel Lehr

32. *Masculinities and Markets: Raced and Gendered Urban Politics in Milwaukee*
by Brenda Parker

www.ingramcontent.com/pod-product-compliance
Lightning Source LLC
Chambersburg PA
CBHW012231230426
43666CB00038B/2888